Making Meaning in the Response-Based Classroom

Making Meaning in the Response-Based Classroom

EDITED BY

Margaret Hunsberger
University of Calgary

George Labercane
University of Calgary

Allyn and Bacon

Boston ■ London ■ Toronto ■ Sydney ■ Tokyo ■ Singapore

Series Editor: Aurora Martínez Ramos
Series Editorial Assistant: Beth Slater
Executive Marketing Manager: Amy Cronin
Editorial Production Service: Omegatype Typography, Inc.
Composition and Prepress Buyer: Linda Cox
Manufacturing Buyer: Julie McNeill
Cover Administrator: Kristina Mose-Libon
Electronic Composition: Omegatype Typography, Inc.

Library of Congress Cataloging-in-Publication Data

Making meaning in the response-based classroom / Margaret Hunsberger and George Labercane, editors.
    p.   cm.
Includes bibliographical references and index.
ISBN 0-205-26760-2 (alk. paper)
    1. English language—Study and teaching.   2. Reading.   3. Reader-response criticism.   I. Hunsberger, Margaret.   II. Labercane, George Donald.

LB1576 .M248 2002
801'.95'071—dc21

                                                                    2001045090

Printed in the United States of America

10 9 8 7 6 5 4 3 2 1   06 05 04 03 02 01

In memory of
Diane Paulsen

Gifted teacher
Insightful student
Warm-hearted friend

CONTENTS

INTRODUCTION

> Response, then, can never be singular; it is always multiple, layered, combining understanding and affect, involving mental images and gestures for which the surface features of words always seem inadequate. For me, and for the children I know, responses are other versions, rediscoveries, sets of possibilities, hazards, risks, a change of consciousness, a social interaction. (Meek, 1990, p. 10)

Reader response theory has, perhaps, been the most influential development in the teaching of English for the past decade. Numerous treatments of the theory have been put forward in a series of writings by notable figures such as Louise Rosenblatt (1978), Wolfgang Iser (1978), and Stanley Fish (1980). This work has reflected an interest in the reading process and with reader-text relationships. Eagleton (1983), in his review of literary theory, raises issues of definitions of literature and corresponding notions of it that have been imported from Europe: hermeneutics, semiotics, reception theory, structuralism, and deconstruction. Freund (1987) also provides a clear and cogent account of the development of reader response criticism in which she focuses on the work of four influential thinkers in the field: Culler, Fish, Holland, and Iser. These, and other accounts, reflect the interest and concern with moving our thinking beyond the work of the New Critics.

Richard Beach (1993) provides further explication of reader response theories from five different theoretical perspectives: textual, experiential, psychological, social, and cultural. His review is instructive in that he presents a comprehensive overview of these perspectives and provides teachers with a number of useful strategies for showing how each perspective reflects its own theoretical framework. Other texts have attempted to show how response can be taught using a variety of pedagogical approaches: Corcoran and Evans (1978) and Hayhoe and Parker (1990), to name a few.

What these reviews and edited versions show is that the field of reader response, as it relates to classrooms, has been evolving in recent years, so that we are now into the second generation of such work. The first generation ushered in new and exciting ideas, often presented dramatically and idealistically. What was evident was the import of these ideas for the classrooms. Teachers were excited by Atwell's (1987) conception of the Readers' Workshop, in which students were encouraged to develop an understanding and deep appreciation for literature by simply being given a text and an opportunity to read. Teachers were admonished to act as guides who "led from behind" while students were to be left alone to read what they wanted. We now know what some of the difficulties are with such approaches and what kinds of issues ordinary teachers encounter when they try to implement a Readers' Workshop in their classrooms. As we enter the second generation in our teaching of response, we need to deal with these issues so that teachers will not abandon the teaching of literature because they feel overwhelmed by the evident difficulties but rather will find renewed vigor in the approaches offered in this book of readings.

The writers here are teachers and scholars, in the sense that each has taught elementary or secondary school and has also done graduate work and given attention to research. Some are university professors. What we have attempted to do is to seek to meld theory and practice, not by offering a section of each, but by using both to show how and why. Some case studies have been included showing what the teacher actually did to develop response and taking an analytical approach to why or how an idea worked, did not work, or partly worked.

The book includes suggested teaching strategies, ideas, and procedures; bibliographies of theoretical and applied sources; children's and adolescent literature; reflective questions within chapters; and other invitations to the reader to reflect on or discuss with other teachers the ideas raised. Our goal has been to develop a set of readings that present evolving ideas in reader response and to show how reader response is being translated into practice in classrooms. Although we believe that the text could serve as an introduction to the area of reader response as it has evolved to this point, our intent is to allow those teachers (or pre-service teachers) who have some acquaintance with the theory to pursue it more fully and thoughtfully. Our bias is against those texts that make reader response sound easy and rose-colored (i.e., "Adopt reader response and your language arts problems will be solved") and those that discuss teaching activities as divorced from theoretical underpinnings and principles. We are biased toward reader-text positions that we think can be reasonably applied in the classroom, such as the views held by scholars like Iser and Rosenblatt.

Finally, to reiterate the aims of this book, we see the necessity to re-vision reader response, to see it as an attempt "to allow readers to take risks in trying out new generic forms, to tolerate uncertainty, to discover that texts have power, and to read against the grain in the spirit of the age, as we teach it" (Meek, 1990, p. 7).

Acknowledgments

We would like to thank the following reviewers for their helpful suggestions: Joyce Bainbridge, University of Alberta; Nancy Falter, Lincoln Public Schools; Penelope Moore, Mountainview School; Allan Neilsen, Mount Saint Vincent University; and Kenneth J. Weiss, Nazareth College of Rochester.

REFERENCES

Atwell, N. (1987). *In the middle: Writing, reading, and learning with adolescents.* Portsmouth, NH: Heinemann.

Beach, R. (1993). *A teacher's introduction to reader response theories.* Urbana, IL: National Council of Teachers of English Press.

Corcoran, B., & Evans, E. (Eds). (1987). *Readers, texts, teachers.* Upper Montclair, NJ: Boynton/Cook.

Eagleton, T. (1983). *Literary theory.* Minneapolis, MN: University of Minnesota Press.

Fish, S. (1980). *Is there a text in this class? The authority of interpretive communities.* Cambridge, MA: Harvard University Press.

Freund, E. (1987). *The return of the reader: Reader-response criticism.* New York: Methuen.

Hayhoe, M., & Parker, S. (1990). *Reading and response.* Milton Keynes, UK: Open University Press.

Iser, W. (1978). *The act of reading: A theory of aesthetic response.* Baltimore: Johns Hopkins University Press.

Meek, M. (1990). Why response? In M. Hayhoe & S. Parker (Eds.), *Reading and response.* (pp. 1–12). Milton Keynes, UK: Open University Press.

Rosenblatt, L. (1978). *The reader, the text, the poem.* Carbondale, IL: Southern Illinois University Press.

CONTRIBUTORS

Richard Beach is Wallace Professor of English Education at the University of Minnesota, Twin Cities. He is author of *A Teacher's Introduction to Reader Response Theories* and coauthor of *Teaching Literature in the Secondary School* and *Inquiry-Based English Instruction*. He is a member of the board of directors of the National Reading Conference.

Paul Boyd-Batstone began his teaching career as a bilingual teacher in the Long Beach Unified School District in Southern California, during which time he initiated a number of innovative projects, including creating a bilingual (Spanish/English) musical of Lynne Cherry's book *The Great Kapok Tree* (Harcourt Brace, 1990). He also began the first Cambodian bilingual program in California and participated in the school district's first Spanish/English gifted and talented program. He is the coauthor of *Crossroads: Literature and Language in Culturally and Linguistically Diverse Classrooms* (Merrill/Prentice Hall, 1997). Currently, he is on faculty at California State University, Long Beach, in the Department of Teacher Education.

Kelvin Broad completed his doctorate in 1999 at the University of Calgary, Calgary, Alberta. He currently holds the position of assistant professor in early childhood education and literacy at Northern Arizona University, Flagstaff, Arizona. Originally from New Zealand, Kelvin has taught in elementary and early childhood settings in New Zealand and Canada. His research focuses on the nature of early readers' aesthetic response to text and the infusion of technology into reader response pedagogy.

Niki Cherniwchan teaches English language arts and French language arts in junior high school in Calgary, Alberta. She holds a master's degree in curriculum studies, with particular attention to teaching text interpretation and writing.

Carole Cox teaches at California State University, Long Beach, where she received the 2001 Outstanding Professor Award. Her publications include *Teaching Language Arts: A Student- and Response-Centered Classroom* (4th ed., Allyn & Bacon, 2002), and *Crossroads: Literature and Language in Culturally and Linguistically Diverse Classrooms* (Merrill, 1997), with Paul Boyd-Batstone.

Patrick Dias is professor emeritus of education at McGill University, Montreal, where he taught and researched writing and response to literature and was founder–director of the Centre for the Study and Teaching of Writing. Publications include *Reading and Responding to Poetry: Patterns in the Process*, Heinemann Boynton-Cook, 1996; *Developing Response to Poetry* (with Mike Hayhoe), Open University Press, 1988; *Writing for Ourselves/Writing for Others* (with Beer, Ledwell-Brown, Paré, & Pittenger), Nelson, 1992; *Worlds Apart: Acting and Writing in Academic* *and Workplace Contexts* (with Freedman, Medway, & Paré), Lawrence Erlbaum, 1999; and Dias & Paré, Eds., *Transitions: Writing in Academic and Workplace Settings,* Hampton Press, 2000.

Joanne M. Golden is a professor of language and literacy education at the University of Delaware, Newark, Delaware, where she teaches courses in children's and young adult literature and the social foundations of literacy. Her publications include two books, *The Narrative Symbol in Childhood Literature* and *Storymaking in Elementary and Middle School Classrooms,* as well as articles on reader response and narrative texts.

Margaret Hunsberger is associate dean in the Faculty of Education at the University of Calgary, Alberta. Her teaching is in the areas of language arts and curriculum study, with a particular interest in text interpretation. She participated in a three-year research project on the responses of upper elementary school students.

George Labercane is a professor in the Graduate Division of Educational Research and the Division of Teacher Preparation at the University of Calgary, Alberta. He is one of the coauthors of *Elementary Reading: Process and Process* and teaches graduate courses in reader theory. He participated in a three-year research project on the response processes of children in an upper elementary classroom.

Rebecca Luce-Kapler is an assistant professor of language and literacy in the Faculty of Education at Queen's University, Kingston, Ontario. Her research, which focuses on writing and interpretation, draws from her experience of teaching elementary to post-secondary students, and from her work as a poet. Her coauthored book (with Brent Davis and Dennis Sumara), *Engaging Minds: Teaching and Learning in a Complex World,* was published in 2000 by Lawrence Erlbaum.

Catherine Ramsden has taught junior high and high school English for twenty-five years and is currently an assistant principal in a large Calgary, Alberta, high school. She earned her master's degree at the University of Nottingham, England, and also served for three years as coeditor of *English Quarterly.*

Dennis J. Sumara is an associate professor of teacher education at the University of Alberta, Edmonton, Alberta. He is author of *Private Readings in Public: Schooling the Literary Imagination,* and coauthor of *Engaging Minds: Learning and Teaching in a Complex World.* His work is developed around studies of literary engagements, with particular attention to the ways they function to create sites for learning. He is currently working on a new book titled *Learning How to Fall in Love: Creating Insight from Literary Engagements.*

David L. E. Watt is an associate professor in the Faculty of Education at the University of Calgary, Alberta. The ideas presented in his chapter stem from a SSHRC-funded research project that investigated the development of aesthetic response among upper elementary students in integrated classroom settings. He can be contacted by email at dwatt@ucalgary.ca.

Making Meaning in the Response-Based Classroom

"Can We Really Read Anything We Want?"

Aesthetic Reading in the Classroom

CATHERINE RAMSDEN
Calgary Board of Education

"I have never finished reading a whole novel for school since Grade Four!" Bill announced boldly to me and his Grade Twelve English class. Trying to maintain my composure at this scandalous confession, I responded with, "But how did you manage in Grades Ten and Eleven?" To which he proudly replied, "In Grade Ten, we did *To Kill A Mockingbird,* and in Grade Eleven *Lord of the Flies,* and I rented the videos."

This flagrant revelation stirred a long-suppressed awareness in my English-teacher soul: the attitudes and practice inherent in Bill's statement were more common than I or my colleagues really cared to admit.

The Challenge

The challenge became to find a better way to develop in my students a heightened interest in and commitment to reading in their lives, but more specifically in English class.

Much has been written (including Farrell and Squire, 1990) about the difference students experience between the reading and responding to literature they do in school and that which they do apart from school. "I read for detail when I read for school. . . . I try to focus on all the little things I know we'll talk about in class. When I read for myself, I just kick back and let the story sort of swallow me up" (Nelms & Zancanella, 1990, p. 44). Louise Rosenblatt describes students as operating on "two separate and distinct planes" (Rosenblatt, 1983, p. 58), one relating to information and ideas about literature handed down from teachers and critics, and the other—not often considered—pertaining to their personal responses to what they have read. My concern here has more to do with their attitudes toward the reading itself than specifically how students are asked to respond to it, but it is naive to consider that the two are mutually exclusive. Also, as I was considering a Grade Twelve English class (with provincewide examinations looming at the end of the school year), evaluation was a necessary (albeit somewhat restrictive) component. It impacts how free students feel to explore and respond as they wish versus what they think the teacher expects. The first consideration, though, was the reading.

The Nature of the Reading

The specific nature of the project emerged from reading Rosenblatt's description and discussion of efferent and aesthetic reading, and from personal reflection about why I enjoy reading and what I would really like my students to take away with them from my English class. Rosenblatt suggests: "The teacher of literature, then, seeks to help specific human beings discover the satisfactions of literature" (1983, p. 26). Also, "Literature provides a *living-through*, not simply *knowledge-about* . . ." (p. 38). She originally expressed these ideas in 1983, and although we teachers of literature have moved some distance in that direction, there is still considerable room for growth and change. When I assign a novel or short story for my students to read, I suspect—rather, I am certain—that many of them do not necessarily experience much "satisfaction" but are more interested in getting the job done and receiving a reasonable (the definition is relative!) mark for doing it. However, acknowledging their understandable concern about the results, I was drawn to Purves' conclusion that an important goal of literature education deals with "habits of mind in reading . . . inculcat[ing] specific sets of preferred habits of reading and writing about that body of texts termed 'literature'" (1993, p. 88).

My objective has been to provide a reading project and an environment that would allow and encourage students to move their reading stance as close to the aesthetic end of the continuum as possible, while still retaining an evaluative component. This was partly to satisfy the need for marks from the perspective of the teacher and students, but moreso to demonstrate that work done related to reading can be personally fruitful as well as "educational." Before describing the specific nature of the project, its implementation, and its results, however, it is important to review the theory and reflection on which it was based.

It is worth considering Purves' assertion that "the problem may be that we err when we even consider that reading a literary work in school is anything like reading for pleasure" (1993, p. 348). This observation apparently suggests that there is no resemblance or relationship between the two. However, he may be proposing that reading for pleasure and reading for assignments are different enough that teachers should pay attention.

In support of aesthetic reading in the classroom, Greco, for example, writes: "Because reading is personal and dynamic, it can trigger self-discovery and self-actualization" (1990, p. 40). She also quotes Iser's description of the reading process as "active and creative" and providing "a theoretical base for focused reader-oriented writing assignments that can excite students about reading literature" (p. 40). My contention is while writing assignments that focus on specific reader orientations can excite them, the same is true for choice of literature to be read. So I began planning the project with the belief that the students should be absolutely free to select their reading material.

When I presented this idea to the students, of course, their questions about the choice of books very much reflected their school experience. Could they really read anything they wanted? I replied by asking them if they felt there should be any limits and was rewarded with their response that their choices should reflect a meaningful use of their time. In other words, *The Cat in the Hat* (their suggestion) would be inappropriate. The issue of rereading also arose, and we agreed that this was an acceptable element of free choice—and, incidentally, an interesting aspect of reading that I could examine through their responses.

That being said, some support for the free choice of texts is perhaps necessary. Probst said it well when he observed that "the fundamental literary experience is intimate, personal, and dependent upon the nature of the individual" (1988, p. 37). Albeit rather obvious, this conclusion is not often considered when assigning literature to be read by students in English classes. I was reminded of it during my Grade Twelve English students' discussion of Timothy Findley's *The Wars.* Their responses were as varied as their personalities, to the extent that one student declared it was the best assigned novel he had ever read, whereas another insisted he disliked it so much that he didn't even want to discuss it. Despite my students' observation that their choices should reflect a valuable use of their time, one concern that arose for me when considering absolute free choice of books to read was the fear that they might choose "junk." Donelson has a delightful way of alleviating that misgiving as he examines the types of books we all read when we were young "but now find reprehensible" and suggests that our students may also "survive their lists of literary horrors, just as we did" (1989, p. 23).

In reader response work, some student choice is critical (Probst, 1990). However, an important consideration is the fact that all reading assignments in English classes do not need to be individual student choice. It is indeed the mandate and responsibility of teachers of English to expose students to a variety of genres, themes, authors, and so forth. However, first we need to create what Prest and Prest call "a dynamic atmosphere of trust, discussion, enthusiasm and acceptance in the classroom" (1988, p. 131). In fact, a good number of students sought my advice, especially those who did not usually read for pleasure. I took great delight in chatting with them about their interests and then recommending some of my favorites, which I was happy to lend them. This created an unexpected additional reward in the relationships that were developing between teacher and students.

Meeting Curricular Needs

Having decided that the project would allow students this free choice of books to be read, I faced a number of significant questions. The most important of these were the amount of time allowed for completion of the project and for reading in class, the nature and weighting of evaluation, and the question of how much background and explanation of my goal I should share with the students.

I confess to feeling anxious about the amount of time we would be spending away from the "curriculum," but my guilt was assuaged when I reflected upon Galda's comment that "allowing students time to be with books in the class-room . . . teaches them to value books" (1988, p. 100). Also, because I had decided that there would be oral and written components to the evaluation (the only teacher demand apart from time), I realized that many of my curricular responsibilities would be addressed. The students would be engaged in prewriting activities, such as small group discussion and one-on-one planning with me; they would have the opportunity to participate in peer editing; and they would be challenged to exercise their creativity and personal and critical response to literature.

The specific nature of the evaluation would be decided by the students. As a result of our collective brainstorming, we settled on a total mark of 100, to be divided between written work and an oral component, which could occur either through a class presentation or one-on-one with me. The breakdown between written and oral work would be decided by each student. However, first we had to determine *what* we would be evaluating. I asked the question, "What does a thoughtful, insightful, aesthetic reading entail?" As I examine that question now, I realize that its wording somewhat influences the possible responses, but I believe that is almost impossible to avoid. The list they brainstormed was:

- vivid description
- what you liked
- recommendation
- enthusiasm
- understanding
- comparisons
- related interests
- thoughts provoked

When discussing *how* we would be able to discern whether any of these elements were present, they again devised a long list of possibilities, including such ideas as seminars, newspaper articles, and posters. I encouraged them to select a book first because it was something they wanted to read and to think about what to do with it later—easier said than done, as it turned out.

With regard to the issue of what to tell the students about the purpose of the project, I elected to introduce them to the concept of efferent and aesthetic reading.

Aesthetic and Efferent Reading

I am tempted at this point to quote Rosenblatt's entire chapter entitled "Efferent and Aesthetic Reading" (1978, pp. 22–47), as this is the basis of my understanding and I highly recommend her explanation. However, time and space preclude such quoting; moreover, articulating my own interpretation will more effectively characterize my application of it. In essence, the difference between efferent and aesthetic reading lies in where the reader's attention is focused. In efferent reading, the attention "is directed outward . . . towards concepts to be retained, ideas to be tested, actions to be performed after the reading" (p. 24). When reading aesthetically, however, the reader is attentive to "what he is living through during his relationship with that particular text" (p. 25).

An important feature of this theory is the fact that these two types of reading exist at opposite ends of a continuum. This is crucial to the argument that aesthetic reading can occur in schools, because the practice, I believe, needs only to move students' reading stance closer to the aesthetic end of the continuum. Purves refers to Langer's suggestion that one "difference between efferent and aesthetic reading in school lies less in the way we read than in the follow-up to the reading" (Purves, 1993, p. 349). Rosenblatt also introduces the idea that the same text may be read efferently and aesthetically. My own experience of reading as a student in school attests to that. I often recall feeling very fortunate that while being absorbed in a good novel, I was actually doing my homework. Rosenblatt contends that, compared with efferent reading, aesthetic reading requires more and continuing attention to the words of the text and their effect on the reader. That suggests a more conscious, active reading than does Nell's description of ludic reading as being *Lost in a Book* (Nell, 1988), which is the kind of reading Purves argues is impossible in the classroom. Rosenblatt proposes that an aesthetic reading may be interrupted by a concern about information being acquired but that this enhances the overall aesthetic reading.

I explained to my students that my objective was to provide an opportunity for them to really enjoy their reading apart from restrictions created by the English class, and I made a point of expressing my confidence and faith in them as individuals who would make worthwhile choices (for them) and be responsibly involved. As I reflect on this, I'm sure that assurance was more for me than for them.

Expectations

The final aspect of the introduction to the students was a discussion of expectations: theirs of me and mine of them. I talked about wanting them to throw themselves wholeheartedly into their reading, especially if we were to devote considerable class time to it. In other words, that time would be for reading, not doing other homework or staying away. I was reassured later when, on a day that I had to be away from school, during the two hours allotted to reading, my substitute reported that they did exactly that with little distraction but for bathroom breaks. When I asked the students about their expectations of me, I had to do a little prodding. This is not something students are often invited to do, and I'm sure it had not really occurred to them that they have this right. Eventually, they expressed their need to be reassured that they really did have all this freedom and that I would be fair in their evaluations. This issue arose several times throughout the project, with students asking questions such as, "Would this be okay?" and "Is this what you want?"

The Project in Action: Benefits and Drawbacks

Thus, the project was launched. I kept some notes as the time passed and noticed some benefits not anticipated and some difficulties not foreseen. The benefits revolved around communication in a number of ways. As Bonnycastle (1991) indicates, in reader response work, participants must discuss or repeat their interpretations and listen thoughtfully to each other; therein lies the challenge and excitement of reader response work. I arranged times for students to conference with me, either as they were reading or when they were finished, and all twenty-six of them met with me at least once to discuss possibilities. For me as a teacher, the by-products of these meetings (as well as the one-on-one oral evaluations later) were innumerable. I came to know these individuals much better, and some of their responses to later studies in English class were much more enthusiastic. Another advantage emerged in the student-to-student communication, first in informal reading discussions, which I scheduled for a few minutes intermittently throughout the project. This idea surfaced after reading Leal's article in which she praised "the benefits of peer-group discussions . . . that enable students to view themselves as resources for information rather than merely objects of instruction" (1993, p. 118). This was also evident in some of the students' oral presentations to the class. For example, a student who read *The Ryan White Story* incorporated information on AIDS. Another presented some fascinating background on Dracula, such as that the original character was based on an historical figure named Vlad the Impaler—a gruesome individual in whose story the students took a ghoulish delight.

A second type of communication benefit came when the students described the project to each other. I overheard one boy explaining "the homework" to a student who had been absent. Her confusion resulted in his seeking clarification from others—definite support for collaborative learning (but that's another topic). Still another variety of communication, both delightful and surprising, involved one of my parenting students (a young woman of nineteen with a two-year-old son). She chose to read some children's literature with a view to thinking about what she would like her child to read. For her oral project, she interviewed four elementary students (from grades three to six) about their reading of *The Lion, the Witch and the Wardrobe* by C. S. Lewis. I was privileged to witness (and videotape) the interview, and I was touched by the sharing of the reading experience among these diverse, and yet similar, readers. Another student concluded her presentation with, "I hope you enjoyed my presentation, and that it inspired you to want to read more on this ancient story about a real man and the myths that surrounded his life."

The difficulties that arose—and there were difficulties—originated from the students' need for assurance that they were headed in the "right" direction, and from the problems they experienced because they were not accustomed to thinking about reading in an abstract way. I also had to deal with the variety of students' needs for time to read, time to work on the project, and requests for permission to work elsewhere than in the classroom (which I granted with my fingers crossed). It is interesting to note how a request like this follows naturally from my attempts to make reading more aesthetic. Being able to choose where we read, and reading elsewhere than in a hard, uncomfortable desk, are normal aspects of personal reading. As we reached the deadline, another problem arose—that of students who had procrastinated or who had had legitimate difficulties completing their work. I had established an atmosphere of flexibility, so I felt it only appropriate to extend the deadline as well. This created some time pressure when planning the next unit.

The Presentations

When the class-presentation dates arrived, I was thrilled with the results. One student divided the class into two societies (based on her novel) and gave them a territorial dispute to resolve. A fascinating aspect of the follow-up discussion, about the stereotypes of males and females, arose as a result of her decision to put all the girls in one group (the aggressors) and the boys in the other (the pacifists). Another presenter engaged the students in a fantasy journey in which he read excerpts from his book, *The Paradise War*, by Stephen Lawhead. His objective was to demonstrate that "the author uses tremendous detail in describing even the minorest [sic] of events, but he doesn't in any way make the scenes boring." Later, when assessing the success of his presentation, he wrote, "When I told them it was over, they opened their eyes and the expressions on their faces were saying, 'But I don't want this to be over!' I heard Ryan say 'Wow!' aside to Jackie." In addition, one of the weakest students in the class (a returning Grade Twelve student who had real writing problems and rarely participated in class discussions) read a book involving business scams, so he researched and presented information about typical scams that occur in everyday life.

The Conferences

The one-on-one discussions I had with students varied in their success. I realize that next time I shall have to be clearer in explaining that they should come prepared to talk about their books rather than relying on me to ask all the questions. Some were very effective, whereas others told me the plot and then waited. However, even the latter group proved insightful when probed a little. Two were of particular interest. The first was a boy who read the *Star Wars* series (written to follow the films) and who knew as much of the technical detail as if it were a science. (His math teacher later told me he had shared his enthusiasm and plans for his project with her.) The second was a boy who had read *Johnny Got His Gun*, by Dalton Trumbo. He brought with him the lyrics and tape of a song by Metallica (a heavy metal band) based on the story. We had a wonderful conversation about the emotion aroused in him as he read the novel and listened to the lyrics written by a group that the general public (me included) views as mindless. This was the same student, Bill, who had previously proudly declared that he had not finished an assigned novel since Grade Four. Because I had labelled him a hard nut to crack, I was especially moved as he shared his feelings of sympathy for the suffering of the main character, his struggle to imagine how he himself would cope with the kind of isolation the injuries of war could cause, and finally, through Metallica's music, his disgust with war in general.

The Written Projects

The written components of the project were also interesting. The most absorbing I deliberately selected to read first because the student had explained her process to me during her conference and I was most impressed. She chose to reflect on her development as a reader by examining books she had read at age four (*Katy and the Big Snow*), eight (*Charlotte's Web*), twelve (*Nancy Drew: Murder On Ice*), and sixteen (*The Firm*). The content and appearance chosen for each book suitably represented her age and insights at the time. She began with large print in crayon and developed through neater print to handwriting and, finally, to a computer printout. Her observations about her reading developed accordingly. Admittedly, she was my top student, but her finished product surpassed all my expectations, especially her attempts to generalize beyond her own experience to make observations about reading development:

> Being able to visualize Katy ploughing out the town helps to involve the child in the book even if he is not actually reading the word for himself. I vividly remember looking at the map on pages 6 and 7 for hours each time we got the book out of the library. This book's main purpose is to begin to develop the mind of a child and to interest him in reading more. . . . One of the first books I remember having read all by myself was the well-known *Charlotte's Web*, by E. B. White. The story is quite descriptive but a large portion of it is dialogue, which helps to keep the reader interested in what is happening. The sentences are beginning to get longer and more complex but are not overwhelmingly difficult. By this time, my child's imagination was developed enough so that it did not need to be stimulated by pictures as often as was necessary before. . . . The Nancy Drew stories, by Carolyn Keene, are known world-wide as favourites of girls in the next stage of life (ages 11–13). The first noticeable characteristic of this series is the appearance of the book. Girls this age do not want to be treated as children any longer and a mature presentation of the book is vital. The reader's maturity is also recognized when the author stimulates an element of fear. She would not do this if she did not think that the reader could distinguish between reality and fantasy. This book is clearly trying to appeal to the maturing mind of a preteen girl and help her through difficult changes in her life. . . . The cover of a book is not nearly so important for older readers and such is the case with the book, *The Firm*, by John Grisham, although a picture of Tom Cruise has never hurt in advertising a product. The diction and choice of sentence structure are obviously directed

towards a mature audience. I was required to use my mind to think out the plot and try to figure out a solution or decide what I would do in this situation. . . . Although there are times during the reading process that this may be doubted, a reasonably happy ending is achieved in all of these books. Katy clears the road; Wilbur lives; Nancy solves the mystery; and Mitchell McDeere escapes the mafia. Although these characteristics may seem insignificant, they are present in most of the books which I read. But the important lesson to remember is that the development of a reader is first seen at an early age. For people to remain interested in books, they need to read books which are suitable to their age group while appealing to their personality. It may take awhile for them to settle on a genre but if such care were taken for each individual, there would be many more happy readers in our society.

Student Responses

Finally, I felt it was essential to acquire some feedback from the students regarding their observations about their reading process and their feelings about the project as a whole. I gave them specific questions to consider because, although I knew these would direct their thinking somewhat, I also know from experience that asking for general observations elicits very vague information.

Reading
1. How did you make your choice of which book to read?
2. How did the reading go (e.g., fast, slow, variable, etc.)?
3. What did you notice about your involvement in the reading?
4. What did you gain from the reading (or rereading)?
5. What were your strengths and weaknesses during this reading?
6. Any other observations/comments about the reading?

The Project
1. How did you feel about the project?
2. What would you change about the experiment itself and about your participation in it?
3. What are the advantages and disadvantages of this process for a Grade Twelve English class?
4. How did you decide how you would be evaluated?
5. Were the consultations useful? If not, how could they be of more value to you?

The responses varied from very thoughtful and thorough to less detailed, resembling an assignment to be completed, but I learned something from all of them. The questions were directed specifically to two areas: experience of the reading, and their feelings about the project. In both cases, student responses reflected a positive view of the overall activity. One of the most pronounced areas was their self-evaluation. They commented on what types of readers they were—emotional, visual, slow, comprehensive. They reflected on how they would carry out the project differently another time (e.g., prepare more thoroughly for one-on-one consultations with the teacher in order to benefit more). One particularly interesting comment came from one of the few students who had not read *Lord of the Flies* in Grade Eleven: "I picked this novel because people told me it was a good book and I knew I would spend my time wisely reading it. Plus my reading is not all that great and neither are my writing skills which reading always helps. Also being a slow reader, I needed a book that I would finish in time to not look dumb." This recognition of the opportunity to learn more and to do well was as heartwarming for me as the students' increased tolerance and acceptance of others' interests and abilities.

The topics of the oral presentations were as varied as the students themselves and, naturally, their choices of books. An avid climber produced a video of a simulated climbing rescue. His classmates responded with a myriad of questions about climbing in general and his experiences specifically. The girl who presented information about AIDS found herself conducting a follow-up discussion on society's responsibility to individuals afflicted with the disease. Regardless of the topic or the effectiveness of the presentation, the students' attentiveness and active participation demonstrated their interest in and consideration of each other. A third critical factor was the sense of ownership revealed in their comments. They appreciated being included in the decision-making process, both in their selection of books and in the nature of the project. This was reinforced by their suggestions of changes that might improve the activity for others later. One suggestion that arose several times was a recommendation to have more time for conferences, both with me and with their peers, "because during the one we had I came up with even more good ideas." They also wanted help with sticking to the deadlines, perhaps with some checks and balances throughout. It was interesting to note that many of their suggestions were accompanied by a self-evaluation such as, "I would have liked a little more structure to the project. That's the main thing I had troubles with, but that was the point of the assignment: to get us to think." Another important result was the attention paid to individual learning styles and rates. Students were able to address these differences on their own.

Student Growth

All of these attitudinal developments could not help but enable the students to grow as readers and as students, but there was also growth in specific English curricular areas. The increase of confidence in oral communication was evident in formal presentations as well as in small group discussions. The small group conferences also fostered their skills in collaborative learning. Because this was a senior-level English course that culminates in a government-department examination worth 50 percent of their final grade, students were quick to acknowledge how this project helped them to prepare for it. They were able to develop their skills in critical analysis of literature. Although I had not directed them to do so, many students found themselves making significant observations about the style of an author's writing, the development of characters, and other "typical" English course requirements. They also—and in much more depth—addressed their personal responses to literature. Their writing, on the whole, was more lively and interesting to read as they cultivated their own voices. There was also a valuable "spin-off" effect on the students' reactions to assigned reading later on in the course. Many of them responded as Rosenblatt describes: "the reader's dominant concern usually continues to be the information to be retained after the reading, yet at the same time he is aware of, is paying some attention to, the actual experiential aspects of the reading, and deriving some satisfaction from them" (1978, p. 36).

Conclusion

The most important conclusion I have drawn is that this project was worthwhile, and I will definitely repeat it. Second, although not less noteworthy, is that it is indeed possible, and desirable, to create an environment and assignment that allows students in an English class to move a good deal closer to the aesthetic end of the reading continuum than they have been previously. There are obstacles to overcome, such as a teacher's need only to teach *about* literature, although to be fair, as Duke (1984) suggests, we do what we have been trained to do. The teacher also must "create situations that provoke students into answering questions of their own in order to arrive at solutions which satisfy them" (1984, p. 4). Indeed, if I haven't read all the books they choose to read, I can't have all the answers. However, none of this will happen if I haven't first established an atmosphere in which students feel safe, in which they can trust me to honor my commitment to them and to respect their choices and decisions.

There are adjustments to be made, of course, but in what good teaching is this not the case? I will take the students' suggestions to heart and, for example, give more consideration to the time factor and to providing more opportunities for talk. However, most important is the fact that all but one of the students did feel that they had read aesthetically based on their understanding of aesthetic reading. I agreed, especially because of their enthusiastic and personal responses to the project as a whole: "I felt that this personal response was a great idea and it just shows how well this assignment went across. Overall this was the most interesting, fun, fascinating and exciting English project that I have ever done." They also benefited in a variety of ways and have connected a positive reading experience with their high school English class. From a teacher's perspective, I have to agree with Margaret Meek (1990, p. 7) when she says, "Would we not be better informed about both literature and learning if we gave them [the students] more responsibility for texts, the undoing and remaking of them?"—and, I would add, the selecting of them.

REFERENCES

Bonnycastle, S. (1991). *In search of authority*. Peterborough, Ontario: Broadview Press.

Donelson, K. (1989). If kids like it, it can't be literature. *English Journal, 78*(5), 23–26.

Duke, C. (1984, April). *The role of reflection, problem-solving and discussion in the teaching of literature*. Paper presented at the annual meeting of National Council of Teachers of English, Detroit, MI.

Farrell, E., & Squire, J. (Eds.) (1990). *Transactions with literature*. Urbana, IL: National Council of Teachers of English.

Galda, L. (1988). Readers, texts and contexts: A response-based view of literature in the classroom. *The New Advocate, 1*(2), 92–100.

Greco, N. (1990). Recreating the literary text: Practice and theory. *English Journal 79*(7), 34–40.

Leal, D. (1993). The power of literary peer-group discussions: How children collaboratively negotiate meaning. *The Reading Teacher, 47*(2), 114–120.

Meek, M. (1990). Why response? In M. Hayhoe & S. Parker (Eds.), *Reading and response* (pp. 1–12). Milton Keynes, UK: Open University Press.

Nell, V. (1988). *Lost in a book*. New Haven, CT: Yale University Press.

Nelms, B., & Zancanella, D. (1990). The experience of literature and the study of literature: The teacher-educator's experience. In M. Hayhoe & S. Parker (Eds.), *Reading and response,* (pp. 34–48). Milton Keynes, UK: Open University Press.

Prest, P., & Prest, J. (1988). Clarifying our intentions: Some thoughts on the application of Rosenblatt's transactional theory of reading in the classroom. *English Quarterly, 21*(2), 127–132.

Probst, R. (1988, January). Dialogue with a text. *English Journal, 77*(1), 32–38.

Probst, R. (1990). Five kinds of literary knowing. *Report Series 5.5*. Albany, NY: Center for Learning and Teaching of Literature.

Purves, A. (1993). Towards a re-evaluation of reader response and school literature. *Language Arts, 70*(5), 348–360.

Rosenblatt, L. (1978). *The reader, the text, the poem*. Carbondale, IL: Southern Illinois University Press.

Rosenblatt, L. (1983). *Literature as exploration*. New York: Modern Language Association.

CHAPTER

2

Reader Response Instruction for Emergent Readers

KELVIN BROAD
Northern Arizona University

The key to successfully reading imaginative literature is the ability on the part of the reader to transform the words into images in the reader's mind.

> It is a transformation with which some readers seem to find no difficulty at all . . . , but for others, perhaps over-concerned with the mechanics of the reading process, it seems to provide great problems, and for them we need to find ways of helping. (Evans, 1987, p. 30)

Instruction directed at assisting readers in effecting this transformation has become an integral component of many classroom programs. Much of this instruction is informed by reader response theories. At the upper elementary and high school levels, students are expected to engage in activities that concentrate their efforts on becoming aesthetically engaged with literary texts (as other chapters in this volume attest). For those teaching in early elementary settings, the questions are: Does reader response-based instruction have a place in early elementary language arts programs? If so, how can reader response-based instruction be woven into the fabric of language arts programs in early elementary settings? The aim of this chapter is to go some way toward addressing these questions.

I begin by briefly discussing approaches to reading instruction at the early elementary level. I outline the predominant emphasis on strategic reading instruction and developing students' decoding skills. Then the literary theories of Louise Rosenblatt (1978, 1991) and Wolfgang Iser (1978, 1989) are explored as they relate to language arts instruction at the elementary level. Next, my focus moves to the integral role teachers play in scaffolding instruction to allow students to become aesthetically engaged with text through the orchestration of oral storytelling events. Also, I discuss in this section the vital importance of teachers being familiar with the myriad of literary works available for children. The nature of young children's aesthetic response is described in the next section. What is of particular interest to me is to examine the type of responses that emergent readers may generate from their engagements with literature. The next section shifts to focus on strategies that teachers can use to develop contexts that will encourage emergent readers to become aesthetically engaged with literary texts. In the final section, I outline instructional approaches for implementing reader response-based literary events in classroom and school library environments.

Bringing Together Strategic-Reading Instruction and Reader Response Instruction

The more we have talked about reading as a tool, the more we may have obscured the delight that comes from personal literacy. (Duke, 1990, p. 443)

Strategic Approaches to Reading Instruction

Traditionally, the early years of school have been considered a time when learning the skills of reading and writing are the focus of language arts instruction. As a result, mechanistic conceptions of reading often predominate at the expense of approaches that encourage students to engage aesthetically with text. This imbalance has not gone unnoticed by researchers; Prest and Prest contend that "in the beginning years of schooling, the emphasis was placed on teaching him [her] how to read words. Little emphasis was placed on his [her] response to literature" (1988, p. 127). Daniel Pennac, in his volume that explores the joys of reading for pleasure, comments harshly about the demise of reading for pleasure in educational settings. He suggests that the school's role has become to "teach mastery of technique and critical commentary and to cut off spontaneous contact with books by discouraging the pleasure of reading" (1994, p. 91). This is particularly true of emergent reading instruction.

Reading instruction in early elementary settings is also guided by expectations society has traditionally held. Many parents expect elementary classroom programs to focus on developing reading and mathematical skills (Graue, 1993). Learning to read is often seen solely as the development of decoding skills. Informed by these expectations, early elementary classrooms often offer contexts that leave little space for the inclusion of instruction that focuses on nurturing literary exploration and encouraging students to engage aesthetically with text. Thus, the mechanistic way in which some children approach text in classrooms is often ". . . forced upon them. It is not so much individual choice or even inferior knowledge but the context of learning which imposes" (Wallace, 1992, p. 60) the way students engage with text in classroom settings. Children's expectations when entering school are that school is a place where they will "learn to read."

The premise of this chapter is not that mechanistic approaches to reading instruction are of no value. To the contrary, we understand that without exemplary instruction that introduces and consolidates skills and strategies for decoding text readers would be unable to unfurl the magic that lurks within the pages of literary texts. The balance of this chapter discusses how teachers can integrate reader response-based classroom practice effectively and authentically as one component of a balanced classroom language arts program. However, for teachers to make the first steps toward implementing reader-response instruction effectively in their classroom they must become familiar with the underlying philosophy that informs reader response.

Reader Response: A Brief Overview

> The meaning is created by readers as they bring the text to bear upon their own experience, and their own histories to bear upon the text. (Probst, 1994, p. 38)

Reader response instruction has its roots in Louise Rosenblatt's (1978, 1991) literary theory. She and other reader response theorists (e.g., Iser, 1978) view the act of reading from a different perspective than those who posit reading as simply the act of decoding ink marks on the page to create words and sentences that will provide the sole, definitive meaning of the text. According to Rosenblatt, the act of reading is a transactional relationship between the reader and the text. "An element of the environment (marks on the page) becomes a text by virtue of its particular relationship with the reader, who in turn is a reader by virtue of his [her] relationship to the text. And at the same time the term transaction, as I use it, implies that the reader brings to the text a network of past experiences in literature and life" (1985b, p. 35). Iser (1978) discusses reading in a similar manner. For him, the reading act occurs when the "convergence of the text and reader brings a literary work into existence; it cannot be identified totally with the reality of the text or with the individual disposition of the reader" (Iser as cited by Cullinan, Harwood, & Galda, 1983, p. 32). Thus, the act of reading is not simply stringing together words into sentences accurately. It also involves the feelings and images conjured up by the words in the mind of the reader.

Rosenblatt describes reading that focuses on feelings and images as aesthetic reading: "The reader's attention is centered directly on what he [she] is living through during his [her] relationship with that particular text" (1978, p. 25). The reader who reads aesthetically not only focuses on ". . . the abstract concepts that the words point to, but also what of those objects or referents stir up personal feelings, ideas and attitudes" (Rosenblatt, 1982, p. 269).

Other scholars also emphasize the importance of aesthetic reading. Wiseman and Many describe aesthetic reading as "when the reader's attention is on the lived through experience of the story and the thoughts, feelings, images and associations which are evoked as the story is read" (1992, p. 66). Extending this description further, Cox and Many contend that aesthetic reading involves the reader's "transaction with the book and the images, feelings, sensations, moods and ideas called to mind from his [her] own reservoir of past experiences with language, literature, and life" (1992, p. 29). Rosenblatt (1978) contends that, during aesthetic reading, the reader creates a personal literary work of art that she terms a "poem." The poem is a creative work that develops not solely from the text or from the reader, but as a result of the transaction between both reader and text. When literature instruction is based on this conception of reading, it becomes a "far more dynamic and unfinalised activity than we might assume from the way literature has been traditionally taught" (Dias and Hayhoe, 1988, p. 21).

Encouraging aesthetic reading in classrooms de-emphasizes the notion of a single, correct reading or interpretation of a text (Spiegel, 1998). It is imperative that teachers accept the idea that each student's reading and interpretation of the text will be unique. Children's interpretations, however, will be connected because they are reading the same text in the same context. Thus, there will be points of contact between student's interpretations. Children must be encouraged to make intertextual connections and to articulate aspects of their personal experiences that are summoned up as they read the text. For emergent readers who are unable to decode print effectively, the role of the teacher becomes pivotal in allowing students to become involved in aesthetic reading of texts.

The Teacher's Role

> The teacher's role is not that of final arbiter of interpretive correctness . . . but rather that of a guide in the development of individual responses to literature. (Harker, 1990, p. 69)

In reader response-based instruction, as in all areas of teaching, teachers play a pivotal role in the outcomes of instruction. This section outlines how teachers of emergent readers (readers who cannot yet read conventionally) become intermediaries between texts and students and how teachers can orchestrate this mediation in ways that live out the reader response philosophy. Also addressed is the importance of an extensive knowledge of children's literature in enhancing reader response teaching initiatives.

Shared Reading: Transaction among Teacher, Text, and Students

One guiding premise of reader response practice is that when readers encounter a text they become involved in dynamic transactions with the text. For emergent readers, the opportunity to become involved in a transaction with text is sometimes hampered because emergent readers cannot yet decode text. This is not always the case; many young children are capable of becoming engaged aesthetically with the text by interpreting the illustrations. To help engage emergent readers in aesthetic reading, teachers serve to bridge the gap between text and students through oral story reading. This approach extends what Templeton terms the "shared book experience" (1995, p. 109), an approach that is already an integral component of many early elementary language arts programs.

In *shared reading* for beginning readers, the teacher reads text to students. However, this reading is not simply a recitation. It involves teachers drawing students into the reading, asking them to join in with the reading. Strategies such as having students join in with repeated phrases, engaging in choral reading, and utilizing oral cloze are used to encourage students to become active participants in shared reading events. "Big Books"—enlarged versions of conventional texts—are often used because they allow students to see the printed text and illustrations from a distance. Shared reading offers an environment in which teachers model many literacy skills (one-to-one pointing, word recognition, reverse sweep, etc.). The group setting can also allow students to become involved in an aesthetic reading event to the degree they feel comfortable. As Rosenblatt suggests, reading of this shared nature allows the "child to adopt the aesthetic stance with pleasant anticipation, without worry about future demands. There will be freedom too for various kinds of spontaneous nonverbal and verbal expressions during the reading" (1982, p. 275).

Now, with such an effective literary experience at teachers' disposal, how can it be modified to encompass a reader response focus?

In shared storybook reading, students become readers by virtue of the narrator, thus the way the narrator presents the story and orchestrates the encounter influences the nature of the emergent reader's engagement. In the shared reading described previously, the students' "reading" focuses primarily on the practice of decoding text and becoming familiar with literacy skills. To transfer to a shared reading that concentrates on nurturing literary response, teachers must change the way shared reading is orchestrated.

Teachers become mediators between text and emergent readers—initiating students' involvement in storybook reading events, supporting or scaffolding their consequent responses, welcoming students into the literary event, encouraging them to become engaged with the text, and building on students' previous literary experiences. Storybook reading events grounded in the reader response approach support each student's lived-through experience with text.

Shared storybook reading becomes a social transaction in which students interpret text within the social milieu of the storybook reading event. The group combines to form what Fish (1980) terms an *interpretive community,* in which students become involved in "the constant activity of choice and revision, the structuring and testing that constitute the total transaction" (Rosenblatt, 1985a, p. 102).

Teachers, along with the text, become an integral component of students' transactions. As narrators, teachers translate written text into a form (spoken language) students can transact with effectively. Translating, however, does not adequately describe the teacher's role. Teachers do more than simply translate; they orchestrate literary events: punctuating the narrative with pauses, questions, and elaboration; modifying the text to enhance the children's understanding; and encouraging children's participation in the story reading event. The talk that develops around the reading becomes a fertile field for response building and growing as naturally as possible (Probst, 1994). Students become actively involved in the literary event. Each student is an individual transacting with the text, but they are not isolated from others in the group. Responses articulated by one student will inform responses of other group members. Students' responses will also guide how the teacher orchestrates storybook reading events.

The term "a happening" (Murphy, 1998; Rosenblatt, 1968) aptly describes shared storybook reading events. The class or group is involved in the same literary happening; however, each individual, although involved in the group happening, is also experiencing his or her own unique literary experience. So, the event becomes, metaphorically speaking, a literary three-ring circus, with numerous individual events occurring as part of the larger literary event. Each individual event will not be totally isolated from those of the other individuals in the group; they will be connected. As Hunsberger suggests "each [reader] will make a personal interpretation. But because the text has a degree of constancy and each reader must attend to the voice of the text, the interpretations will have some aspects in common and cannot be entirely idiosyncratic" (1989, p. 120). With group storybook reading, the closeness of the interpretations may be accentuated because the interpretations are emerging from a single context. However, through careful attention to students' responses, teachers can encourage students to follow the pathways their personal responses take them, and thus the diversity of the overall response of the classroom will be cultivated.

The aim of response-based shared reading is for students to become involved in a variety of forms of response. These forms may include, according to Cox and Many, "students imagining themselves in a character's place in the story events; questioning or hypothesizing about the story; extending a story or creating new stories; making associations with other stories and their own life experiences; and mentioning feelings evoked" (1992, p. 33).

By using carefully selected questions, teachers can challenge students to go beyond the text and participate as active responders. Teachers design global questions that encourage students to delve into their personal experiences of the text: Questions such as:

- While you were listening to this story, did it remind you of anything that has happened in your life?
- Was there a special part of the book that brought back a memory for you?
- Does the story remind you of anything you, your family, or your friends have done?

Questioning and probing must emerge naturally from the text and students' responses. This will occur most effectively when teachers possess a sound knowledge of the literature they will be reading with children. With this knowledge, teachers make informed decisions about what texts they use in their classrooms. Such knowledge is acquired through a number of avenues. Reviews published in literary magazines, educational journals, and newspapers provide a guide to books that may be appropriate material for reader response instruction. Also, consulting with fellow teachers or the school librarian and spending time browsing the shelves in libraries and book stores will help teachers develop familiarity with literature that is available for children.

Teachers must preread books that sound "good" from reviews, then critique them in light of particular questions, such as:

- Does this text offer opportunities for students to explore diverse pathways as they engage with it?
- Do the illustrations tell a story in themselves without support of the text?
- Are there aspects of the text that will connect with students' previous personal and literary experiences?
- Does this text offer opportunities for students to make predictions or extensions?

Teachers' stances as readers are also extremely important to the type of instructional context that unfolds in the classroom. Koeller contends, "teachers who are 'non-readers' [i.e., those who choose not to read] can have a lethal effect upon reading interest" (1981, p. 554). Teachers should endeavor to talk about books as if they are "frequent and familiar friends" (p. 555). Demonstrating a familiarity and affinity with children's literature helps communicate to students that reading can be a lifelong pursuit and that reading is not simply a quest for answers. Students also see their teacher as a partner in the reading pursuit rather than an all-knowing expert.

The following section will outline the form of responses that emergent readers are likely to articulate as a result of their engagement with literary texts.

The Nature of Young Readers' Responses

As Marcus and I shared Burgess's *The Little Father* (1989), he read the lines:

> *But everywhere that Michael went, his father went of course.*
> *If Mr. Master couldn't walk, he rode on Michael's horse* (p. 85).

On completion he commented, "It is sort of like Mary had a little lamb where it says everywhere that Mary went the lamb was sure to go." With this comment, Marcus makes a rudimentary attempt to respond aesthetically. A number of the elements of Marcus' statement are similar to responses that researchers have considered aesthetic response. Rosenblatt (1978) suggests that aesthetic response includes paying attention to "the sound and rhythm of the words in the inner ear, attention to the imprints of past encounters with these words and their referents in differing life and literary contexts" (p. 26). Marcus's statement can be interpreted as his attention to sound and rhythm in the words and their associations with other stories.

Students in their first years at school are in the initial stages of becoming literate. They are developing proficiency at creating representations using conventional written English, and they are becoming effective decoders of print. However, these skills are at varying stages of completeness and hamper children in their quest to read texts aesthetically. They struggle simply to read text conventionally. Students' writing and printing abilities also stifle their articulation of their lived-through experiences with text in written form.

In contrast to this struggle to respond to text as they read and to write down responses, most young children are practiced in creating oral, pictorial/artistic, and dramatic representations. Preschool and early elementary environments, be they the home, some form of early childhood institution, or school, offer children many opportunities to utilize these forms of representation. Although teachers must move students toward utilizing written response, these other modes of response allow students who are not yet accomplished writers to become actively involved in creating and articulating their personal responses to text. Teachers need to encourage children to use these forms of representation to articulate responses to text as stepping-stones toward written forms of response.

Children's artistic representations can be used as an intermediate step toward written response. Once students complete their artistic response, teachers can act as scribes, recording students' verbal descriptions of their artistic representations. These records form the basis for further discussion and represent a model for students' future writing and reading. Stimulus for students' creation of artistic representations should grow out of global questions relating to a particular text—questions that allow students to explore personal evocations. For example:

- I want you to think about the things you thought about while we read this book.
- What pictures came into your mind?
- Did the story remind you of anything? Places you have been? Activities you have participated in?
- Did you feel like you were in the story with the characters?
- Where are you?
- What can you see around you?
- Who is with you?
- How did you feel when the character . . . ?

Teachers cannot predetermine the creative medium students use to exemplify their response; instead, teachers must "avoid undue emphasis upon the form in which the student's reactions are couched" (Rosenblatt, 1976, p. 67). The text and the nature of the literary journey will guide the medium students utilize for articulating their responses. Thus, teachers must offer students a variety of materials to use to articulate their responses.

In early elementary settings, spontaneous responses will often occur outside language arts instructional periods. For example, particular movements in a physical education class may connect with students' interpretations of how a character from a particular text moves. Such responses should be nurtured by praising how connections have been made and exploring these connections further. This allows students to see that literature permeates all areas of the curriculum and is not confined to language arts programs. Students' responses may not only encompass verbal dialogue. Young children will often respond physically in an attempt to articulate their experience of the text. They will live out dramatically the way they perceive particular characters to move or behave. This is a continuation of children's early childhood experiences. Children in their preschool years play out their creative experiences as an effective means of articulating their literary understanding to others (Broad, 1995). They recreate stories as they see them, improvising to suit their lived-through experiences with the text.

Nurturing Literary Response in School-Based Contexts

When talking to and teaching prospective teachers, I am often asked to focus on the "practical"—what happens in the classroom—and not to bother too much about the theory. However, it is difficult to address one without alluding to the other. In the area of reader response, a number of scholars have gone some way to marrying theory with classroom practice. Their work serves as an excellent guide to assist nurturing literary response in school-based contexts.

Rosenblatt applies her literary theory to school-based instruction. She posits two major initiatives for dealing "with the young reader's responses without inhibiting the aesthetic experience" (1982, p. 276). First, a "truly receptive attitude on the part of teachers and peers—and this requires strong efforts at creating such trust—can be sufficient inducement to give spontaneous verbal expression to what has been lived through" (p. 276). It is essential to effective reader response instruction for teachers to create climates in which students feel secure and confident that personal responses to text will be accepted without ridicule. Each student's creative response should be considered both unique and valuable. Secondly, Rosenblatt advises teachers to use questions that are "sufficiently open to enable young readers to select concrete details or parts of the text that had struck them most forcibly. The point is to foster expressions of response that keep the experiential, qualitative elements in mind" (1982, p. 276).

Robert Probst (1990) utilizes Rosenblatt's (1976) *Literature as Exploration* to inform the development of what he terms "principles of instruction," underlying principles for reader response-based teaching at any level:

- Create a feeling of security in the classroom situation and the relationship with the teacher.
- Allow students the freedom to deal with their own reactions to the text.
- Provide the time and opportunity for an initial crystallization of a personal sense of the work.
- Avoid undue emphasis on the form in which the students' reactions are couched.
- Find points of contact among the opinions of students.
- Use the teacher's influence to dwell on the vitality and influence of the literature.
- Although free response is necessary, it is not sufficient. Lead students to reflection and analysis.

In the following section I discuss instructional initiatives that allow teachers to weave these principles into the fabric of literature-based activities in school library and classroom contexts.

The School Library: A Haven for Engagement with Literature

"By going beyond the classroom to the library, reading horizons and children's perceptions of reading are broadened." (Zaidi, 1979, p. 41)

It would be difficult to find a more appropriate context than the school library to utilize as part of reader response-based programs at any level. Libraries offer a literary sanctuary removed from, but still connected to, the classroom. They are environments within the schools in which teachers can promote reading as a pleasurable, risk-free pastime and the lifelong reading habit can be nurtured. Public libraries may also fulfill this purpose, with the added benefit that students become aware that engagement with literature goes beyond the school and into the community. This section discusses literary activities teachers can implement in the text-rich environment of the library, activities that nurture children's aesthetic exploration of literary texts.

For students in the early grades, visits to the school library should be a regular ritual. These visits are not for the sole purpose of borrowing books. In fact, borrowing is a secondary concern. As discussed earlier, whether we like it or not, the classroom is infused with a particular culture and part of this culture is that texts will be used in particular ways. The library possesses a culture that can be different from the classroom, a culture in which expectations for engaging with text are different. It is a context that implores teachers to allow literature to work its magic on readers.

Students can participate in shared reading in the library in a similar manner to that outlined more fully earlier in this chapter. The nature of the library environment—immersed in literature—provides an excellent setting for shared readings to unfold. Well-designed libraries offer cozy nooks where teachers and students can "cuddle up" with a good book, away from the stresses (either real or imagined) of the classroom. Involving students in whole-class literary discussions can form the precursor to students becoming independently involved in similar explorations with text in small groups or pairs.

Moving on from whole-class or group literary events guided by the teacher, teachers can instruct students to participate in browsing, an activity that encourages students to read in aesthetic ways and to move toward independent literary reading. Dias and Hayhoe describe browsing as a communal activity in which students "can be allocated 20 minutes to relax with poetry [or in this case any literary text] the only obligation being to read silently for a while and then to read to one another and chat about what has been read" (1988, p. 83). Once the children become familiar with book browsing routines, they become a "ritualized exploratory behaviour" (p. 82). With young children, teachers must pay careful attention to familiarizing students with the expectations of browsing. Initially, the time spent will be less than the twenty minutes outlined by Dias and Hayhoe. However, five- and six-year-olds can become accomplished at this activity and embark on a myriad of personal and shared journeys through text.

In a class of emergent readers, some students are more capable of participating in browsing than others. This is a result of five- or six-year-old students already having accumulated diverse literary experiences, depending on the social and cultural contexts they have experienced. Those who are capable will launch themselves at the shelves looking for something to capture their interest. These children are familiar with literature and libraries. They use books in appropriate ways, turning the pages carefully and using their rudimentary literacy skills. This ability to interact with literature appropriately has developed through authentic interactions with print during the preschool years, both at home and in other settings (e.g., day care and kindergarten).

Other students, however, have few experiences with literature in their preschool years. These children are not familiar with literature or libraries. For many reasons, they have little experience of books, book sharing, or book reading before they come to school. Books have been a rarity in their lives. Some students may be aware of the particular behavioral expectations within the school environment but unfamiliar with the protocols for using books and unaware of the stories and experiences awaiting them within each book. Others may be disruptive, throwing cushions, disturbing other children, and displaying other inappropriate behaviors. These children do not yet understand the contemplative nature of books. They see books as objects of action. They will "have to learn that books are for reading, not eating, throwing, chewing or building towers" (Snow & Ninio, 1986, p. 122).

These less-experienced students require guidance; otherwise, browsing will become a time when they simply fool around and garner no educational benefit. Modeling the type of behavior students should become involved in during browsing is an effective means of supporting students' initial attempts at browsing. Teachers should bring a group of three to five children who have been observed to be using ineffective browsing techniques together with a selection of books (three to five should be enough). Initially, teachers display the front covers of the books to the group. They give a brief introduction to break the ice. For example, "I have chosen some books for us to read together today. I chose them because they are favorites of mine and I think that there are parts of these books that you will enjoy too. Are there any of the illustrations on the covers that you find interesting, that make you want to look at the story inside?" With this question, the students are directed to the texts and they are asked to bring their own experiences to bear on the conversation by articulating their reasons for choosing a particular book. As students put forward their selections and reasons, teachers can build on them with statements such as: "I like that illustration too, but for a different reason than Jessie.

It reminds me of those warm, windy days that we sometimes have here in the summer." By allowing the students to put forward their ideas first, the notion is generated that what the teacher contributes is of no more value than the students' contributions.

The group then starts to "read" one of the books. This will not be a conventional reading in which the written text is read. Instead the group will interpret the illustrations to create their reading of the text, although the teacher may make some reference to the text. Teachers should make response-like connections in which elements of the text are connected to aspects of students' lives or aspects of other texts. For example, in John Burningham's (1970) rollicking adventure *Mr. Gumpy's Outing*, the event when all the animals, along with Mr. Gumpy, fall into the river could be compared with too many children climbing onto a tire in the playground and, when one child overbalances, everyone falls off. Conversations like this allow students to experience elements of their personal lives being interwoven with elements of the text.

In this modeling activity teachers must be careful not to force their personal interpretations of the text on students. It is quite possible that students may interpret the information provided by the illustrations differently from a reading in which a reader utilizes information from both the written text and the illustrations. Also, what the students bring to the text from their experiences will be different from what the teacher brings. As Probst (1990) argues, "students must be free to deal with their own reactions to the text" (p. 31). With this modeling, students can be guided toward independent browsing as they become aware of the nuances of browsing activities and how to engage with text appropriately.

However, we cannot leave reader response isolated in the library environment. Teachers must transfer the dynamic engagement with text that occurs in the library setting into the classroom context as an integral component of their language arts program.

In the Classroom

> The literary text must not be reduced to an exercise or drill, but must be allowed to live as a work of art, influencing the reader to see, think, and feel. (Probst, 1994, pp. 37–38)

Teaching children to read has been a cornerstone of school-based education since the time that schools became an integral component of society. However, in recent years, as educators have developed programs that highlight learning to read through engagement in authentic reading experiences, some elements of traditional reading instruction have become off-limits for teachers who utilize literature-based reading instruction. These elements include ability grouping for reading instruction (Eder, 1986; Rosenbaum, 1980) and the use of packaged reading resources. This section outlines how teachers can utilize these components of reading instruction while maintaining the integrity of the reading act and living out the reader response philosophy.

Packaged Reading Materials in Reader Response Instruction

The use of packaged materials in reading programs has suffered from the backlash against using basal reading series in classroom programs. However, within the past decade or so, the nature of packaged materials has improved markedly. Previously, authors had written simplified texts with restricted vocabulary, but current series have asked authors to create authentic texts that mirror many characteristics of quality trade books. These texts exemplify literary texts, depicting interesting, exciting events and utilizing vocabulary that replicates natural language. "The vocabulary is not 'controlled' in the sense of a mathematical formula whereby new words are introduced at a predetermined rate. Instead, the control lies in the repetitive nature of the text which arises naturally from the story" (Smith & Elley, 1994, p. 27).

It is not the fact that these "little books" are components of a packaged series that "basalizes" them. Instead, it is how teachers utilize these texts that dictates the type of reading experience students have with them. If teachers use questions with one correct answer derived solely from the text, then students will read the text in that fashion—searching for the "right" answer. Consequently, any lived-through experience they may have with the text will be relegated to the periphery of their reading. In contrast, if students are encouraged to share the connections they make between their personal experiences, other texts, and the text being read, students will undertake a different reading. Teachers must develop an approach that allows students to enhance their strategic reading abilities and encourages them to engage aesthetically with each text.

Grouping Students

At the early elementary level, many teachers have shunned grouping students for reading instruction because groupings are often based on reading ability, resulting in the grouping being seen as a form of labeling. However, in reader response research with older students, placing students in groups has been lauded as an effective way of enhancing readers' responses to text (e.g., Moss, 1998; Leal, 1993; Eeds & Wells, 1989). Group reading and discussion allow students to become involved in "grand conversations" (Eeds & Wells, 1989) about texts and to work as "interpretive communities" (Fish, 1980), collaborating to help one another elaborate on their personal responses. The group setting also provides "a less threatening platform from which to explore . . . meaning" (Leal, 1993, p. 117). In some cases the groups observed in research investigating reader responses have each contained an adult who has, to varying degrees, assisted the students in their responses to text. It may be contended that it was the presence of the adult that allowed the literary discussion groups to work so effectively.

With early elementary-level children, the presence of the teacher in small literary discussion groups is imperative. In these discussion groups, teachers encourage students toward higher levels of aesthetic engagement with texts. For this to happen, the composition of small groups will vary from day to day. Some days, groups will be relatively homogeneous and the activity will be similar to the instruction described in the library for students who require assistance in browsing. A book from a series that can easily be read in one sitting may be used in this activity. The book should be selected with both the students' reading abilities and the book's potential to evoke response in mind. Some attention may also focus on developing students' strategic reading skills in these reading events. In this way, students begin to recognize that engaging aesthetically with text is an integral component of the act of reading.

Another day, groups may be more heterogeneous and may be formed because a particular group of students is interested in reading a particular text. Some children may be able to read the text conventionally, whereas others may have yet to develop the reading skills necessary to read the text effectively. With this type of group, the teacher may ask those who are capable of reading the text to take turns or to read chorally. Those who are unable to read the text will listen, and the teacher will elicit their responses during associated discussion about the text.

Exploring Text

Many students' initial responses are re-creations of the text—a replaying of the events of the story. However, once students are comfortable with this, teachers can encourage students to go beyond the text to create new texts. One way of doing this is to address the "blanks or gaps which occur in the text" (Labercane, 1990, p. 145). An example of a blank is a story focusing on the viewpoint of one character at the expense of another; that is, one character's story is not told. Thus, the blank is what that character's story might have been. When gaps are addressed, students' attention is drawn away from the accepted reading of the text to create a new reading from another point of view. This encourages students to imagine themselves in a character's place in the story event (Cox & Many, 1992).

Take, for example, Pat Hutchins' (1968) *Rosie's Walk,* which simply recounts the journey of Rosie the hen around the farm. However, it is the portrayal in the illustrations of the unsuccessful attempts of the hapless fox to capture Rosie that engage children with the text. After an initial reading, teachers can encourage students to fill the gaps left in the written text—gaps that are obvious in the illustrations. The following questions could be used to encourage students to re-create the text from the fox's focus:

- Which character in this book makes the story exciting/funny?
- Whose story do the words tell?

- Think of yourself as the fox. What would you be thinking or saying in this story?
- How would you feel if you were the fox? at the start? at the end?
- How would you feel if you were Rosie the hen?

Examples of texts that portray stories from another point of view may be used to portray how students can look at a story from other viewpoints. For example, many traditional stories have been rewritten from different viewpoints (e.g., *The true story of the 3 little pigs*, Scieszka, 1996).

Students' responses may also go beyond the text in other ways to what Probst (1992) describes as responding "from" the text. For example, in response to hearing the lines about the organ grinder in *The Potato Man* (McDonald, 1991), James, a seven-year-old, wrote the following:

> The organ grinder man reminded me of an old house in B.C. In the house there's a winding up thing that makes music. You put a disc in to make music. On each disc there is only one song and there's about one hundred discs altogether. You can make the music go slow, fast, or medium. You can put the music fast or medium if you're dancing.

Despite what appears to be a "tenuous connection with the text . . . those reflections might be extremely valuable" (Probst, 1992, p. 118). By engaging in the act of associating two relatively disconnected life experiences, this young reader is dabbling in the initial stages of response to text. Teachers, by accepting these initial forays in response, will pave the way toward more elaborate forms of response.

These activities encourage students to become involved in many literary activities considered to be signs of aesthetic response; for example, "imagining themselves in a character's place in story events, questioning or hypothesising about the story, extending a story or creating new stories" (Cox & Many, 1992, p. 33).

Conclusion

This chapter suggests that reader response-based instruction can be an integral component of early elementary language arts programs. By using methods informed by reader response philosophy, teachers can build on the joyful transactions with text that many students have experienced in their home and/or preschool environments. Also, by immersing students in reader response activities, early elementary teachers prepare students for reader response-based environments they will experience in the balance of their school-based education. Most importantly, reader response approaches allow young readers to see literature as something they can experience at a personal level, rather than something disconnected that is to be endured and completed. Life and literature will be seen as inextricably connected, each interwoven with the other.

REFERENCES

Broad, K. (1995). *An exploratory study of emergent storybook reading: A Rosenblattian approach.* Unpublished masters thesis, University of Calgary, Alberta.

Burgess, G. (1989). The little father. In C. Braun and P. Goepfert (Eds.), *Along the smoky hills* (pp. 82–87). Toronto, Ontario: Nelson.

Burningham, J. (1970). *Mr. Gumpy's outing.* London: Jonathon Cape.

Cox, C., & Many, J. (1992). Toward an understanding of aesthetic response to literature. *Language Arts, 69*(1), 28–33.

Cullinan, B., Harwood, K., & Galda, L. (1983). The reader and the story: Comprehension and response. *Journal of Research and Development in Education, 16*(3), 29–38.

Dias, P., & Hayhoe, M. (1988). *Developing response to poetry.* Milton Keynes, UK: Open University Press.

Duke, C. (1990). Tapping the power of personal response to poetry. *Journal of Reading, 33*(6), 442–47.

Eder, D. (1986). Organizational constraints on reading group mobility. In J. Cook-Gumperz (Ed.), *The social construction of literacy* (pp. 188–155). Cambridge, UK: Cambridge University Press.

Eeds, M., & Wells, D. (1989). Grand conversations: An exploration of meaning construction in literature study groups. *Research in the Teaching of English, 23*(1), 4–29.

Evans, E. (1987). Readers recreating texts. In B. Corcoran & E. Evans (Eds.), *Readers, texts, teachers* (pp. 22–40). Upper Montclair, NJ: Boynton Cook.

Fish, S. (1980). *Is there a text in this class? The authority of interpretive communities.* Cambridge, MA: Harvard University Press.

Graue, M. (1993). Expectations and ideas coming to school. *Early Childhood Research Quarterly, 8,* 53–75.

Harker, J. (1990). Reader response and the interpretation of literature: Is there a teacher in this classroom? *Reflections on Canadian Literacy, 8*(2&3), 69–73.

Hunsberger, M. (1989). Students and textbooks: Which is to be master? *Phenomenology and Pedagogy, 7,* 115–126.

Hutchins, P. (1968). *Rosie's walk.* New York: Macmillan.

Iser, W. (1978). *The act of reading: A theory of aesthetic response.* London, UK: Routledge and Kegan Paul.

Iser, W. (1989). *Prospecting: From reader response to literary anthropology.* Baltimore: Johns Hopkins.

Koeller, S. (1981). Twenty five years advocating children's literature in the reading program. *The Reading Teacher, 34*(7), 552–556.

Labercane, G. (1990). The possible world of the reader. *Reflections on Canadian Literacy, 8*(4), 145–152.

Leal, D. (1993). The power of literary peer-group discussions: How children collaboratively negotiate meaning. *The Reading Teacher, 47*(2), 114–120.

McDonald, M. (1991). *The potato man.* New York: Orchard Books.

Moss, J. (1998). Literary discussion and the quest for meaning. *Teaching and learning literature with children and young adults, 8*(1), 99–109.

Murphy, S. (1998). Remembering that reading is "A way of happening." *Clearing House 72*(2), 89–96.

Pennac, D. (1994). *Better than life.* Toronto, Ontario: Coach House Press.

Prest, P. & Prest, J. (1988). Clarifying our intentions: Some thoughts on the application of Rosenblatt's transactional theory of reading in the classroom. *English Quarterly, 21*(2), 127–133.

Probst, R. (1990). Literature as exploration and the classroom. In E. Farrell & J. Squire (Eds.), *Transactions with literature: A fifty year perspective* (pp. 27–37). Urbana, IL: National Council of Teachers of English.

Probst, R. (1992). Writing from, of, and about literature. In N. Karolides (Ed.), *Reader response in the classroom: Evoking and inventing meaning in literature* (pp. 117–127). White Plains, NY: Longman.

Probst, R. (1994). Reader response and the English curriculum. *English Journal, 83*(1), 37–44.

Rosenbaum, J. (1980). The social implications of educational grouping. In D. Berliner (Ed.), *Review of research in education* (Vol, 8, pp. 361–401). Washington, DC: American Educational Research Association.

Rosenblatt, L. (1968). A way of happening. *Educational Record, 49*(3), 339–346.

Rosenblatt, L. (1976). *Literature as exploration.* New York: Noble and Noble (Original work published in 1938 by Appleton-Century).

Rosenblatt, L. (1978). *The reader, the text, the poem: The transactional theory of the literary work.* Carbondale, IL: Southern Illinois University Press.

Rosenblatt, L. (1982). The literary transaction: Evocation and response. *Theory into Practice, 21*(4), 268–278.

Rosenblatt, L. (1985a). Viewpoints: Transaction versus interaction—a terminological rescue operation. *Research in the Teaching of English, 19*(1), 96–107.

Rosenblatt, L. (1985b). The transactional theory of the literary work: Implications for research. In C. Cooper (Ed.), *Researching response to literature and teaching literature: Points of departure* (pp. 33–53). Norwood, NJ: Ablex.

Rosenblatt, L. (1991). Literary Theory. In J. Flood, J. Jensen, D. Lapp, J. Squire (Eds.), *Handbook of research on teaching of English language arts* (pp. 57–62). Urbana, IL: National Council of Teachers of English.

Scieszka, J. (1996). *The true story of the 3 little pigs.* New York: Penguin Putman.

Smith, J., & Elley, W. (1994). *Learning to read in New Zealand.* Auckland, New Zealand: Longman Paul.

Snow, C., & Ninio, A. (1986). The contracts of literacy: What children learn from learning to read books. In W. Teale & E. Sulzby (Eds.), *Emergent literacy: Reading and writing* (pp. 116–138). Norwood, NJ: Ablex.

Spiegel, D. (1998). Reader response approaches and growth of readers. *Language Arts, 76*(1), 41–48.

Templeton, S. (1995). *Children's literacy: Contexts for meaningful learning.* Boston: Houghton Mifflin.

Wallace, C. (1992). Critical literacy awareness in the CFL Classroom. In N. Fairclough (Ed.), *Critical language awareness* (pp. 59–92). London: Longman.

Wiseman, D., & Many, J. (1992). The effects of aesthetic and efferent teaching approaches on undergraduate responses to literature. *Reading, Research and Instruction, 31*(2), 66–83.

Zaidi, L. (1979). From the primary reading program to the library. In D. Monson & D. McClenathan (Eds.), *Developing active readers: Ideas for parents, teachers and librarians* (pp. 36–43). Newark, NJ: International Reading Association.

3

Challenging the "I" That We Are:

Creating Liberating Constraints with Reader Response Practices

DENNIS J. SUMARA
University of Alberta

Art is the realization of a complex emotion.

—Jeanette Winterson (1995, p. 111)

In recent months I have been asking my teacher education students to bring one-half of a pair of old shoes to class. I tell them that, although this need not be a shoe that they still wear, it must be one for which they continue to feel an attachment. I ask that this shoe be concealed in a bag and that it not be shown to other class members. At the beginning of class, the students are told to pile their bags of shoes in the middle of the room. I do not explain why they have been asked to bring a shoe; however, I do say that there will be an activity that develops around it later in the class. What is the significance of an old shoe?

Interpreting Cultural Objects

Several years ago while visiting Amsterdam, I spent a day at the Van Gogh museum. Because I had read the German philosopher Martin Heidegger's (1977) essay "On the Origin of the Work of Art," in which he provides a description and interpretation of Van Gogh's painting "Old Shoes," I was curious to see the original. In that essay, Heidegger suggests that the work of art retrieves elements from already-lived experience and, by re-presenting in a new form, makes that experience significant. What is usually the uninterpreted ground of experience becomes the figure. As Madeleine Grumet (1988) suggests, "It is the function of art to rearrange experience so it can be seen freshly" (p. 81).

As I stood in front of Van Gogh's painting, I began to notice things about shoes that I had not noticed before. Like all shoes that have been worn, these shoes had inscribed in them the mark of the wearer and the history of the wearing. I found that in order to come to an understanding of this painting I had to overcome my desire to dash around the museum looking at everything and, instead, had to stay in one place for a while meditating on this painting. Jeanette Winterson (1995) writes about the importance of moving slowly when in the presence of the work of art: "For myself, now that paintings matter, public galleries are much less dispiriting. I have learned to ignore everything about them, except for the one or two pieces with whom I have come to spend the afternoon" (p. 8). Interpreting the work of art requires that time be made so that a relationship with it can be developed. As I stood in front of the painting, I imagined the old peasant woman that Heidegger described and, at the same time, was reminded of other persons who wore shoes. I thought about the white "clinic" shoes that my mother dutifully cleaned with white, liquid roll-on polish before setting out each day for work at Park's Dry Cleaners. I remembered how these shoes always sat at the foot of the stairs leading to the kitchen of the modest bungalow that my parents, both immigrants from Europe, built from discarded materials from the old municipal hospital shortly after their arrival in Lethbridge, Alberta, in 1952.

Developing a relationship with this painting meant engaging in an act of interpretation. Interpreting the painting meant invoking my own memories. Of course, it was not only the associations amongst the shoes in the painting that I interpreted; it was the relationships announced by shoes. The shoes that I remembered were not just *any* shoes—they were my mother's shoes. At that moment I became positioned in the middle of memories that had been collected by my developing relationship with this painting. The painting announced what I call a *commonplace location* for the interpretation of past, present, and projected experiences. Not only was I now thinking about events from the past in relation to my current situation of viewing the painting, I was wondering about events that had not yet occurred. Assembled before the painting "Old Shoes" was a multiplicity of selves: those from the past, the present, and the not-yet-lived. The painting was what Maurice Merleau-Ponty (1962) would call a "cultural object":

> Just as nature finds its way to the core of my personal life and becomes inextricably linked with it, so behaviour patterns settle into that nature, being deposited in the form of a cultural world. Not only have I a physical world, not only do I live in the midst of earth, air and water, I have around me roads, plantations, villages, streets, churches, implements, a bell, a spoon, a pipe. Each of these objects is molded to the human action which it serves. . . . In the cultural object, I feel the close presence of others beneath a veil of anonymity. *Someone* uses the pipe for smoking, the spoon for eating, the bell for summoning, and it is through the perception of a human act and another person that the perception of a cultural world could be verified. (p. 347)

The relations that we form with others are always mediated by the cultural objects that surround us and others—cultural objects that carry a trace of the histories of their use. Getting to know others depends on understanding the way in which their experience and their actions are mediated by objects. It is impossible to make clear distinctions between persons and the things that surround them. Nor is it possible to understand things in the absence of knowledge about how they are used. Heidegger (1977) suggests that one cannot know about things by merely looking at them; knowing about them means having an understanding of how they are used, an understanding that can only occur in the relationship developed when subject and object become engaged in use. The painting, like a pair of shoes, is an historical object that has participated in the lived experiences of the painter and of those who have viewed the painting. This suggests that in order to understand present experience, we must not only study the history of experience but, as well, we must study the *things* that mediate experience.

I could not gaze at the picture of the shoes without thinking about my reading of Heidegger's essay. I wondered what prompted him to believe that these shoes belonged to an old peasant woman. I could not tell, merely by looking, whether these were men's or women's shoes. At the same time, I could not look at the painting without thinking about his interpretation. The essay "On the Origin of the Work of Art" existed with the painting. More specifically, my *memory* of reading that essay existed alongside my present viewing of the painting. I was experiencing what writers such as Julia Kristeva (1984) and Roland Barthes (1974) have called *intertextuality*—a moment when several experiences are collected in one place. Like all newly collected experiences, these required some interpretation.

It is not surprising that I thought of my mother's work shoes when looking at this painting. Like the woman Heidegger describes, my mother worked long hours on her feet. I remember how, as a child, I noticed how worn her work shoes became. I remember how these shoes came to represent, for me, the work life she lived. It is also significant that my mother, like Heidegger, spoke German as her first language. Perhaps my attraction to Heidegger's writing is, in part, an attraction to a way of thinking to which I am genealogically and experientially attached. Whether this is so or not, it seems clear to me that the intertextual associations and the eventual interpretations of my reading of Heidegger's essay, my viewing of Van Gogh's painting, and my memories of my mother and of my childhood relationship with her announced a new commonplace location that required further interpretation.

Like visual works of art, literary texts function as cultural objects. And, like other cultural objects, the literary text comes to represent the histories of its use. The literary text, when read, also mediates and collects the experiences and the interpretations of the reader. In order to interpret the text the reader must develop a relationship with it. This relationship may remain superficial—a simple comprehending of the details of the text as these are understood in relation to the reader's own knowledge. Or, this relationship may become more complex. In order for this to occur, the commonplace location announced by a reading of the text must be allowed to develop more fully. It must become enlarged with new associations arising from specific reading and writing practices.

Creating Generous Commonplace Locations

After asking my students to pile their bags of shoes in the middle of the room, I begin class by reading them Mem Fox's (1985) children's book titled *Wilfrid Gordon*

McDonald Partridge. The main character in this book is a little boy named Wilfrid who learns from his parents that his good friend, ninety-six-year-old Miss Nancy, has "lost" her memory. Because Wilfrid does not understand what this means, he asks his parents and a few of the residents at the senior citizens' home where Miss Nancy resides the question, "What's a memory?" They tell him that memory is something: that you remember that is warm, that is from long ago, that makes you cry, that makes you laugh, and that is as precious as gold.

Once Wilfrid learns that memory is important, he becomes concerned that Miss Nancy has lost hers. He decides to help by collecting things that are meaningful to him: a box of sea shells, a puppet, a medal given to him by his grandfather, a football, and a fresh warm egg. He carries these specially selected objects to Miss Nancy and, one by one, hands them to her. As she and Wilfrid examine the objects, she begins to remember: the blue speckled eggs she had found in a bird's nest in her aunt's garden, going to the beach as a child, a big brother who had gone to war and never returned, and a puppet she had shown to her sister. As she remembers, she tells Wilfrid the stories connected to these memories.

Like Patricia Polacco's (1988) *The Keeping Quilt* and Phoebe Gilman's (1992) *Something from Nothing,* this children's picture book shows the way in which certain cultural objects mediate interpersonal, intertextual, and intergenerational memories.[1] The objects that Wilfrid brings to Miss Nancy create a location for the retrieval of memory, for the evocation of stories announced by these memories, and for the interpretation of them. For me, the book itself began to function as such a cultural object. As I continued to pass it around to friends and to enter into discussions with them about it, the book continued to provide a focal point, a collecting place for my and others' interpretations. These interpretations were not just of the book; like the conversations between Miss Nancy and Wilfrid Gordon, these conversations came to include many memories and events that were announced by our shared reading of the book. This children's picture book and my responses to it became part of the commonplace location that had been created with my viewing of Van Gogh's painting and my reading of Heidegger's essay. It was within the commonplace location that I began the process of interpreting already formulated knowledge and the process of creating new knowledge. Deciding to incorporate this book into my teaching, then, was not merely the addition of a text into my teaching practices, it was the incorporation of a complex set of relations and interpretations that existed with my relationship with this book.

It is important to understand that the commonplace location does not exist "in" the work of literature or "in" the reader. Nor does the commonplace location exist in what Rosenblatt (1978) has called the "transaction" between reader and text. The commonplace location, in itself, is not a thing; it cannot be captured as an object. The commonplace location is an idea that represents the complex and ever-evolving intertextual relations that collect around a particular interpretive activity. Reading is one such activity. During and after reading, many associations are made with the text. As reading occurs, the reader is reminded of other experiences. At the same time, as the reader begins to interpret the new reading in relation to what is remembered and associated, these memories and associations change. It is the process of memory and re-memory that is mediated by the reading and interpreting of the text. Although this occurs with all texts that are read, the literary text has the poten-tial to create more elaborate and intricate interpretations.[2]

Wolfgang Iser (1978, 1993) has suggested that this is so for two reasons. First, when a text is "announced" as fiction, the reader understands that she or he must read it as fiction. This means that the reader suspends disbelief, allowing the implausibilities in an imaginative text to be accepted and, as a consequence, creat-ing an interpretive position for the reader that is fuller than those developed with other texts. Second, literary texts have more "gaps and spaces" for the reader to negotiate. Barthes (1974) calls this a "writerly" text, in which the reader must "write in" information in order for the text to become meaningful. The work of lit-erary fiction, then, has the potential to immerse the reader in a more elaborate and imaginative experience and, therefore, usually allows for a more intricate and complex commonplace location for interpretation.

When literary texts are shared with others, the commonplace location creates opportunities for interpersonal and intertextual interpretation. As a cultural object that bears the mark and trace of its own history, the work of literary fiction, like other cultural objects (such as the objects that Wilfrid Gordon brought to Miss Nancy), mediates and collects various remembered, lived, and projected experi-ences. As I am reading *Wilfrid Gordon McDonald Partridge* to my teacher education students, I do so in order to begin the process of individual and collective interpre-tation. I understand that as I read this particular book to them they will begin to make connections between the cultural objects that the characters in the book use to mediate experience and cultural objects that they remember. As well, I under-stand that this shared reading of a literary fiction will become part of the collective commonplace location that we inhabit as a group of readers. I also understand that, in order to make the responses that come to be included in these shared read-ings more generous, I need to intervene in the reading process with specific response practices.

Creating Liberating Constraints
with Reader Response Practices

After reading *Wilfrid Gordon McDonald Partridge* to the students, I ask that they do a five-minute timed writing that begins with the prompt: "As I listened to the story I was reminded of. . . ." In her books about living a writer's life, Natalie Goldberg (1990, 1993) suggests that timed writings are necessary to unleash thoughts and ideas that are bubbling below the surface of our conscious daily experience. Because most of my students have fears about writing, following Rebecca Luce-Kapler (see Chapter 5), I have begun to use structured timed writing as a way to begin the process of capturing layers of response to literature so that these become materially present and available for interpretation. Adapting techniques used by both Goldberg and Luce-Kapler, I explain to students that these timed writings consist of continuous, uninterrupted writing that is meant to reveal the various associations that a reader has made to a particular literary work. I explain that it is important for the writer to "suspend judgment" and not censor or edit what appears on the page. I also explain that, although these writings will eventually become part of a collection of material that is interpreted, they are not writings that students are required to share publicly. Although the timed writings often reveal deeply personal, surprising, and sometimes troubling insights to the writer, these function as material for later work, rather than material that is publicly disclosed or subject to the evaluative gaze of the teacher; therefore, students seem able to participate fully in the timed writing activities.

Although this timed writing is a form of response to literature, for me it is not the most significant aspect of the response experience, but only the first in a series of "collecting" activities. Immediately after this writing practice, I ask students to move with me to a shared reading of another work of literature. In the sequence of reading and responding that is associated with the "old shoes" activity, I follow the Mem Fox book with two poems from Michael Ondaatje's (1989) poetry collection *The Cinnamon Peeler.* The first poem, "Light," expresses the experience of interpreting intergenerational memories through the activity of looking at old photographs. The second poem, "Her House," describes the way in which a person's house becomes inextricable from her sense of self-identity.

Although I believe that students need to have opportunities to respond personally to literature, I also strongly believe that these responses need to be developed within forms that I call "liberating constraints." Like the literary text, these forms function to condition students' experiences but not overly constrain them. As well, they situate students in experiences that are, at the same time, familiar and strange. Although reading and responding to poetry in class is familiar, the specific response practices that I use are less familiar.

Because I have an audiotape of Michael Ondaatje reading "Light," I play it rather than orally reading the poem myself. Students are asked to follow along with photocopies of the poem that I hand out. I play the recording three times. The first time I ask students to follow along without making notes. The second time I ask them to underline, circle, or in some other way, mark words or phrases that are interesting to them. After this second reading, I ask them to choose *one* word or phrase and, on a clean sheet of paper, copy the entire line of poetry in which the chosen word occurs. A ten-minute timed writing follows, beginning with the prompt: "This line of poetry is interesting to me because. . . ." I then ask that they reread what they have written and underline or circle anything in the passage that represents some new learning or insight. I do this so that students begin to identify the way in which new learning emerges from associations made in response to the reading of literature. Following this, I play the poem again, asking students to mark on their copies anything that has new significance or interest for them. Once again, I ask them to identify an interesting word or phrase, to copy out the line, and to engage in a timed writing. As with the previous writing, students are asked to examine this writing and to select words or phrases that represent new ideas or new thinking.

Although at this point students are already producing a great deal of writing in response to the repeated oral readings of the poem, I refrain from asking for any sharing or discussion. I do so for two reasons. First, much of this response is not fully formulated. Although associations have occurred and interpretations have been made, these are usually only tentative. It is true that with each successive reading of the poetry the students become more deeply involved with the poem and the interpretive location developing around it; however, without making the explicit move to include other texts and other experiences, these responses are overly personalized and, as a consequence, often not interesting for others. Second, even though I believe that response to literature should include opportunities for students to explore personal associations they are making to the reading of literature, I also believe that these responses must be, in some way, resymbolized before they are made available for public examination. Just as the poet or the novelist must work to reinterpret her or his experience and knowledge into a new form, so, too, must the student who is engaged in interpretive work within the commonplace locations that are created around the reading of literature.

Therefore, rather than discussing this poem and our successive rereadings of it, I move into another reading and responding activity, this time using the poem "Her House." I choose this poem because, like "Light," it shows the way in which the objects that circumscribe our experience become inextricable from our sense of self and cultural identity. Again, I move students through at least three readings of the poem, the latter two followed by a timed writing that is initiated with a specific writing prompt. Sometimes the prompt asks that students elaborate a word or phrase of interest; other times, I ask them to respond to a particular idea or issue raised by the poem. Regardless of the sort of prompt used, the structure of the response seldom varies. I have found that this "constraint" helps to "liberate" students from the "write whatever you want" model that, for many, is paralyzing. Also, the prompt coupled with the timing of the writing oftentimes elicits associations that are surprising to students. It is this, I find, that helps produce more imaginative written responses that become important in the next stage of response interpretations.

Because I am able to work with teacher education students for long stretches of time (always at least three hours, sometimes a morning and an afternoon consisting of a total of six hours), I feel able to slow down—to conduct repetitions of readings and responses to the same reading—knowing that there will be time for the synthesizing, resymbolizing, and continued interpretations that occur with these various reading and writing practices. When I do this work with elementary or high school students, I use the same sorts of activities over a minimum of a two-week period. Over the years I have learned that this way of structuring response can only work if the teacher is able to and prepared to slow down the usual trot through the curriculum.

Learning to See Freshly

Jeanette Winterson (1995) explains that the familiarity of the everyday often prevents writers from producing work that functions as art:

> The more familiar a thing becomes the less it is seen. In the home, nobody looks at the furniture; they sit on it, eat off it, sleep on it and forget it until they buy something new. . . . Our minds work to continually label and absorb what we see and to fit it neatly into our own pattern. (p. 143)

Although the literary work must, in order to be understood, use familiar elements from the reader's world, this familiarity must be interrupted. Winterson suggests that good writers deliberately try to create conditions in their lives that will help them see familiar things in new ways. I have come to believe that, in addition to providing these skills for writers, we must provide them for readers. Although schools are becoming more and more proficient at teaching students to read, they are not very adept at teaching students *how* to read. This is especially true in secondary schools. Although students are taught how to hunt for metaphors, symbols, and themes, they are not usually taught how to develop a meaningful relationship with a literary work.

In my work with readers of all ages (from elementary school to graduate school), I discuss with the students with whom I read the *manner* and *conditions* of reading that, I believe, create more interpretive locations for response. For example, I suggest to students that although familiar forms of fiction are pleasurable and comforting and oftentimes provide the kind of "escape" that we desire in our reading of fiction, these forms do not challenge us to see things in new ways. If literature is meant to rearrange our familiar worlds, then it, in itself, must immerse us in an unfamiliar form. These forms (such as the literary work of Virginia Woolf, Toni Morrison, Michael Ondaatje, and Jeanette Winterson) are often difficult to read. They must be read slowly. And they must be reread. The first reading only provides a general sense of the geography of the text. It is in successive readings that the needed relationship begins to form between reader and text. This relationship is necessary for the continued development of the commonplace location.

In addition, I suggest to students that the reading and rereadings are more interesting if some trace of these readings is made. Because many readers dislike interrupting their reading to write in a reader response journal (I am such a reader), I ask that they keep track by making notes directly in the book. If these are books that the reader does not own, I ask that they use sticky notes to mark places of interest and that they write on these notes. With poetry, I generally provide photocopies of the poem that will be studied so students can make a variety of markings on the page. Whether students mark directly on the text or on sticky notes that eventually become part of the text, these "traces," when read during a rereading of the text, become very interesting for the readers. Not only do the readers begin to understand how knowing the contents of the entire work affects their original interpretations, depending on the amount of time between the readings, they come to sense how they, as readers, have changed since the previous reading. Making successive markings over a period of days and weeks has proven to be a most interesting way for my students and me to notice how our interpretations of literary works coevolve with our senses of individual and collective identities.

Even if all the responses are made in one day, as is the case with the two poems "Light" and "Her House" that I discussed previously, readers become aware of how quickly and dramatically their responses to, and interpretations of, a work of literature change. They also become aware of how their timed-writing activities come to coexist with their reading of and response to the literary work. With each successive wave of rereading and timed writing, the response becomes increasingly complex. It is these rereading and rerehending processes that, I believe, create beginning conditions for the interruption of the familiar, because with each successive response new and more unusual associations are made. The *Wilfrid Gordon McDonald Partridge* book and the Ondaatje poems are concerned with the way human experience is circumscribed and mediated by things and with how these things are inextricable from our memories. Not surprisingly then, many of the students begin to write about personal and family objects that have meaning for them. They also begin to make associations between these objects and specific personalities and events that they associate with these objects. Because I do not want students to remain for too long in the narrow band of the personal, I move into the shoe activity as a way to interrupt the familiarity of these readings and the response evoked.

Fictionalizing Acts

After removing all of the old shoes from their bags and heaping them into a shoe mountain, I ask students to select one shoe that is not theirs and that they do not recognize as anyone else's in the room. I then ask that they examine this shoe, paying close attention to details of the construction and marks of wear. I ask that they not communicate with one another while doing this. After approximately five minutes, I ask them to place the shoe on the desk or table directly in front of them and to move into a twenty- to thirty-minute writing that begins with the prompt: "This shoe is interesting to me because. . . ." Before allowing them to write, I encourage them to focus on the shoe while they are writing, but not to feel constrained by the shoe. Although they will begin by attending to the shoe, oftentimes the various associations that they make while writing will move them into a topic that is related to, but not necessarily directly concerned with, the shoe.

Once this timed writing is completed, I ask them to reread what they have written and mark passages, phrases, or images that are interesting to them. I also ask them to identify some portion of the writing that they would be willing to read to the rest of the class. At this point, of course, students become very interested, not so much in their own writing, but in what others may have written about their shoe. Before beginning the reading, I ask that students rearrange their desks or tables into a circle. I also ask that they place the shoe that they have been writing about on the tabletop in front of them, and, most importantly, I ask that no students identify their own shoe. Students then begin to read what they have written about the shoes. In every instance, the writing not only reveals descriptive details about the shoe but also speculations about the possible histories of the shoe. Although the writers are usually unaware of the shoe's owner or lived history, they create detailed descriptions and expositions of possible situations, possible events, and possible relationships: A high-heeled, white, ladies' sandal participates in a wedding ceremony on a sailboat; a chewed-up thong becomes complicit in a robbery; and a scuffed, brown hiking boot goes trekking in Nepal. All of these situations, of course, are enacted by very specific characters who, for the most part, are given interesting and well-developed personalities.

After these writing and reading practices around the "old shoe," I ask students to engage in a ten-minute reflective writing that begins with the prompt: "Hearing _____'s writing about my shoe has provoked me to think about. . . ." This, of course, becomes a very interesting response activity since the writer is responding to someone else's interpretation of an artifact that has personal significance to her or him. Although the just-disclosed writing about the shoe was wholly fictional, it now necessarily exists alongside each person's own memories of that shoe. Once this writing is completed, I ask each student to identify the shoe they have brought and to say a few words about why they selected it, including something about the shoe's history. Although this sharing generates a great deal of laughter, it also opens up a very interesting interpretive space. Some of the students, for example, are amazed at how close the invented situations were to their memories of the shoes' histories. Even when the invented narrative and the remembered narratives are very different, the writer and the shoe owner become complicit together in developing new interpretations of the shoe. And so, although Marla's white high-heeled shoe had not been part of a wedding on a sailboat, but rather had been worn to a high school graduation, the two stories suddenly existed together and, in interesting ways, began to become involved with one another. Marla suggested, in fact, that she would never be able to look at her old, white high-heeled shoe without remembering the story that Jeff had constructed around it. The telling of a fictionalized story participated in the continual evolution of memories that were evoked by the shoe. Also, because the invented story and the remembered story now coexisted, each participated in the ever-changing commonplace location announced by the shoe. I use these various reading and writing activities, and the interpretations sponsored by these activities, to help all readers begin to understand how their remembered and fictionalized interpretations of literary texts and other cultural objects participate in the complex act of identity formation and re-formation.

Inventing and Discerning

At this point in the unit of study, I ask students to revisit all of the products of their various writing practices that have accumulated around the reading of *Wilfrid Gordon McDonald Partridge* and the poems "Light" and "Her House" and from the shoe activities. I ask them to choose *three* images or ideas from these writings and to represent each in one sentence. One of these should emerge from the children's picture book, one from one of the poems (or some combination of the two), and one from the shoe activity. I ask them to write these three sentences on a fresh sheet of paper. I then ask them to examine these three sentences and imagine what relationships there might be among them. This often seems very strange to them because the three images or ideas they have chosen are seldom obviously connected or related. However, despite the difficulty and ambiguity of the task, I insist that students make the move from these various personal and interpretive responses to some resymbolized form of them. I call this writing activity *intertextual chaining,* and the connections that they make between these sentences *intertextual links.* Because students now must work to make sense of these often-disparate ideas, I allow them several days to work on it, asking that they create a short piece of writing that explains and interprets what has emerged for them by juxtaposing various interesting ideas that have come from their responses.

What is the significance of this assigned interpretive writing? As I have explained, the very reading of and responding to the literary text announces a complex set of relations and interpretive possibilities that I have called the *commonplace location.* In order for this commonplace location to function as a site for "seeing freshly," the responses must become resymbolized into something more akin to a work of art. I believe that the commonplace locations that develop around the reading and response to literary works of art are, in themselves, meant to become generous places for such creation, particularly when these are developed around intertextual reading and response activities such as the ones I have just described. By collecting together layers of written response from multiple readings of a literary work, the reader creates a material form that represents associations and interpretations that have been made. Although these are often, in themselves, very interesting, in my view they are insufficient. In order for these responses to become useful and productive for the reader and for those who are interested in the reader's responses, they must become resymbolized.

It is this process of resymbolization that transforms the responses produced in the various timed writings into a form that allows a more complex interpretation of the relationship between the reader and the text to develop. In important ways, it is this new form that, in itself, begins to function as a literary work, inviting further response and further interpretation. If, as Iser (1993) suggests, readers produce new knowledge about themselves through engagements with literary texts, then that new knowledge begins to function alongside existing knowledge. Because the reader's sense of identity emerges, in part, from perceived and interpreted knowledge about the world, response to reading alters a reader's sense of self. As the text is interpreted, the reader is interpreted. Iser (1993) also suggests that what the reader has to say about the text is not nearly as interesting as what the text says about the reader. Adding interpretations of a literary text to one's store of knowledge contributes to one's evolving sense of self in the present world. At the same time, this knowledge participates in the process of reinterpreting memories of past events and projections of future events.

The various timed writings that I ask students to accomplish, then, are not merely fragments of response that exist alongside the life of the reader. In interesting ways, these responses represent the emergence of the reader's evolving sense of self. Crafting these responses into a new form is necessary, but it is not easy. As Winterson (1995) suggests, making something new requires that particular knowledge and skill be readily available. She writes:

Invention is the shaping spirit that re-forms fragments into new wholes, so that even what has been familiar can be seen fresh. Discernment is to know how to test the true and the false and to reveal objects, emotions, ideas in their own coherence. The artist is a translator; one who has learned how to pass into her own language the language gathered from stones, from dreams, from the body, from the material world, from the invisible world, from sex, from death, from love. A different language is a different reality. (p. 146)

Invention requires discernment. It requires that the inventor understand that a new language, a new way of representing the familiar must be developed. Because I teach literature in the context of English language arts settings, I insist that students struggle with the difficulty of transforming their initial responses into a form that functions as a literary text. This does not mean that they must write poetry or short stories or plays from their responses (although they may, and, indeed, some do). It does mean, however, that like the painter and the poet, they must learn to discern what elements from their responses can be juxtaposed in a manner that creates a generous location for another reader's interpretations. Just as the juxtaposing of the shoe activity with the children's book and the Ondaatje poetry created what I would call a "literary" learning experience for them, I ask that they juxtapose elements of their response for the reader in their resymbolized work. Because students often do not know how to begin this process, I assign the intertextual chains as the next layer in the response activities. Although I usually ask students to do only one chain (using three sentences from three of the other responses activities), I also mention that they might like to try this with two or even three sets of three. Usually, students require some practice making intertextual links between ideas.

Interrupting Familiar Patterns

The intertextual chaining activity is still not the final step in the resymbolizing of response process. Once students have completed to their satisfaction one of these "chained" writings, I ask that these be read to the class. Because I want students to choose language precisely, I ask that their readings be limited to three to four minutes. These oral readings become highly ritualized affairs. Usually, I set aside a large chunk of time for these readings. Whether in the university or the school setting, I try to allow for an entire morning or afternoon. My usual procedure is to ask each student to read what he or she has written to the rest of the class. I tell them that they are not allowed to say anything at all about what they are about to read. They are not to contextualize it, apologize for it, or defend it. They are simply to read it. While each person reads, others in the class listen carefully, jotting down any words that represent associations they are making as the reading is occurring. Following the reading, I ask each person in the class to engage in a one- to two-minute timed writing in which each person responds to what the person has read. I explain that these responses are not meant to be congratulatory, nor critical. Rather, the responses should represent associations and connections that the reading announced for them. Once short responses have been made, they are passed to the reader. Because I time the reading and the response practices, each presentation takes no more than five to seven minutes. Also, because each student moves through the same process of reading, responding, and collecting notes related to the reading, the morning or afternoon of reading and response becomes an intense and very focused experience of thinking.

At the end of all the readings, I ask all students to spend fifteen minutes writing out their interpretations of the morning's activities. I ask them to make special note of any common themes that seemed to have occurred in the writing, including any connections they made for themselves that they found interesting. Finally, I conduct a whole-class discussion of what new ideas and images have been produced that morning. I also ask that they identify the particular *conditions* that helped all of us to see and understand in new ways.

As the final stage in the response process, I ask that students take home all of their notes to read and reread several times, making further notes about ideas and associations that are interesting and helpful to them. The notes from others, their responses to them, their notes resulting from the experience of listening to others' writings emerging from the shared reading of other texts, and their own intertextual chain writing then function as a new set of texts from which they are to create some new writing. Because by this point students have had a great deal of practice generating experimental and response writing and have had many opportunities to share their own and listen to others' responses to the various literary texts studied, they have fewer fears and anxieties about continuing to write from these experiences.

Inventing a New Reader

Theorists such as Appleyard (1990), Grumet (1991), Hunsberger (1985, 1992) and Rosenblatt (1938, 1978), who have pondered and interpreted the experience of reading literature, suggest that these events are transformative for the reader. Because the literary text positions readers in a world that is simultaneously familiar and unfamiliar, new insights and interpretations arise. Although this new knowledge emerges from a fictional experience, like all experiences, it becomes encoded into the reader's memory and begins to function as a lived reference point. What is imagined is often as influential as any other experience.

However, in order for the literary text to do its work, the reader must be able to establish a meaningful relationship with it. This does not mean merely comprehending the plot or being able to identify figures of speech. It also does not mean simply providing an immediate personal response to a first reading. Meaningful relationships with literary texts take time to develop. They require a more prolonged engagement. This means that the text needs to be read more than once. It also means that some "trace" of the various readings must become materially present for further interpretation. For those of us who work in public education institutions this need is difficult to fulfill because, of course, there is a strong desire to "cover the curriculum" by touring through as many texts as possible. I believe, however, that as difficult as it may be, these demands must be strongly resisted. If we are to help our students learn to think, we must teach them how to see with new eyes, to hear with new ears. Learning to perceive freshly cannot be imposed or willed on oneself or others. As any artist knows, it requires that a particular set of conditions be created and a particular set of skills learned.

It is my view that it is the teacher's responsibility, not only to teach students to read, but to teach them *how* to read. Although we are becoming better at teaching how to read in the content areas, I believe that we still have much to learn about how to teach students to read literature. The sequence of reader response activities that I have described in this chapter is one I have been developing to help create conditions for more imaginative and creative readings. I have learned that students cannot simply be told to be imaginative and creative with their responses. Conditions and forms must be created to make this work possible. Particular skills and strategies also must be taught.

Teaching Response

Although I have described a specific sequence of activities that I do with adults in pre-service teacher education classes, all of the techniques and skills can be adapted to readers of any age. I have used these approaches to reader response from Grades Five through Nine. Graduate students of mine have used them with children through elementary and secondary school. Although the procedures are modified, there are common features in all this teaching.

First, literary texts must be read and responded to more than once. By examining the trace (the response) of a previous reading, readers begin to notice how dramatically their interpretations have changed. Most importantly, they begin to notice how their readings of literature have influenced their real lives and senses of self-identity.

Second, a literary text must be read alongside other literary texts, as well as alongside other cultural objects. These intertextual readings help to construct a broader and more complex commonplace location for interpretation. When accomplished with groups of readers in the classroom, these intertextual responses facilitate complex interpersonal relations among student readers and their teacher.

Third, written or oral responses to literary texts must have form. They must have structure. By offering prompts, by timing responses, by reading and interpreting one response in relation to another using intertextual chaining, teachers help students to become positioned in interpretive locations that function as liberating constraints. It is within such locations that students begin the process of making unique forms emerge from their literary readings.

Fourth, students' responses to literary texts must, at some stage, become resymbolized into a form that functions like a literary text. This does not mean that they need to create a novel, a short story, a play, or a poem. It does mean, however, that they must learn to create new forms to express familiar ideas. It is the resymbolization process, the creation of new form, that comes to represent more fully the complexity of the commonplace locations that students have developed through their shared reading of literary texts in the classroom.

Finally, it is important for the teacher to understand that, although students must be given opportunities to respond in many different ways, the responses must be contained in a structured form. The response activities and forms that I have described in this chapter differ from the "hunt for the literary device" that is still commonly used in English language arts classrooms; they also differ from the open-ended response journal method that has become common. Although I do feel that both of these are still useful, I strongly believe that the teacher, like the literary artist, must create specific liberating constraints in order to facilitate the production of interesting, imaginative responses to literature. In so doing, teachers not only create the possibilities for understanding, they also create possibilities for transformation. This, in my view, should always be the primary reason for including shared readings of literature in the classroom. As Winterson (1995) suggests: "True art, when it happens to us, challenges the 'I' that we are" (p. 15).

E N D N O T E S

1. Three recent Newbery award-winning young adult novels are also developed around the idea of memory, interpretation, and intergenerational knowledge. They are Cynthia Rylant's (1992) *Missing May,* Lois Lowry's (1993) *The Giver,* and Sharon Creech's (1994) *Walk Two Moons.* I have used all three alongside *Wilfrid Gordon McDonald Partridge, The Keeping Quilt,* and *Something From Nothing* with young adult and adult readers. Together these six works of literature provoke an interesting commonplace location for interpretation.

2. I develop this idea much more fully in my book *Private Readings in Public: Schooling the Literary Imagination* (1996).

R E F E R E N C E S

Appleyard, J. A. (1990). *Becoming a reader: The experience of fiction from childhood to adulthood.* New York: Cambridge University Press.

Barthes, R. (1974). *S/Z.* New York: Hill and Wang.

Creech, S. (1994). *Walk two moons.* New York: Harper Collins.

Fox, M. (1985). *Wilfrid Gordon McDonald Partridge.* Brooklyn, NY: Kane/Miller.

Gilman, P. (1992). *Something from nothing.* Richmond Hill, Ontario: North Winds Press.

Goldberg, N. (1990). *Wild mind: Living the writer's life.* New York: Bantam Books.

Goldberg, N. (1993). *Long quiet highway: Waking up in America.* New York: Bantam Books.

Grumet, M. (1988). *Bitter milk: Women and teaching.* Amherst, MA: University of Massachusetts Press.

Grumet, M. (1991). Lost places, potential spaces and possible worlds: Why we read books with other people. *Margins 1*(1), 35–53.

Heidegger, M. (1977). *Basic writings.* San Francisco: HarperCollins.

Hunsberger, M. (1985). The experience of re-reading. *Phenomenology + Pedagogy, 3,* 161–166.

Hunsberger, M. (1992). The time of texts. In W. F. Pinar & W. M. Reynolds (Eds.). *Understanding curriculum as phenomenological and deconstructed texts.* (pp. 64–91). New York: Teachers College Press.

Iser, W. (1978). *The act of reading.* Baltimore: Johns Hopkins University Press.

Iser, W. (1993). *The fictive and the imaginary: Charting literary anthropology.* Baltimore: Johns Hopkins University Press.

Kristeva, J. (1984). *Revolution in poetic language.* New York: Columbia University Press.

Lowry, L. (1993). *The Giver.* New York: Bantam Doubleday Dell Books.

Merleau-Ponty, M. (1962). *Phenomenology of perception.* London: Routledge.

Ondaatje, M. (1989). *The cinnamon peeler.* Toronto, Ontario: McClelland and Stewart.

Polacco, P. (1988). *The keeping quilt.* New York: Simon & Schuster.

Rosenblatt, L. (1938). *Literature as exploration.* New York: Appleton-Century.

Rosenblatt, L. (1978). *The reader, the text, the poem.* Carbondale, IL: Southern Illinois University Press.

Rylant, C. (1992). *Missing May.* New York: Orchard Books.

Sumara, D. (1996). *Private readings in public: Schooling the literary imagination.* New York: Peter Lang.

Winterson, J. (1995). *Art objects: Essays on ecstacy and effrontery.* Toronto, Ontario: Alfred A. Knopf.

4

Reading as Rewriting

PATRICK DIAS

McGill University

The major contention of this chapter is that classroom practices in the teaching of literature need to be more properly aligned with guiding principles which one can properly draw from now well-established reader response theory and research. I have dealt elsewhere at some length with the implications of reader response theory for classroom practice (Dias, 1992), particularly as exemplified in the work of Louise Rosenblatt (1978). In this chapter I shall focus largely on one common-sense notion that has almost every teacher nodding in agreement, but whose implications are often negated in practice: in curriculum guidelines, classroom practices, and the ways we approach assessing response to literature. In *The Reader, the Text, the Poem: The Transactional Theory of the Literary Work,* Louise Rosenblatt argues that ". . . no one can read a poem for you. Accepting an account of someone else's reading or experience of a poem is analogous to seeking nourishment through having someone else eat your dinner for you and recite the menu" (1978, p. 86).

"Poem" is Rosenblatt's convenient term for a reader's evocation of a work of literature. She is arguing that someone else's account of a literary work cannot substitute for our own reading, our own transaction with the actual text. We realize the powerful implications of her statement when we consider that we can never as adults read a poem or story through the consciousness of a ten- or fifteen-year-old. We know too much that prevents us from seeing what it is they see. Our lived experiences, as well as experiences given us by our reading and viewing, intervene to blind us to the possible evocations the text offers them.

Can we recall or relive the experience of our first reading of Anne Frank's diary so we can be in touch with what our students are living through? What happens then when we match our experienced and repeatedly tested readings of Blake's *Tiger,* for instance, against their seemingly naive but refreshingly current (can there be any other kind of reading for our adolescent readers?) readings? Do not our ever-so-gentle nudgings toward the preferred reading signal to our students that we hold the correct answers to the questions we ask? As teachers, we need to remind ourselves continually that our own readings, however expert, can only deny the validity and value of our students' readings. This is a vital concern if we see our responsibility as teachers of literature as one of cultivating lifelong readers, rather than one of handing over our expert readings, of eating and digesting their dinners for them.

Throughout Rosenblatt's work we are made aware that the "poem" is not just *there* in the words on the page, but is uniquely evoked by each reader in each rereading. As Terry Eagleton, the British literary critic, puts it, "we never read the same poem twice" (1983). That unique evocation of a story, for instance, is conditioned by the circumstances in which it is read or heard and the knowledge and associations we bring to our reading, including other readings that may have preceded it. Thus my reading of Hanif Kureishi's *The Black Album* cannot but call up memories of his *The Buddha of Suburbia* and the film *My Beautiful Launderette.* If I choose to read *The Black Album* again at some future time, my experience of that novel will hardly be the same as the one arising from my first reading. Other texts, films, and life experiences will have intervened. Yet many of our teaching practices seem to operate on the premise that each and every one of our readers, faced with the same text, is evoking more or less an identical experience of the "poem."

Quite obviously we cannot and should not expect our students to adopt a seemingly objective stance that enables them to shed their personal experiences and understandings (some may read these as personal biases) to arrive at a commonly agreed-upon reading. Jerome Bruner in his *Actual Minds, Possible Worlds* reminds us:

> Obviously, it will always be a moot question whether and how well a reader's interpretation "maps" on an actual story, does justice to the writer's intention in telling a story, or conforms to the repertory of a culture. But in any case, the author's act of creating a narrative of a particular kind and in a particular form is not to evoke a standard reaction but to recruit whatever is most appropriate and emotionally lively in the reader's repertory. (1986, p. 35)

What if we made it our agenda as teachers of literature not to guide our students toward the one preferred reading but rather to create the contexts whereby our students can "recruit whatever is most appropriate and emotionally lively in . . . [their] repertory"? However, Bruner goes on in the same passage to say:

> So "great" storytelling, inevitably, is about compelling human plights that are "accessible" to readers. But at the same time, the plights must be set forth with sufficient subjunctivity to allow them to be rewritten by the reader, rewritten so as to allow play for the reader's imagination. . . . In the end, one is asking how a reader makes a strange text his own. (p. 35)

Here Bruner recalls a passage from Italo Calvino's *Invisible Cities*, an exchange between Marco Polo and Kublai Khan, in which Marco Polo has been telling the Khan about the cities he has known and is told at the conclusion of his account that he has in every one of his accounts been speaking really about Venice. Bruner goes on to point out how our accounts of our experiences, and, for our purposes, of the texts we read and retell, will inevitably be composed in terms of the maps we carry of the world. Each new experience as it is shaped and placed provides a new map or a modification of an older map, a coloring in, a revision of boundaries here and there, and as we encounter new experiences, we draw for the narratives we compose on our stock of maps. It is in this way that "a reader makes a strange text his own."

I have drawn on Bruner at some length because he provides two key guidelines for the kinds of changes we need to contemplate if we are to engage students more fully in realizing their independence as readers. What if we work to organize our classrooms and our teaching in ways that enable students to "recruit whatever is most appropriate and emotionally lively in . . . [their] repertory" and to tap into the "subjunctivity" of texts so they can be rewritten by them, allowing them thus to make those texts their own? What would a program of work deriving from these not-too-unreasonable expectations look like?

In what follows I describe some activities that would compose such a program in the hope that, as teachers try them and adapt them to their specific situations, they will develop a fuller repertory than the sample outlined below. What is crucial in the success of such a program is that students begin to recognize that they are indeed being allowed full ownership of their own readings and that they do indeed have the capabilities that are the common inheritance of all those who read for pleasure. This will take time because there are so many past admonitions to shake off. At all cost, there must be no shifting back and forth between activities that engage them as readers in their own right and activities that constrain and smother that freedom.

In *Young People Reading: Culture and Response* (1991), Charles Sarland speaks of finding oneself in the text and finding the text in oneself. By this he means approximately what both Rosenblatt and Bruner identify as central in readers' transactions with literature: the need to acknowledge that readers compose the texts they read, that literary texts afford the potential of being filled in and completed by the reader (Wolfgang Iser's [1978] notion of gap-filling is certainly relevant here), and that it is eventually our own selves, our own worlds, we are writing. As teachers we need to work our way carefully into realizing the full impact of such notions. The great danger is that we reduce them to something like, "The poem or story is whatever you want it to mean," or "There is no one right meaning; whatever you think the poem means is correct!" Such statements suggest irresponsibility and dereliction of duty (and are particularly disturbing to parents), but these statements are also misguided.

Literary texts do impose constraints on interpretation, and it is working within such constraints that affords us the pleasure of reading. None of us would want to read if a text could mean anything we wanted it to mean. It is because we may have missed some of those constraints in developing our own accounts that we turn to other readers to question and confirm our readings. "Oh yes," we say, "I hadn't noticed that. How much that changes what I thought!" That is why the program I suggest has as its ground an understanding that a classroom constitutes a community of readers—several small communities in interdependent dialogue—with the teacher a nondirective, though interested, spectator. But more of that next.

Contexts for Reading Literature
in the Classroom

What are the necessary conditions that enable fuller, engaged responses to literature, responses that indicate that students are in fact finding themselves in the text and the text in themselves? As I have indicated, the foremost condition is that the teacher as experienced and expert reader step out of the transaction as mediator between readers and the literary work. The teacher is far too powerful a reader to be overseeing (literally) their readings, volunteering an opinion here or suggesting a way into the text there. A teacher's comments count as commands, however benign and nonauthoritarian we may wish to be. Students need time and opportunity to explore and find their ways into the text, to consider several hypotheses, to stray from the text, to advance to seemingly outrageous readings, to find their way by indirection and error. It is the travelling that matters, not the arriving.

I have compared the directive teacher to a tour guide who is concerned that his charges stay on the prearranged itinerary, see what is worth seeing according to the brochure, and not stray away into beckoning byways. The tour guide points where they must look lest they miss a prized feature, and hurries by sections with a brief summary account ("We do not have time to tarry; the tour must go on."). You see, the tour guide has been there already and does not sense the need of first-time visitors to look again, question, and wonder. It is not surprising then that those herded travellers will never be able to find their way around independently when they return to visit the city they were so carefully shown. In contrast, those who were encouraged to explore on their own in collaborative groups will have taken a wrong turn several times, will have consulted maps, shared their doubts and discoveries, and found unexpected points of interest. They may have missed some of the tourist highlights, but they will have come to know the city in ways that will allow them to revisit it profitably. They also will travel increasingly on their own. (Of course, they will have sensibly stayed within the tour book's general guidelines of where tourists ought and ought not to wander; they do not need the tour guide to tell them that.)

Unlike the tour guide, the nondirective teacher resists at all costs the desire to nudge students in the right direction ("right" as determined by the teacher). Students who are developing confidence as readers of literature need to assert their right to be wrong without risking the intervention of the reader over their shoulder. At what cost do we intervene to always set things right? At the cost that students will have been corrected but will not likely trust themselves as readers without one tentative eye on what the teacher wants. I am, of course, thinking of the vast majority of students who do not view themselves as readers and who do not trust their own responses in that role. For those who worry that there will be hundreds of students wandering around with "wrong" interpretations of a poem or a story, I say that poems and stories are expendable; the developing readers' efforts to make sense for themselves aren't. One can always return months or years later with more discerning eyes to those "misinterpreted" stories and poems. And I also add, with apologies to Tennyson (and because I relish the line), 'tis better to have read and erred than never to have read at all.

The teacher's prime responsibility in the nondirective classroom is to set up the occasions for reading by selecting appropriate texts and by setting up groups for the joint inquiry to negotiate those readings. It is important that the texts challenge readers and justify the joint effort within and among groups. I have developed a procedure that facilitates such collaborative work, and I refer readers to accounts elsewhere (Dias, 1995; Dias & Hayhoe, 1988). Key aspects of that procedure require that groups report back on the results of their discussions in plenary sessions and that tasks be designed such that groups are genuinely interested in and depend on the reports of other groups and have a stake in their success. Thus, in the tasks suggested below, all work is done in small groups (four to six members), and all groups are involved in the same task, engaged by the same question. All groups report back to the large group, building on, acknowledging differences, and generally complementing one another's efforts. The keys to success in such work are the students' convictions that they are truly relied on to make sense for themselves, that they have the resources within and among themselves to do so, and that the teacher will value their effort whatever the outcome. If, as teachers, we feel the slightest misgiving at having let seemingly gross misreadings go by, we need only to remind ourselves that our students encounter on their own outside the classroom a vast sea of print, audio, and video that we assume no responsibility for their reading correctly. Perhaps the best preparation for that world lies within a classroom community that allows them to assume responsibility for and take the measure of their own reading. Of course, such "uncorrected versions" remain far more lively in the reader's memory than do the approved versions that have been wrapped up for them by the teacher. Perhaps they are more likely to revisit such unfinished texts.

I asked earlier: What if we work to organize our classrooms and our teaching in ways that enable students to "recruit whatever is most appropriate and emotionally lively in . . . [their] repertory" and to tap into the "subjunctivity" of texts so they can be rewritten by them, allowing them thus to make those texts their own? What would a program of work deriving from these not-too-unreasonable expectations look like? What I have outlined thus far are the grounding assumptions for such work. I now describe some sample activities.

Rewriting Activities

Writing an Ending

Students read a short story with the last paragraph or so deleted. The students are expected first individually and then collectively to work out a likely version of such an ending.

The teacher might begin by reading the story aloud to the whole group and, if time permits, asking groups to nominate someone to read aloud within the group. The teacher indicates how much (number of lines) has been deleted. Students individually begin to write their versions of a likely ending or notes toward such an ending. Within the same session or in a following session, students read out their proposed endings within their groups, discuss their appropriateness, and work together to draft an optimum version, something that will accord well with the preceding text. I generally ask students to write in such a way that the seams don't show, so that it is difficult for most readers to tell where the actual author ends and their ending begins.

Final versions are presented in plenary session. Each group provides explanations if necessary and receives comments from the class. The teacher does not comment other than to commend each group's efforts. The intention, as in all such tasks, is that students ought not be looking to the teacher to validate their efforts. The teacher then presents the actual conclusion, which the class then is in a position to examine critically and compare with their own efforts.

An appropriate story for such an exercise is one that can be read aloud in fifteen to twenty minutes, one in which such a deletion is feasible, and one that allows students to work out a fitting and credible conclusion. Teachers will notice how carefully the students examine the story, paying heed, among other things, to aspects of plot, character, dialogue, and diction. At no time have I intervened to "teach" any of those terms. I recall a particular Grade Six class in which students in their group discussions were scrupulously insistent on using dialogue because that was the prevalent mode in which the story had been presented. It was especially exciting, for instance, to overhear a seemingly inexperienced eleven-year-old reader argue within her group that in the setting they had assumed for the story, a woman would not have had the option of leaving her abusive husband to move into a shelter, as some members of the group were proposing as a way of solving the problem. As they considered the various endings in terms of the one offered by the actual author, they became aware of the constructedness of stories, that the writer had chosen an outcome from among a few likely outcomes, and that the ending was not inevitable.

Such an exercise, in which the readers' rewriting of the text becomes salient and therefore open to discussion, can be further extended by offering another class the several group-authored endings together with the writer's ending, without identifying the latter as such. The class in groups has to decide which ending is the original ending and say why they think so. They can also discuss their own preferred ending from among the ones they have been offered. Such an exercise can generate another engaging follow-up in reverse, in which this class can write endings to another story and challenge the original class in a similar way to sort out the endings. The prospect of external readers gives some edge to the challenge of writing a "seamless" ending.

Thomas McKendy (1987) has designed an exercise using poetry that has interesting parallels with the story-ending task. Students individually or in groups select a short poem that has a decided form and rhythm. Their task is to write two substitute stanzas for the original last stanza, and then to challenge the class to decide which among the three is the original ending and to say why they think so. In this case, the prospect of challenging other readers drives the task: Each imitator must work from within the poem to decide how it works and the prospective endings that might be put forward as legitimate alternatives.

From Story to Play

This exercise works well with both short stories and long fiction. Choose a section of the text that appears mostly in the form of dialogue or reported speech. Students, individually and then working together in groups, rewrite that section in the form of a play or part of a play. Because their scripts will be performed as a play reading by another group, they are asked to pay close attention to providing a clear text in the form of a proper play script. A sample page from a published play is always helpful.

The challenge is to translate narrative into dialogue and stage action without diverging from the developing plot and characters as they understand them. It is important that the story or section of the novel allows for the participation of at least two, and preferably more than two, characters. Discussions I have witnessed focus on how such and such character would speak and whether the narrative is fully represented in the script. As with the other activities suggested here, what is most rewarding for students is to see other groups confirm their own readings or suggest other interpretations and extensions that they had not thought of but are now primed to consider and evaluate.

Having other groups perform their script allows students to discover the gaps in their own text. Such gaps reveal how much literary texts rely on readers to complete them and how such completions are not rigidly controlled by the cues signalled by the text. Groups seeing their scripts performed are invariably delighted by how the performance presents a reading they had not envisaged as potentially present in their text.

From Play to Narrative

In contrast to the previous activity, this exercise requires students to recast in the form of a narrative a section of a play they have read. The narrator can be one of the characters, or it can be written from an omniscient stance. As in the previous exercise, the teacher's responsibility is to find a section of the play that particularly lends itself to such an activity, that challenges but does not frustrate. Students should be cautioned against merely summarizing the action and should be reminded how narrative can be just as lively as drama. In preparation, groups can practice with very short sections of a play, reading aloud their drafts, so that they become aware of the several options open to them in translating dialogue into narrative. The teacher should select a section of a play that affords such translation and allows for a compact narrative.

Thus, a short section from Shakespeare's *Julius Caesar* may begin with Cassius as he stands outside the stadium where Caesar has been offered the crown. Students may experiment with telling the story in the person of Cassius ("I wondered if anyone had noticed me leaving; Casca, I am sure, had glanced anxiously at me once or twice as the tomfoolery went on.") or in the third person ("The noise around the stadium could not drown out the cheers that erupted inside. Casca winced each time a cheer rose and fell, torn between. . . ."). The longer section can begin with the scene in Brutus' tent just before the ghost of Caesar appears, challenging writers to set the mood of the scene and incorporate somehow Brutus' sense of his impending defeat. As with the other activities, students do the preliminary writing individually before getting together in their groups to pool resources.

Of course, narrative is not the only form into which a section of a play can be rendered. Students, again individually at first and later in groups, can begin to sketch out the storyboard for videotaping a short scene from a play or a narrative, presenting their effort to the large group as a preliminary to refining it, and then going on to produce the actual video. In this case, students may work on a common text or choose or be assigned appropriate scenes.

I have insisted thus far that all groups work on a common text. There are several reasons for this, of which the most important is that students come to realize the variety of readings each text affords. Moreover, individuals whose timid offerings have been turned down by their groups may find their contributions validated in the work of other groups. This is a precious resource for such individuals to find their voices within their groups. It also is a resource for dominant group members, who begin to realize that there is much value in attending to others and that they do not really have to carry the ball in order to accomplish anything. Moreover, other groups take over the task teachers always feel the need to fill: the task of providing feedback. In all my experience of such work, I have time and time again been reminded how much more appropriate and to the point are the comments provided by the class members, and how much better received than if they had come from me. Moreover, it is they who have wrestled with the task and can therefore offer the most appropriate and pertinent assistance. These are only the beginning points of a larger rationale for such collaborative work.

Imaginative Entry

The teacher selects a critical moment in a story or a novel and has students write a stream-of-consciousness account of one of the participant's thoughts during that moment or episode. As a group exercise, this allows students to draw on each other's insights into character and situation. The length of the soliloquy will depend on the episode chosen. Peter Adams (1989) provides examples of some imaginative work in this mode: one involves writing an epilogue to a novel and another, reconstituting a "gap" in a novel. Several teachers have had students keep a diary or a journal in the voice of one of the characters in a novel. It is important in all such work that the students do not see such tasks as interesting busy work, a new spin on an ancient teacher habit. The task must engage their imagination and their desire: To recall Bruner (1986), they are engaged in rewriting the text and, to recall Sarland (1991), finding themselves in the text and the text in themselves.

Subtexts

A technique used by many directors in rehearsing a cast, subtexting involves presenting (in our case, writing) the thoughts of characters in a play (including silent onlookers) so as to differentiate what they say publicly (if and when they speak) from what they feel and think privately. Not everything a speaker says or a listener hears calls for a subtext; however, in most cases it is a matter of finding out what's behind the words. When our hero affords a warm greeting to a newly arrived guest, "I am so glad you've come; I hope you'll stay longer than you did on your last visit," the subtext might be: *I don't think your coming here will improve matters. I now know what I did not know before.*

When the teacher has identified a particularly rich section in a play—a few lines or a page will do—students in groups, after some improvisation on key lines and exploratory discussion, write out the subtexts and present the group's version to the class. Characters speak their actual lines with their shadows following immediately with the subtexts. These presentations allow students to discover how similarly and variously readers interpret seemingly unambiguous texts and situations.

Gap-Filling

For reasons of economy, form, or in order to maintain the flow of a story, writers don't tell us everything, which is all to the good because it allows readers to remain active in constructing the story. Thus we are told that, in effect, the two kissed and made up. Everything in the story points to such reconciliation, so we are not surprised, nor do we want to know who said what to whom in the process. We are not privy to lives of characters outside what we are given in the story; on the basis of our own lived experience, we assume what we need to assume. A character goes to school daily, but we don't often get told about the teacher or with whom this character ate lunch. We assume that life outside what we are given in the novel goes on in its normal way and we will be told if it doesn't when it matters to the story. And so it goes with minor characters in novels, who are often stereotypical so they will not distract from the main characters. The butcher is the butcher and no more; grandfather goes on in his grandfatherly ways. If a seemingly minor character, like the butler, is drawn with more than the usual detail, we suspect that such a character will quite likely move to center stage.

In recognizing gaps and asking students to reconstitute them, we are making overt their role as coconstructors of the tale with the author. The action of the story is composed by readers in terms of their own experiences, and characters are understood in terms of aspects of the people they know or have read about. Someone is fatherly or motherly, or doing poorly in either role, only in terms of what readers know (have experienced and have read) of fathers and mothers and caring.

When we have identified a gap in a story and ask students to add a paragraph or two to reconstitute the gap, they know they must remain consistent with the story so far and with what is to come—that characters must stay in character. This exercise allows them to display their understanding of the story, not by retelling the story, but by rewriting parts of it. Done in groups, this exercise allows students to draw on their varying experiences to decide what so-and-so would say and do, and whether a particular sentence is consistent with the way the author's style has come through to them. This is a challenging exercise and can be invigorating as well, if the moments are well-chosen and if students have learned to trust their own and one another's intuitions.

The Teacher's Role

Throughout this account I have implied how inhibiting the teacher's authority as an informed reader can be, and I have suggested that, apart from setting up the contexts, the teacher must at all costs stay out of the role of arbiter of the correct reading. It is not enough to say, "I don't have the answers." Students do not trust such responses; the teacher is a teacher by virtue of what she or he knows. Rather than assert one's peripheral role and ignorance, it is the teacher's role to help students realize their own power as readers and to help them to relish that power, so that the question of what the teacher thinks does not enter into their working out of the tasks the teacher has discovered for them.

Yet the teacher's role remains major and challenging. It is to find appropriate literary texts, to define engaging tasks, and then to back off. We know the story or the poem we read and experience is not identical with the story or poem our students read. It is not our job to hand over our versions to them, however much we believe that our versions more accurately and responsibly reflect the text.

Looming in the background of all such work and threatening to redirect it is the teacher's role as evaluator and grader. My argument simply is that I must describe the kinds of work that respect our understandings of how readers read and respond to literary texts and what kinds of teaching are most likely to engage them and develop lifelong habits of reading. My experience is that teachers approaching the teaching of literature in these ways will amass volumes of evidence that reflect what their students do and can do as readers. Released from the role of being at the center of the classroom—what I have often called full-frontal teaching—teachers have all the time they need to monitor their students' development as speakers, readers, and writers, and as participants in collaborative work. My experience is also that students become far more aware of their processes as readers, writers, and participants in group work and are able to discern what they have accomplished and what they need to do. They can thus be better prepared coparticipants in their own evaluation.

REFERENCES

Adams, P. (1989). "Imaginative Investigations: Some nondiscursive ways of writing in response to novels." In J. Milner & L. Milner (Eds.), *Passages to literature: Essays on teaching in Australia, Canada, England, the United Kingdom, the United States, and Wales.* Urbana, IL: National Council of Teachers of English.

Bruner, J. (1986). *Actual minds, possible worlds.* Cambridge, MA: Harvard University Press.

Dias, P. (1992). Literary reading and classroom constraints: Aligning practice with theory. In J. Langer (Ed.), *Literature instruction: A focus on student response.* Urbana, IL: National Council of Teachers of English.

Dias, P. (1995). *Reading and responding to poetry: Patterns in the process.* Portsmouth, MA: Boynton-Cook Heinemann.

Dias, P. & Hayhoe, M. (1988). *Developing response to poetry.* Milton Keynes, UK: Open University Press.

Eagleton, T. (1983). *Literary theory: An introduction.* Oxford: Blackwell.

Iser, W. (1978). *The act of reading: A theory of aesthetic response.* Baltimore: Johns Hopkins University Press.

McKendy, T. (1987). Arguing about taste: An introduction to poetry, *English in Education, 21*(3), 44–49.

Rosenblatt, L. (1978). *The reader, the text, the poem: The transactional theory of the literary work.* Carbondale, IL: Southern Illinois University Press.

Sarland, C. (1991). *Young people reading: Culture and response.* Buckingham, UK: Open University Press.

Dancing through Light: Learning to Read and Write Poetry

REBECCA LUCE-KAPLER

Queen's University, Kingston

> *Only after the writer lets literature shape her can she perhaps shape literature.*
>
> —Annie Dillard (1989, p. 69)

Beginning writers searching for advice are often given two suggestions: first, read widely and, second, reread in close detail the kind of literature you want to write. This surprises some people because they believe that reading literature while writing will lead to plagiarism and the loss of one's own creative vision. Yet in other arts, such as painting and dancing, learners often emulate experienced artists. Beginning painters develop a feel for shadow and shade, experimenting with hues while following their instructor's lead and samples of finished work. Dancers stretch and twirl their bodies in front of mirrors, comparing their progress to that of their teacher. When we teach writing, however, we often overlook insights from the teaching of other arts because we envision writing as having a more pragmatic than artistic function. If, instead, we use these insights, students are encouraged to emulate published writers. This participation in the rich, intertextual dialogue within the field of literature changes students' reading and writing of texts.

As American writer Natalie Goldberg explains, to read aloud the work of great writers is to take on the voice of inspiration, to breathe their breath "at the moment of their heightened feelings" (1993, p. 22). In describing the close relationship between reading and writing, Annie Dillard notes that Hemingway studied the novels of Hamsun and Turgenev, Thoreau examined Homer, and Welty explored Chekhov. "By contrast," Dillard tells us, "if you ask a twenty-one-year-old poet whose poetry he likes, he might say, unblushing, 'Nobody's.' In his youth, he has not yet understood that poets like poetry, and novelists like novels; he himself likes only the role, the thought of himself in a hat" (1989, p. 70).

What experienced writers have long known and practiced can be a key for our teaching reader response to literature in school. In reading poetry, for instance, students are introduced to a variety of aesthetic forms that they can use as models for their own response. By writing poetry, they learn how to read poems: the rhythm of the words, the significance of the line breaks and arrangements, the imagery, and the unity. Reading, responding, and writing become part of a recursive working that leads students to a deeper understanding of the literature that they read and write.

In coming to understand my own work as a writer, I can make connections between the role of response in my writing and the teaching of response to poetry. In this chapter, I explore my poetic practice by asking how I make writing decisions, how I work with and respond to other texts, and what inspires my thinking. Then I describe how I have enacted some of these practices in an English language arts classroom through reading of and responding to poetry. Finally, I suggest ways teachers can encourage students to move beyond monologic responses to poetry—those first, personal reactions to the reading—to responses that are more complex and dialogic. This complexity emerges through the intermingling of experience with various texts, an intertextuality that enriches the students' written responses.

The Practice of Poetry

For the past year, I have been submerged in a poetry writing project exploring the life and work of Canadian painter and writer Emily Carr. Most of my mornings begin with the writing of new poems and the revising of those in progress. However, my work also has three other dimensions that involve responses to literature or art: the reading of others' poetry, the exploration of aesthetic form, and the reading of a variety of texts about Emily Carr. My relationship with these other texts and the experience of responding to aesthetic forms such as paintings or poetry move me to places in my writing that are unexpected and exciting. To have to sit every day at my desk and try to coax poems onto the page would be difficult. Instead, by moving between a variety of experiences and responding to those experiences, my writing takes on a dynamic feel of being immersed in a bubbling stream. This dynamic motion creates a rich source for poetry, as revealed in one of my journal entries:

> As I worked on the Emily poems today, I got the strong sense of how intertextuality works for me. As I began to work on the baby stories from Emily's life, I remembered a poem about a baby that was in my novel and this was based on a photograph in the book *The Last Best West* which was about pioneer women on the prairies. That seemed to fit the tone of what I was trying to do. Then I remembered the story about the child whose legs had to be broken to fit a coffin—that story came from somewhere I don't remember but I used it in my novel as something happening to a character and then I used it again in a slightly different form this time. As I was writing this, I could feel texts flying through my head from all over and connecting to the work I was doing. It was almost visceral.

This awareness that our words come from many places, that they are not wholly dependent on the single writer, is described by Bakhtin:

> Every word smells of the context and the contexts in which it has lived its intense social life; all words and forms are inhabited by intentions. In the word, contextual harmonies (of the genre, of the current, of the individual) are unavoidable. (cited in Todorov, 1984, pp. 56–57)

Only in this dance between aesthetic forms, other texts, and my own experiences does the language begin to become populated with my own intentions; I struggle for harmony and my poetry emerges.

Perhaps the best way to illustrate this poetic practice is to follow the writing of one of my poems, "Trying to Find the Space to Paint Among All These Humans." Although it is impossible to be aware of all the traces of texts and experience that threaded through my thinking in writing this particular poem, examining the more obvious aspects still can give a sense of the experience. My intention was to write a poem that would trace Emily Carr's development as an artist. I wanted enough imagery to suggest the complexity of the process and yet leave room for readers to form their own impressions.

I was reading several texts about Emily Carr: her own autobiographical writing (*Hundreds and Thousands* [1966] and *Growing Pains* [1946]) and three biographies (Blanchard, 1987; Shadbolt, 1990; Tippett, 1979). From these sources, I jotted down words and quotations. For aesthetic models, I viewed some of Carr's paintings, thinking about how their composition might inform my poetic form, and I studied the style of Michael Ondaatje's *The Collected Works of Billy the Kid* (1970). This book is a series of prose and poetic pieces and pictures that characterize Billy through carefully chosen detail so that, from few words, readers can sense a fully developed character.

I felt immersed in a *heteroglossia,* a term used by Bakhtin to express the plurality of language that resists unification. I was aware that the "word in language is half someone else's" (1981, p. 293), that it came from other places and contexts. Emily's voice mingled with those of her biographers and the words of journalists, artists, family members, and friends. The language of Billy the Kid and other characters from within that book threaded through the voices from Emily. Within this rich dialogic possibility with voices speaking to voices speaking to me, I began with a first-level response, making notes and writing impressions in my journal. This dialogue among several texts encouraged me to play within the writing, to begin linking my own memory and experience as another thread of the heteroglot and to reshape the language with my intentions. The interplay between others' words and my own held a creative tension that began to suggest a poem. As Kristeva notes, "Bakhtin was one of the first to replace the static hewing out of texts with a model where literary structure does not simply *exist* but is generated in relation to *another* structure" (1986, pp. 35–37).

But the poem was not written yet. How could I move beyond merely imitation or collation of a series of quotations? How could I imbue the language with my meaning, as well as other meanings? How could I shape a new text from the intermingling voices? Bakhtin explains that language can be so overpopulated with others' intentions that expropriating it for one's own use is difficult. A writer must apply existing ideas to new material, find other ways of presenting images, and change the context while working among the traces and threads of others' intentions. This creative tension arises from a dialogue in which words oppose or "interanimate" each other as my intentions coexist or challenge previous ones (Bakhtin, 1981, p. 354).

As I read my first-level responses to those other texts, I saw the traces of their words and aesthetic forms, and yet I saw something new arising from the context of my experiences. Like Michael Ondaatje, I wanted to intersperse some actual historical quotations throughout my poetry, making the heteroglossia more visible and changing the way the poem is read. I decided this poem would use ideas from what I'd read, as well as my own vision in speaking of Emily's artistic process. I began to write the poem:

> *When Father died I was still at school getting into a great deal of trouble for*
> *drawing faces on my fingernails and pinafores and textbooks*
> wondering about the curve of a dog's ruff the curl of his fur
> and how to shimmer eyes with tears that float across the surface.
> I found a stick in the charred remains of a barnyard junkfire
> ripped open a brown-paper sack to draw Carlow
> his eyes, his ruff.
> Years later
> after Father died
> I found the drawing among his letters from England
> some Bills of Lading
> "Emily–Age 8" he had written
> when I thought no one else had watched
> me cross the threshold

The italics in this excerpt indicate Emily's actual words taken from her autobiography, a format established early in the poetry collection. The incident described in my poetry echoes other things said by Emily. For instance, in her autobiography, she tells the story about trying to draw the dog and later relates how the picture was found among her father's belongings. Although she never states how she feels about the picture being there, I began to imagine what she meant; I read between the lines and shaped the event. For Emily, this occasion might have been a sign that someone had noticed that she had artistic talent—this attention in a family in which she struggled all her life for recognition. With my imagining her insight, I then chose details and arranged them for that end.

There is a range of intertextuality at work in this poem, which can be characterized as falling between the coordinates of citation and significance. Citation directly evokes other texts for the reader—a horizontal reading, of which my direct quotation is an example. Significance affects the semantic structure of the poem—a vertical reading, in which words, themes, and contexts mingle with my intentions and are less attributable to specific sources (Guillen, 1993).

Intertextuality that affects a poem vertically begins to blur the boundaries between the "fictitious and the natural, the novel and the autobiography, the original and the replicated, the self and the other, written and read, broken and whole" (McHugh, 1993, p. 71). We can no longer tell with any certainty what has arisen from texts or experience and what I have constructed in a new context to imbue the words with a different meaning. The poem moves beyond imitating texts to finding a unity of its own. As Bakhtin tells us, along the way of writing a poem, the writer continually encounters someone else's word: "Each takes new bearings from the other; the records of the passage remain in the lag of the creative process, which is then cleared away (as scaffolding is cleared away once construction is finished)" (1981, p. 331). My writing, then, becomes a dialogic practice emerging from many texts.

Dancing in the Triquetra

This movement between forms, texts, and experience suggests a triangular rather than a linear, sequential process. Triangulation has been a term that some theorists have used in describing the process of coming to understand in writing and reading. (For example, see Berthoff, 1990; or Kent, 1993.) However, the triangle seems too closed to entirely explain the process I am engaged in. In the movement between aesthetic forms, other texts, and my experience, I weave and dance back and forth, often intuitively. This openness of process provides for multiple connections both within and beyond the emerging poem. Yet this dance is not without structure. As Grudin suggests, in his exploration of creativity, the imagination needs both "control and exuberance, precision and ambiguity, exacting professionalism and childish fun" (1990, p. 50).

I approach my poetic practice at regular times, using certain established routines; I create parameters through aesthetic forms and texts. These boundaries take away the fear of wandering aimlessly or becoming lost in the heteroglossia. Instead, I have a range within which to play the possibilities. To begin to visualize a process that embraces both precision and ambiguity, control and exuberance, I stretch and loop the triangle until it becomes a *triquetra,* a pattern of poetic dance (See Figure 5.1).

The triquetra is an ancient trinity symbol formed by three interlaced arcs that resemble the petals of a chrysanthemum. A circle runs through the arcs, connecting

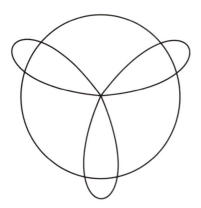

FIGURE 5.1   Triquetra

them even as the points of the petals extend beyond the circle. There is movement in such an image—not only within the protective circle of imagination, where lines run through the center and each is joined to the other, but also outside the circle, where the petals reach out to invite other texts. The back-and-forth weaving suggests the process and practice of writing poetry. As Mary Oliver writes:

> The poem is not nailed together, or formed from one logical point to another, which might be retrievable—it is created through work in which the interweavings of craft, thought, and feeling are intricate [and] mysterious. (1994, p. 117)

How, then, can we invite our students to participate in such a dance?

Exploring the Triquetra of Poetry

One of the criticisms directed toward reader response theory is the tendency to focus "on the reader's holistic response to the overall text rather than to the ongoing experience with the text" (Beach, 1993, pp. 21–22). In teaching reader response, we sometimes ask students for this holistic response to a literary text by working only with their own unexplored and unchallenged personal knowledge. Although this touchstone can be a good beginning, we must do more than leave them in this "state of interpretive narcissism" (Harker, 1990, p. 71). When we ask readers to return to the writing changing the perspectives or enhancing their experiences each time, we highlight and enrich the context that surrounds and connects to the text, and we open up the heteroglossia within which the poem lives. By creating occasions in which students can experience the disciplined practice of exploring a poem more fully, teachers help them move beyond the routine daydream response into a fully exercised imagination. In the process, the connections between students' lives and literature are deepened, and they are invited to add threads to the intertextual relationship.

One of my poetry lessons that best exemplified this process used Earle Birney's poem, "David." Although we explored the poem in different ways, including viewing the film version and having discussions about friendship, the most intriguing and powerful images in the students' writing occurred after an experience of climbing. All of them had visited the mountains, but none had ever been rock climbing. When I heard that our school was renting a portable climbing wall at the same time as we were reading "David," I decided it would be a good opportunity for students to have a firsthand experience.

They had been reading poetry for several weeks, and before going to climb the wall, we discussed what poetic form they might try writing after the experience. The students revisited the climbing experiences of the characters in the poem, pointing out the short bursts of fear and energy, split-second decisions, breathtaking beauty, and the exhilaration before the tragic decision. What kind of poem would convey those feelings? I asked. They decided that haiku might capture the brief intensity, and they agreed that during and after their climbing they would write the short poems. We also listed other reading they had done that might connect to this experience, poems such as Margaret Avison's "Banff" and Earle Birney's "High Rockies," and a nonfiction piece about mountain climbing.

The three petals of the triquetra were in place: other texts, an aesthetic form, and now actual experience. This triquetra circled through "David" and worked to produce poems that were powerful in their intensity and imagery. Students wrote about clinging to a rock face, fear, excitement, cold winds, tired muscles, and dangling above the world. Clearly, through the experiences of the text and the small, indoor climbing wall, their imaginations were rich with imagery.

Afterward, when we returned to Earle Birney's poem to compare their experiences, they found other images within the long narrative that spoke to their haikus. One student revealed a basic theme in the poem when she wrote:

> *Wail of mosquitoes*
> *Shreds of the shattered storm clouds*
> *Last day of my youth*

Within the narrative poem, students began to see how the individual images evoked their imagination and how those pictures worked to connect them immediately to the story. When students collectively displayed their haikus drawn from the poem and from their own experiences, there was a sense that these, too, told a story.

Revisiting the poem and then writing in response began a dialogue of craft. What students learned through their own writing is how poetry can be written, and as they returned again to the text, they had a greater awareness of this poetic craft. This knowledge is what is needed to carry an "individual's ideas to the far edge of familiar territory" (Oliver, 1994, p. 2) in poetry. We do not begin as writers with a fully developed style and the ability to use our experiences at will in our writing, but through practice and opportunity for a triquetric response and a dialogue of craft, we learn to both write and read poetry.

Within this process of enriching the context of the poem and the students' experience lies the notion of boundaries. Although the petals of the triquetra reach outward, the circle and petals still define the space, representing parameters given to the students. Jill Pirrie, an English teacher in Great Britain whose students have had phenomenal success in national poetry writing contests, agrees with the importance of creating a specific space in which students write. In describing her teaching, she explains:

> Paradoxically, the teacher must set boundaries, impose constraints, in order to set free. When we ask children to imagine, we are, above all, asking them to remember with a special intensity. Only then do we establish an authentic starting point for their writing. And so, two clear problems emerge:
>
> 1. How do we transform the limited, "ordinary" experience of the child so that he turns to it as a source of interest and excitement, willing to relive it in a state of total involvement?
>
> 2. How, having achieved this involvement, do we help the child towards a position of detachment from which he can apply his craft as conscious artist, subject to the rigour of his discipline? I have found that these problems can be resolved only through a literature-based curriculum. (1987, p. 1)

Again, we come full circle: the writing is connected to the reading to the writing to the reading. Our role as teachers, Pirrie suggests, is one of narrowing down rather than opening up. In the narrowing down, students' imaginations become anchored in reality and open to possibility. Ted Hughes, in *Poetry in the Making*, agrees.

> I doubt if much would come of just "snow" as a subject. But there are an infinite number of categories within the general concept "snow," and it is the teacher's job to help the pupil narrow the idea down to a vivid memory or fantasy. (1967, p. 40)

How can we narrow the possibilities for students? If we think about using aesthetic form, other texts (intertextuality), and student experience as a way of approaching a response to a poem, we can begin to establish parameters for our students.

By exploring the three aspects individually in the next sections, I do not mean to suggest a separation between them. Like the petals of the triquetra, they all arise from the same loop. Nor would I suggest that a teacher should choose only one focus for a poem. I think it's important to recognize that aesthetic form, intertextuality, and experience are present every time we write a poem and that we can revisit and rework our writing by emphasizing one aspect without excluding the others.

Poetic Practice in the Classroom

Aesthetic Form

Aesthetic form is what draws us to the reading of poetry, creates the sense of awe or exhilaration within us, and becomes part of our memorable experiences. By attending to the uses of language in the poem—its imagery and texture, form and style, stories and themes—readers can begin to appreciate the aesthetics of poetry and develop their own aesthetic practice in the writing of poems. The place to begin is through careful reading and exploration of published poems that can provide a framework for students' own observations and experiences. This exploratory quality is a characteristic of aesthetic achievement. As Grudin tells us,

> Again and again the quest for fullness of an idea has led artists to revolutionary insights into phenomena natural and human. Without undue extension, the exploratory quality of art may be understood as having a character similar to well-practiced analysis. (1990, p. 41)

After reading a poem, the student's first-level response in a journal is a useful starting place. This writing captures those fresh impressions that validate the student's relationship with the text. Jill Pirrie suggests that asking students to launch into the writing of a poem after a first reading can be an expressive moment for them. "I have found," she writes, " . . . that it is immediately after having made a literary connection within a text that a child finds that he has something worthwhile to say" (1987, p. 56). Afterwards, returning to the poem with a teacher's guidance can offer further expressive moments and extend the exploration into further aesthetic work.

For instance, poems often reveal interesting ways of using language. One exercise I created for myself began with Lorna Crozier's poem, "Repetitions for My Mother." The poem opens with the poet's wish for her mother's immortality and continues through a listing of what the narrator wants from her mother. When a list of images ends, she repeats the line "I want her. . . ." This repetition of language creates a rhythm in the poem that draws you into language like a jazz improvisation to a sequence of notes (McKean, 1992, p. 150). I've written several poems using this technique: one with the line "I'd like to live a slower life" and another using a quote from Emily Carr, "Oh, God what have I seen? Where have I been?" During this process, whenever my writing stops, I repeat the line and another stream of language begins.

Poems that are extended metaphors also can be an interesting exploration of language for students. For example, Mary O'Neil's poem, "Fingers," which compares the digits to antennae, could prompt students to discover other metaphors for their fingers, or they could choose a metaphor to describe an entire character. I often begin this exercise by asking people to respond to a list of words, such as a musical instrument, a place, an animal, and so on, with the first word that comes to their mind. I then ask them to choose one of the metaphors and create a poem beginning with the line "I am a _____."

Asking students to explore the imagery and texture of a poem extends this exploration of language in specific ways. For instance, reading a poem like Elizabeth Bishop's "The Fish" or "Pear Tree" by H. D. reveals the sensory power of poetry, its ability to make us present in the poem in a visceral way. Asking students to choose something they know well and having them begin to list images of it that connect to all five senses is a way they can start writing their own evocative piece.

Poetry also offers specific forms and style, which students can use as scaffolding for their writing. For example, they may write a mixture of prose and poetry, as Michael Ondaatje does in *The Collected Works of Billy the Kid* (1970). A more specific response to form can occur through a line-by-line writing (McClatchy, 1992, p. 155). A poem of about ten or twenty lines can be retyped with space left between every line. Students then write their own lines between the original lines in response. At the end of the exercise, the original poem is deleted, with only its echo remaining in the student's poem. Roo Borson's "Rain Song" is a good example of a piece that works well for this exercise.

The themes within a poem also can be a way for students to respond. Elizabeth Bishop's "In the Waiting Room," which explores a child's realization that she does exist as an individual, became an idea that I adapted (Muske, 1992, p. 80). Using a specific time and place as she did, I created a poem describing a moment when I first realized my connection and place in my family.

Every poem can offer a poet a different writing dimension. By learning to read poems as writers of poetry, we can practice our craft and learn to be explorers of the aesthetic.

Exploring Intertextuality

Intertextuality surrounds us and connects us to our reading and writing of literature. Listening to or discovering the heteroglossia from which our writing arises is important for the reader and writer of poetry because, as Kristeva suggested, literary structure is generated in relation to other structures.

When the aesthetic form of a poem is investigated, other texts can be used to extend the understanding or to compare the differences in craft. We also can listen for the echoes of other texts in the poetry. And not only poems. A very broad view of texts can include all genres, movies, music, conversations, and the students' experiences. For example, when my students studied "David," they also viewed the Atlantis Films' version and listened to a slide talk given by a woman who had spent time in the mountains near Banff, Canada. When they climbed the wall, I played Andreas Vollenweider's (1984) music "White Winds" as accompaniment to the experience.

Students are able to see intertextuality clearly when they read a poem written in response to another poet's work, such as Koch's poem "Variations on a Theme by William Carlos Williams," written with Williams' poem "This Is Just to Say" in mind, or the Mendes and Shimizu poem "inappre ciation of eecumm ings," responding to cummings' poem "in Just-."

Reading poems that connect thematically, students can feel immersed in multivoices speaking about the same issue. For example, the theme from "In the Waiting Room," described earlier, is developed differently in "Great Things Have Happened." Michael Ondaatje's poem "Light," which explores his memories of family, can begin a journey through other poems about family, such as Zieroth's "Father," or Aubert's "Me as My Grandmother."

Students also can make intertextual connections among one poet's body of work. Ondaatje has written many poems about family that could be read together. Besides "Light," his poems "To a Sad Daughter" and "Bear Hug" offer compelling images of child–parent relations. Another example is Joy Kogawa's writing about being a Japanese Canadian such as "When I Was a Little Girl" and "Woodtick," and this reading could extend to her novel *Obasan* (1981).

Once connections are made, students begin to realize the rich context from which reading and writing emerges, and as they write in response, their voices become threads in the intertextual tapestry.

Student Experience

By teaching students how to mine their experiences for connections to their reading and by offering enriching experiences in school, we can begin to broaden their personal response to literature. As Robert Probst points out:

> The reader must appropriate the text, not by slavishly submitting to it, attempting to do nothing but absorb it, but rather both submitting and reflecting, by both accepting the visions offered in the text and testing them against his or her own and others. (1989, p. 5)

Exploring the text, attuning to the intertexuality, and comparing these visions to their own are all part of the triquetra of connections students must make; otherwise, the importance of reading and writing literature is lost and holds no meaning for them. Jill Pirrie writes:

> If it is not already known it cannot be the subject of imaginative writing. Further, it has been said many times that we know what we think only as we try to write it down. . . . (T)hrough the very act of writing the poetry, the children came to realize what was already "in their bones". . . . The poems they wrote made the implicit explicit and gave intuitive feelings external reality. (1987, p. 70)

This connection to their experience is important for understanding, but so is the opportunity to write and discover that connection.

We come to know and remember the world through our senses; thus, we can stir our students' memories through the senses or we can stir senses through the memory. One technique I have used with writers is to bring in objects to smell, such as gum, spices, licorice, scented stickers, and soap. For sight and sound, I offer a variety of pictures and play some music. I also have pieces of fruit, candy, and vegetables to taste and I choose a variety of objects they can touch. They explore this sensory world until a memory emerges that they want to write about. Afterward, the students return to the sense exploration, searching for or elaborating on another memory, continuing the process, and eventually writing evocative poems.

Another technique, which uses memory to stir senses, begins with a reading of Margaret Atwood's poem "This is a Photograph of Me." I ask students to bring a photograph of a place they know, a picture from which they are absent. As they closely examine the photograph, I ask them to describe it using sensory description, so that a reader could visualize the setting. While writing, I ask them to think about where they are in relation to the picture and to write their presence/absence into the picture poem as Atwood does. As students write through this exercise, they begin to explore their sensory relationship to this place.

Students, like other poets, need to observe the world closely and be encouraged to look and look again at objects, to experience what they are seeing. What are the precise details that they will remember? What makes this object unlike all others? What words evoke the image? Learning how to keep a writer's notebook or field notes of observations can be an important tool for relating their experiences to poetry, and reading poetry that illustrates the keen eye of the poet highlights the importance of observation. Some examples are Lorna Crozier's "September" or Theodore Roberts' "The Blue Heron." Other poems, such as May Swenson's "How Everything Happens" (based on a study of a wave), Maxine Kunin's "400-Meter Free Style," or John Updike's "Mirror," carry the observing into the form of the poem.

Teachers can help their students make further connections by arranging activities or events that will kinesthetically connect them to poetry, such as climbing, dancing, or drawing. Experience can be deepened for students, even by something as simple as a time for dialogue that gives them an opportunity to share experiences with each other and, in the speaking, uncover further connections.

There are many possibilities for revealing the richness of a poem and its context so that students will see literature as related to their lives and will be able to write what has nestled "in their bones."

Dancing the Triquetra

Poetry offers a discipline of form and craft that we can bring to students in the classroom. From the abundance of poetry available, we can encourage students to learn from established poets and to immerse themselves in a heteroglossia that will support their growth, rather than asking them to depend entirely upon their own personal responses. We can do so assured that we're following the practice of great poets. J. D. McClatchy reminds us that:

> All poets have debts outstanding. It's how we learn, how we adore; we come to ourselves by putting those selves into the hands of masters. With experience we learn how to disguise our thefts (sometimes by flaunting them). It is how we both continue and extend a tradition. (1992, p. 157)

Reading and writing literature help students develop comfort with language, learn its facility, and use it to find meaning in their experience and uncover their thinking. When the teacher makes necessary literary connections for students, their self-awareness grows and, in turn, their self-acceptance. As Jill Pirrie reminds us, "Only then can we turn outward—articulate, expressive, whole" (1987, p. 50).

E N D N O T E

With few exceptions, most of the poems referred to can be found in resources approved by the Alberta (Canada) Department of Education for secondary English language arts: *Imagine* (Iveson & Robinson, 1993), *Inside Poetry* (Kirkland & Davies, 1987), *Literary Experiences* (Oster, Iveson, & McClay, 1989a, 1989b), *Poetry in Focus* (Cameron, Hogan, & Lashmar, 1983), *Sunburst* (MacNeill, 1982), and *Through the Open Window* (Paustian, 1983). See References for information.

R E F E R E N C E S

Bakhtin, M. M. (1981). *The dialogic imagination.* Austin, TX: University of Texas Press.

Beach, R. (1993). *A teacher's introduction to reader-response theories.* Urbana, IL: National Council of Teachers of English.

Berthoff, A. (1990). *The sense of learning.* Portsmouth, NH: Boynton/Cook Publishers.

Blanchard, P. (1987). *The life of Emily Carr.* Vancouver, BC: Douglas & McIntyre.

Cameron, B., Hogan, M., & Lashmar, P. (Eds.). (1983). *Poetry in focus.* Toronto, Ontario: Globe/Modern Curriculum Press.

Carr, E. (1946). *Growing pains: An autobiography.* Toronto, Ontario: Irwin.

Carr, E. (1966). *Hundreds and thousands: The journals of an artist.* Toronto, Ontario: Irwin.

Crozier, L. (1992). *Inventing the hawk.* Toronto, Ontario: McClelland and Stewart.

Dillard, A. (1989). *The writing life.* New York: Quality Paperback Book Club.

Goldberg, N. (1993). *Long quiet highway: Waking up in America.* New York: Bantam Books.

Grudin, R. (1990). *The grace of great things: Creativity and innovation.* New York: Ticknor & Fields.

Guillen, C. (1993). *The challenge of comparative literature.* (C. Franzen, Trans.). Cambridge, MA: Harvard University Press.

Harker, W. J. (1990). "Reader response and the interpretation of literature: Is there a teacher in the classroom?" *Reflections on Canadian Literacy, 8,* 69–73.

Hughes, T. (1967). *Poetry in the Making.* London: Faber and Faber.

Iveson, M., & Robinson, S. (Eds.). (1993). *Imagine: Poetry anthology.* Scarborough, Ontario: Prentice-Hall.

Kent, T. (1993). "Interpretation and triangulation: A Davidsonian critique of reader-oriented literary theory." In R. Dasenbrock (Ed.), *Literary theory after Davidson.* University Park, PA: Pennsylvania State University Press.

Kirkland, G., & Davies, R. (Eds.). (1987). *Inside poetry.* Don Mills, Ontario: Harcourt Brace Jovanovitch.

Kogawa, J. (1981). *Obasan.* Markham, Ontario: Penguin Books.

Kristeva, J. (1986). *The Kristeva reader.* Oxford, UK: Basil Blackwell.

Luce-Kapler, R. (1996). "Emily Carr: Finding space to paint among all these humans." *Event 25*(1), 41–43.

MacNeill, J. A. (Ed.). (1982). *Sunburst.* Scarborough, Ontario: Nelson Canada.

McClatchy, J. D. (1992). "Writing between the lines." In R. Behn & C. Twichell (Eds.), *The Practice of Poetry.* New York: HarperCollins.

McHugh, H. (1993). *Broken English: Poetry and partiality.* Hanover, NH: University Press of New England.

McKean, J. (1992). "The props that assist the house." In R. Behn & C. Twichell (Eds.), *The practice of poetry.* New York: HarperCollins.

Muske, C. (1992). "In the waiting room." In R. Behn & C. Twichell (Eds.), *The practice of poetry.* New York: HarperCollins.

Oliver, M. (1994). *A poetry handbook.* New York: Harcourt Brace.

Ondaatje, M. (1970). *The collected works of Billy the Kid.* Concord, Ontario: Anansi Press.

Ondaatje, M. (1989). *The cinnamon peeler: Selected poems.* Toronto, Ontario: McClelland and Stewart.

Oster, J., Iveson, M., & McClay, J. (Eds.) (1989a). *Literary experiences: Volume 1.* Scarborough, Ontario: Prentice-Hall.

Oster, J., Iveson, M., & McClay, J. (Eds.). (1989b). *Literary experiences: Volume 2.* Scarborough, Ontario: Prentice-Hall.

Paustian, S. I. (Ed.). (1983). *Through the open window.* Toronto, Ontario: Oxford University Press.

Pirrie, J. (1987). *On common ground: A programme for teaching poetry.* London: Hodder and Stoughton.

Probst, R. (1989). "The river and its banks: Response and analysis in the teaching of literature." In J. O'Beirne Milner & L. F. Morcock Milner (Eds.), *Passages to literature: Essays on teaching in Australia, Canada, England, the United States and Wales* (pp. 3–15). Urbana, IL: National Council of Teachers of English.

Shadbolt, D. (1990). *Emily Carr.* Vancouver, BC: Douglas & McIntyre.

Tippett, M. (1979). *Emily Carr: A biography.* Toronto, Ontario: Oxford University Press.

Todorov, T. (1984). *Mikhail Bakhtin: The dialogical principle.* (W. Godzich, Trans.). Minneapolis, MN: University of Minnesota Press.

Vollenweider, A. (1984). *White winds.* [CD]. New York: CBS Records.

Connecting with Poetry: A Reader Response Perspective

6

JOANNE M. GOLDEN
University of Delaware

Ms. Carr is reading aloud to her students Eloise Greenfield's poem "My Daddy," in which a son expresses great admiration for his father's ability to sing the blues while accompanying himself on the guitar. The son emphasizes that in his eyes, his daddy has star quality even though he is not famous. As Ms. Carr reads, Ronald chimes in, reciting parts of the poem from memory.

> **NATE:** It sounds like he's bragging about his daddy.
>
> **JAMES:** And he says he may not be on TV, but he loves him like a favorite star.
>
> **REGGIE:** People don't think he's the best, but in his eyes he is.
>
> **MARCUS:** It sounds like the poem was a song because it kept on repeating itself.
>
> **EDDIE:** He's proud of his father.

These responses of seventh-grade students to Eloise Greenfield's poem "My Daddy" illustrate important reader response processes of constructing, interpreting, and personalizing literature. Reggie and James engaged in constructive processes when they identified the characters of the speaker and his father, translated the poet's lines that the speaker thinks his father is a star, and inferred that others don't think he is because he does not appear on TV. Several students participated in the interpretive process when they commented on the speaker's actions as well as his emotions toward his father. Nate, for example, viewed the speaker as bragging about his father, Ben contended he felt pride, and James commented on his love for his father. These observations indicate the students have moved beyond the literal translation of information to interpreting the speaker's stance toward his father. Students personalized literature by relating their knowledge, experiences, interests, and other aspects of self. When Ronald joined in with Ms. Carr, he illustrated his familiarity with the poem. If he had not previously heard it,

Thanks to Donna and Bruce Canan for their assistance with this chapter.

his comment might indicate his ability to predict information. Marcus showed his knowledge of music by comparing a repetitive element of the poem with that of song. This discussion shows that even a brief exchange can provide insights into how students respond to literature.

The purposes of this chapter are to look at how students' responses to poetry inform us about processes of constructing, interpreting, and personalizing poems, and to consider ways of extending these responses. The premise is that teachers can view their classrooms as meaning-making environments that generate students' responses. Observations of the nature of the interactions between students and literature and the influence of other participants' perspectives on reader response offer a guide for creating contexts that not only facilitate development of students' response strategies, but also increase their enjoyment of reading.

The Classroom Context

Seventh graders in an urban middle school participated in poetry-reading experiences with their two English teachers. Their responses are used as a basis for exploring the processes of constructing, interpreting, and personalizing literary texts and for considering ways of developing these responses. It is important to note at the outset that Ms. Carr's and Mr. Blair's goal for this project (as reported in conversation) was to read aloud poems for enjoyment and to provide a forum for articulating open-ended responses. Therefore, this chapter is not intended as a critique of their approaches for extending responses or analyzing poems, nor as a set of generalizations about how the seventh graders responded to poetry. Rather, the intent is to explore how any event that provides engagement with literature can offer teachers insight into students' thinking and ways of helping them learn how to extend their responses. Poems were selected by both the teachers and the students from Michael Strickland's (1993) anthology, *Poems that Sing to You*, which Ms. Carr had recently discovered at a professional conference.

Response Strategies

Constructing the Poem

The first of three response strategies central in the reader's interaction with literature is constructing the poem, or building a textual world. This process concerns how the reader assembles the work during the reading act through strategies of translating, inferencing, predicting, and integrating information. In his discussion of building textual power, Scholes (1983) refers to this process as reading, the act of creating a text within a text.

After listening to Langston Hughes' "The Juke Box Love Song,"[1] students responded to both narrative and lyrical aspects of the poem. In the poem, the

---

[1]From *The Collected Poems of Langston Hughes* by Langston Hughes, Copyright © 1994 by The Estate of Langston Hughes. Used by permission of Alfred A. Knopf, a division of Random House, Inc.

speaker tells of how he could take his love through the Harlem night to a restaurant where they could dance to music from a jukebox. Tana responded by retelling the poem as an event:

> **TANA:**   Okay, I think they called it "Juke Box"—what was it called?
>
> **FRANCIE:**   "Juke Box Love Song."
>
> **TANA:**   "Juke Box Love Song" because he had a girlfriend and he was in love with her, and they, and he took her to Harlem to a restaurant and there was a jukebox there and he played that song and danced with her.
>
> **ANDY:**   I think they was slow dancing and listening to the music.

These responses give information about how two students offered responses that could be developed. Tana's utterances could be extended by asking her other ways in which the love relationship is apparent as told from the speaker's perspective: for example, "my sweet Harlem brown girl," "we," and "your love song." Tana and Andy could be encouraged to explore other ways the speaker expressed his love through actions, such as "take the Harlem night and wrap around you" and "take neon lights and make a crown." Another aspect to consider is that Tana and Andy viewed the dancing as an event that happened, whereas the speaker is proclaiming what he could do: "I could take the Harlem night . . ." (Strickland, 1993, p. 8). Students could be asked to look more closely at how the language of the poem offers information about whether the event actually occurred.

In the same discussion, Angie focused on the poetic element of imagery in response to Ms. Carr's question, "What does this poem mean for you?"

> **ANGIE:**   I got a picture in my head about the setting and it kind of made me think about what the girl looked like, and like how the restaurant looked inside and how the jukebox was looking like.
>
> **MS. CARR:**   Thank you very much. And what was the picture that came into your mind?
>
> **ANGIE:**   A restaurant with a brown and red jukebox and a young girl like around our age with brown skin was sitting at the table with the person.

Angie linked into the imagery of the poem, picturing a scene that Ms. Carr asked her to describe. To extend her response, Angie could be asked to comment on why she thought the girl was "around our age" and why the juke was "brown and red." Is it like one she has seen in her neighborhood, for example? Other students might be asked if they envisioned the restaurant in similar or different ways, or if they formed images of other scenes in the poem.

Students could also convey their visual imagery through art by selecting media that represented their mental pictures. To portray the cityscape, colored chalks might be used for the "crown of neon lights," or a collage could be made from scraps of different-textured cloth, pieces of wallpaper, or pictures cut from magazines. To depict dancing to the jukebox, students could create a diorama with different-colored papers or a tempera painting. To enhance their responses, they could share their visual representation with classmates, explaining how the poem evoked their image and influenced their choice of what to represent and how to represent it.

Students' responses to "Juke Box Love Song" in another class section reflected a different angle. They tapped into how Mr. Blair read the poem.

MARKITA: You made it seem like a story.

MR. BLAIR: She said I made it seem like a story. But you don't think it is a story though?

STUDENTS: Yeah; no.

MR. BLAIR: But does it tell a story?

NARKITA: You're supposed to sing it—like the blues.

MR. BLAIR: Oh, you want me to put more rhythm and rhyme?

LEROY: Yeah, like Mylo did.

This segment illustrates that Markita and Leroy expected the poem to be read musically, like poetry, rather than nonmusically, like prose. The students' perspective could be probed more fully, and they could be asked to read the poem aloud in a musical manner. Differences between proselike and songlike renditions could then be examined in greater detail as a way of examining poetic elements. Sound imagery, conveyed by the poet through words such as "rumble" of the city's subways, buses, and taxis, could be reproduced in the class by percussion instruments, sound effects created by the students, or sound recordings. Students, as the speaker says, can "tone their rumble down" for the "love song." Percussion instruments can "take Harlem's heartbeat" and "make a drumbeat." Students could bring in recorded songs to accompany dancing to dawn. They might research the Harlem renaissance and learn that Langston Hughes wrote poetry during the time that blues music became a popular musical genre. Dancing to the music of the jukebox is a central aspect of the poem's musicality.

To build on the students' awareness of musical elements in poetry, the teacher could offer opportunities for individual and choral reading performances. These experiences could lead to a consideration of how oral performance affects understanding and how multiple performances—and interpretations—can be generated in this way. For example, students could experiment in pairs or small groups with various techniques, such as different individuals reading alternate lines, one student echoing the reading of a line by another, or several students engaged in unison reading of particular lines. When groups or pairs listen to each other's performances, they can discuss how different choral readings affect their responses to the poem.

In addition, the links students make between music and poetry could be extended by involving them in listening to blues music and comparing and contrasting its elements with those of the poem. The music of Bessie Smith and other blues singers can be compared to the poem in terms of meter. Does the "drumbeat" of the city reflect the rhythm of blues music? Does the repetition of the phrase "dance with you" suggest a blues pattern? Similarly, in "Daddy's Song," mentioned earlier, one line is repeated four times. Marcus compared it to a song for this reason. In addition to rhythmic patterns and repetition of lyrics, blues music is intensely personal (Kamien, 1996). This personal aspect is conveyed in the power of love between two people shown in both poems. Students might compose poems using the patterned structure of rhythm and lyrics to convey feelings they have about a subject.

Interpreting the Poem

During interpretation, the reader is making meaning out of a poetic text. Interpretive processes reflect readers' "descriptions or conceptions" of literature (Beach & Hynds, 1990). Responses focus on determining themes, the speaker's stance toward the subject, the emotional content of the poem, and the poet's purpose for writing the poem, among other considerations. Scholes (1983) refers to these responses as creating a "text upon a text." To produce such a text, the reader moves from a level of constructing the work to a more general level of "thematizing" the poem.

One way that students responded interpretively in the class discussions was to comment on the speaker's state of being or attitude toward the subject, especially if it were to another character. In Harrison's poem "The Musician,"[2] an omniscient speaker tells of a street-corner musician playing his violin for passersby who do not stop or look: "He stands with his eyes closed. There's only his music . . ." (Strickland, 1993, p. 38). After hearing Ms. Carr read the poem, Tana commented on the musician's state of being and how he survived:

> The man seems like he's got his own little world like—he's got his own little world somewhere else like he lives in his world all by hisself in this exotic world in his head and his music's everything to him.

Tana's observation that the man is in his own "exotic world" illustrates that this world is unique to the man and that music plays an important role in it. She could be asked to consider whether the man actually lives in the world and, if not, how his music helps him to survive the actual world in which he lives. His music is "not a place to stay or food or growing old" but "a thin blanket that wraps around him . . . to protect him[self] from the cold." Because interpretation involves assessing the emotional content, Tana could consider how she thought the musician felt in his world, how the passerby felt, and how the speaker felt about the street musician playing his one song.

To engage more fully in the interpretation of the emotional content of the poem, students could participate in composing *dialogue* poems (Dunning and

---

[2]Reprinted by permission of author.

Stafford, 1992), in which one student role-playing a passerby converses with another student role-playing the street musician about how the musician feels. Students might also respond by creating a poem that assumes the street musician's perspective of his world. A *question–answer* poem is another form for generating students' poetic responses to a poem. Students could apply these approaches in composing an exchange between a passerby and the street musician, the two lovers in "Juke Box Love Song," or the father and son in "My Daddy."

An interpretation of the speaker's attitude toward practicing the horn and toward her mother for making her do so is evident in three students' responses to Harrison's poem "Practice." In the poem, the speaker protests to her mother about having to practice the horn: "why practice practice practice? But nothing helps. . . ."

> DORIAN: I think she should tell her Mom like what Shara says because . . . she says she don't like it and she should get something she do like.
>
> TYREL: I think she's afraid of her Mom.
>
> MS. CARR: You think she's afraid of her Mom? What makes you think she's afraid of her Mom?
>
> TYREL: If she isn't scared of her, why is she doing it?
>
> LOUIS: She's getting tired of her Mom always telling her to practice, practice, practice.

Each of the students focused on an emotion experienced by the speaker. Dorian observed that she didn't like to practice her horn. Tyrel considered the speaker's fear of her mother, and Louis indicated how tired she was of hearing her mother. To build on these responses, students could be asked to examine if there is a pattern in the use of the words "practice practice practice" (they occur in lines 4, 8, 12, 16, and 20) and whether it affected their interpretation of the poem. In Line 20, the words are presented in capital letters.

Repetition of the word *practice* reinforces the aggravation the speaker felt when she was reminded to practice the instrument over and over again. Students could explore how repetition functions in this poem compared with the poems with the blues pattern—that is, the repetition of the single word practice to accentuate the speaker's reaction, as opposed to repeated lines of stanzas in blueslike poems to express other emotions. Students might also write a poem about their personal experiences with and attitudes toward practicing, such as warm-up routines for sporting events, academic exercises in classes, or preparing for music lessons.

Responses to Giovanni's "kidnap poem"[3] provide interesting insights into students' perceptions of how the poet engages the reader and the relationship between the poet and speaker. The first lines of the poem are "ever been kidnapped/by a poet/if i were a poet/i'd kidnap you. . . ."

---

[3]Copyright © Nikki Giovanni, reprinted by permission of author.

EDDIE: . . . he'll put you in the story.

RAY: You have to read between the lines.

EVA: Why would it say that—"if I were a poet"—that is a poet.

MR. BLAIR: Well, that's a good point—why would she say that?

LENA: she pretending she's someone else . . . like a child bringing her boyfriend home to see her mama.

Effects on the reader are noted by Eddie, who observed that the author "puts you into the story," and Ray, who commented that "you have to read between the lines." Other responses focused more directly on interpreting the poem itself. Eva's question concerning why the poet would say "if i were a poet" prompted Lena to conjecture that perhaps the poet is pretending to be someone. Phrases such as "love song" and "show you off to Mama," or a personal experience, may have influenced her view that the speaker is "bringing her boyfriend home to see her Mama."

The metaphor of a poet as a kidnapper of a reader could be linked into Eddie's observation that the reader is put into the story. Eddie could explore the poem to find examples of how he was drawn into the poem. Phrases such as "put you in my phrases and meter," "lyric you in lilacs," and "ode you with my love song" (Strickland, 1993, p. 22) are possible responses. Eva's question and Lena's response create an opportunity for students to examine the distinction between the actual poet, Nikki Giovanni, and the speaker of the poem, who is not a poet.

In addition, it would be interesting for students to find poems that "kidnapped" them to collect in a book and read to their classmates. To prepare the way for this, students could brainstorm words or phrases that are suggestive of the word kidnapped, thereby discovering its connotations and accompanying emotions. Language such as absconded, snatched away, swept up, captivated, or captured, for example, might reflect connotations. Following this, students could identify specific music, works of art, speeches, or scenes in nature that transported them. These experiences would provide a prelude for immersion in poetry for the purpose of identifying a poem that kidnapped them. Students could share their poem with other students or write a journal response on aspects or features of the poem that created this effect for them. It would be interesting for the class to consider whether poems that spoke to individuals shared any similarities in form or content with other poems. The students' observations in this section show how interpretation focuses on the emotion conveyed in a poem, which is revealed in the attitudes of the speaker toward the subject.

Personalizing the Poem

In responding to poems, students reveal their personal attitudes, values, beliefs, experiences, and knowledge as they connect the text to self and to other texts (Beach & Hynds, 1990). When a reader experiences the effect of a poem by linking it to self or to the world, the respondent creates a text beside a text. Certain poems may evoke such responses more than others, and particular readers may experience different effects depending on what they bring to the reading situation.

Some poetry invites students to identify with the speaker. For example, Shara in the discussion on Harrison's "Practice" stated what the speaker should do based on her reaction in the same situation:

SHARA: I think she should tell her mother how she feels.

MS. CARR: You think she should tell her mother how she feels? Why?

SHARA: 'Cause I wouldn't want to be sitting up there practicing all day.

As noted previously, Dorian agreed with Shera that the speaker should tell her mom, so she can solve her problem by finding something she does like. Douglas, from a different section, implied that he didn't have the same problem as the character because "my parents don't like me to practice."

From these three responses, it is apparent that students personalize poetry in both similar and different ways. Shara stated what the character should do and projected how she would act in the situation; Dorian also said the speaker should tell her mother, but for the purpose of finding something she enjoyed; and Douglas contrasted the speaker's dilemma with his own situation. Besides the direct extension of asking students if they can relate to the experience of practicing music or anything else (students could also be asked to consider the mother's point of view), should kids occasionally be required to do things that parents think are good for them? Further, the students might look more closely at the poem to explore whether the speaker actually did tell her mother she did not want to practice (multiple interpretations are plausible):

> *I tried to tell her I'm not bright*
> *So I could practice half the night*
> *Forever and not get it right* (Harrison, in Strickland, 1993, p. 40)

and what could be done because "nothing helps, not even tears. . . ."

Judgments about characters' behaviors and what they should do are also evident in Latisha's responses to "The Musician." Following Tana's interpretation of the musician in the previous section "as living in his world in his head," Latisha judged other characters' reactions to him:

LATISHA: I don't like it when people walk past him and turn they heads and put the coins in because. . . .

MS. CARR: Okay, you don't like it when people walk past and put their coins in because it doesn't sound right?

LATISHA: Because they turn they heads—because they don't pay any attention to him.

MS. CARR: What do you think people should do?

LATISHA: They should be more respectful.

MS. CARR: What should they do though, do you think?

LATISHA: Stop and listen.

Latisha's responses show her compassion toward the musician in her expression that passersby should be respectful of the man by stopping and listening to his music. This view could provide the basis for students to discuss street musicians they have encountered. Do they stop and listen? What do they notice about the music, the musician, and their own feelings about the musician? What do they notice about passersby? Is their reaction similar to that of the speaker? Further, students might research how and why street musicians choose their venues, either by investigating secondary sources or by interviewing a street musician. They might report their own experiences or research findings in class or express their views of street musicians evoked by the poem through various art media. Because the musician in the poem seems lost in his own world, students could identify and share music that pulls them into their own worlds. This focus is similar to that of the "kidnap poem," which could be referred to for comparison.

Responses also inform us about students' prior knowledge. As noted in the beginning of the chapter, Ronald predicted the last line of the poem because he had heard it before, whereas Marcus showed his knowledge of music by comparing the repetitive pattern of song to that of the poem. After hearing "Jazz Fantasia," Rashon commented that "Jazz like makes you feel different ways." Markita, as noted earlier, linked "Juke Box Love Song" to blues music because both emphasize the element of rhythm.

Responses can also reveal what students like about poetry. Richard's response to "New Year's Eve," read by Francie, reflected a personal connection with the topic, whereas other students commented that they just liked it.

RICHARD: Oh, I like that.

MS. CARR: Okay, why do you like that?

RICHARD: Because I know—I like New Year's because I know my birthday's on the way.

Students also indicated their liking of poetry because of certain elements. Walter, in response to "Boogie Chant Dance," said, "I like it 'cause it has rhythm to it . . . a beat to it." There are several ways to link into students' poetry preferences in the classroom. Because several students commented on links between music and poetry, this connection could be extended by asking students to bring in and play for the class jazz and blues music, which highlight the repetition and rhythm they observed in the poetry. Students could discuss their favorite musical and poetic elements and find poems utilizing these elements. These poems could be collected in books, placed on a collage, read to the class, and accompanied by students' statements about what they liked. If a particular poet were popular, his or her work could provide the basis for a more in-depth exploration.

The illustrations above show us some of the ways in which we can learn about students' attitudes, values, knowledge, experiences, and interests by listening in on their responses to poetry.

Conclusion

The primary observation regarding reader response to poetry apparent from this exploration is that both the reader and the text are central in the creation of the poem. The poet provides cues pertaining to imagery, meter, and the speaker, for example, which guide the reader in constructing the text. In interacting with the text, the reader interprets its emotional content and, in some cases, personally connects with it. By providing opportunities for students to articulate their responses to poetry, we can observe their response strategies and determine ways in which we can develop these strategies. Students' responses also inform us about the potential influence on response of certain instructional processes, such as reading aloud, whole class discussion, literature circles, and the role of the teacher. Study of classroom events offers a basis for analyzing the roles of the poet's words, the student, and the teacher in the meaning-making process (Golden, 1992). Information from these observations can serve as guides for creating different forums for students to articulate their responses, for examining different tools for observing students' responses, and for designing approaches for developing students' response strategies.

REFERENCES

Beach, R., & Hynds, S. (1990). Research on response to literature. In R. Barr, M. Kamil, P. Rosenthal, & P. D. Pearson (Eds.). *Handbook of reading research, Vol. 2,* (pp. 453–489). White Plains, NY: Longman.

Dunning, S., & Stafford, W. (1992). *Getting the knack: Twenty poetry writing exercises.* Urbana, IL: National Council of Teachers of English.

Golden, J. M. (1992). Inquiries into the nature and construction of literary texts: Theory and method. In R. Beach, J. L. Green, M. L. Kamil, & T. Shanahan (Eds.), *Multidisciplinary perspectives on literacy research* (pp. 275–292). Urbana, IL: National Council of Teachers of English.

Kamien, R. (1996). *Music: An appreciation* (6th ed.). New York: McGraw-Hill.

Scholes, R. (1983). *Textual power.* New Haven, CT: Yale University Press.

Strickland, M. (1993). *Poems that sing to you.* Honesdale, PA: Boyds Mills Press.

7 Conducting Media Ethnographies:

Understanding How Response Groups Construct Meaning

RICHARD BEACH
University of Minnesota

Several years ago in my television/film methods course at the University of Minnesota, one of my students, Cheryl Reinertsen (1993), completed a project in which she analyzed how a group of her adolescent daughter's female friends viewed each week the two television programs *Beverly Hills 90210* and *Melrose Place*. These programs revolve around male/female relationships: fidelity, marriage, sex, relationships in the workplace, conflict resolution, and so forth. Cheryl observed the group discussions of the programs and interviewed various group members about their perceptions of the group meetings. Based on her observations and interview transcripts, she extracted a number of patterns in the group's responses to these programs. She found that members applied their own beliefs and attitudes to judge the characters' actions. They "liked Donna because she is nice and she doesn't do anything wrong; Andrea because she doesn't care only about her clothes and appearance; Billy because he is true and the most caring, ideal, and sensitive; Jo because she is her own person and she stands up for herself; [and] Matt because he is a peacemaker and serves other people" (p. 8). They "disliked Amanda because she is anorexic, out for herself, ruthless and arrogant, and Kimberly because she's a weakling" (p. 9).

For Cheryl, these judgments consistently reflected what she characterized as middle-class assumptions about family, work, and sexual behavior. Group members believed that the characters are often irresponsible in not being concerned with their education or future career. For example, in one episode of *90210*, a female college student becomes engaged to an older man. The group shared their displeasure with her decision to become engaged: " 'She likes him just because he's rich.' 'She should stay in college.' 'She's too young.' 'Wait until her parents find out. They will really be mad' " (p. 14). For Cheryl, these comments reflected a cultural model in which "college age students should not be engaged because they are too young. If they do get engaged, they will drop out. Education is important, love can wait" (p. 22).

Cheryl learned a lot about the response process from conducting this study. She recognized the power of the group in shaping individual members' responses. Through sharing responses valued by their peers, group members affirmed their allegiance to the group's shared beliefs. She also recognized that the group's judgments of characters' actions reflected the middle-class values of her own home and community.

Given her experience, I have assigned small-scale media ethnographies in my college classes. Students have studied book clubs, Internet user groups, television/film viewers' peer or family group discussions, rock/jazz festivals, literature classrooms, and responses to a particular genre. Although my students are at university level, I believe that these studies could be conducted by upper-elementary and secondary students, with some modification of activities to accommodate for students' ability levels.

From conducting these studies, students are learning how the meanings of responses are constituted by a unique set of social and cultural practices specific to a group or community. They are also learning inquiry strategies for investigating a phenomenon—selecting a topic, posing questions about that topic, observing behaviors, interviewing, analyzing responses, and organizing findings for a final written report. To model these inquiry strategies, I provide students with sample published media ethnographies, along with unpublished student reports, such as Cheryl Reinertsen's study. We discuss these studies, focusing on the research methods employed and the possible difficulties involved in conducting the studies.

In this chapter, I will describe the various steps I go through in having students complete these studies, along with illustrative examples of some students' work (I include excerpts from one student's study of responses to "Christian" romance novels in the appendix). I then conclude with thoughts on how all of this ties into response-based instruction.

Understanding Groups as Microcultures

Before students select a topic or begin their research, it is important that they have some understanding of the basic goal of this research, which is to study groups as microcultures. In studying groups as microcultures, students can understand how responses are social practices whose meaning is constituted by group cultures. According to Edgar Schein (1985), these practices include:

- sharing a common language and conceptual categories
- defining norms and boundaries for appropriate interpersonal behavior
- recruiting, selecting, socializing, and training members
- allocating authority, power, status, and resources
- dispensing rewards and punishments
- coping with unpredictable, stressful events

Schein notes that these practices are evident at three levels: artifacts, values, and assumptions/paradigms. Artifacts are visible behaviors that reflect a cultural climate or style. He cites the example of a workplace in which the doors to offices are always open and in which there is a lot of discussion and argument, behaviors that reflect an "open" culture. In a culture, members cite certain values to justify their behavior. The head of the workplace will order the doors to be open because communication is highly valued. Less visible are the underlying assumptions or paradigms that members take for granted, for example, the assumption that members need to test out their ideas with others in the group.

Understanding a group or institution as a microculture requires students to adopt the perspective of an outsider, or Martian, and begin to perceive their familiar world as suddenly strange. Students practice adopting a Martian perspective by going out as teams to different restaurants, stores, athletic events, classrooms, ceremonies, and so forth and recording their observations of peoples' behavior, language, and appearance. They are then asked to adopt a Martian perspective and to interpret the meaning of these phenomena as if they were alien strangers who had no prior knowledge to explain people's behavior. To understand group behavior, students discern norms and conventions that constitute appropriate behavior for a group or institution. They are more likely to be able to define these norms and conventions as an outsider than as an insider.

Once students begin to understand the idea of focusing on behavior as a cultural phenomenon, we discuss various groups in a school (or in the case of my students, groups they recall from high school). Students list the different groups in their school, the characteristics of each group, and how groups often define themselves in opposition to other groups. We look at some excerpts from Penelope Eckert's ethnographic study, *Jocks and Burnouts* (1989), of a large, suburban high school, in which she found that students who perceive themselves as "burnouts" define their roles through behavior, dress, and language that conflicts with the middle-class, academic, bureaucratic culture of the high school designed to serve the pro-school "jocks." To bolster their peer-group image as resisting the jocks, the burnouts often do not participate in extracurricular activities.

Teachers working with middle/junior high students may want to look at examples from Margaret Finders' (1996) study of early adolescent female groups, *Just Girls: The Literate Life and Underlife of Early Adolescent Girls.* In that study, group members solidified their allegiance to their own group by deliberately responding in ways opposed to social practices of members of an opposing group. The girls who perceived themselves as the "social queens" valued practices opposed by the "tough cookie" girls, and vice versa.

Students, therefore, respond in ways that reflect their rejection of groups whose beliefs and attitudes they oppose. For example, in responding to Richard Peck's (1989) story, "I Go Along," about differences between "advanced" and "regular" students in a small-town high school (Beach, 1995), high school students equated being members of an "advanced" or "honors" class with the middle-class values of working hard and delaying immediate gratification. In the story, Gene, a member of a regular English section, decides to accompany the advanced students on a field trip to a poetry reading at a neighboring college. Gene ends up being the only student from the regular class who goes on the trip. On the trip to the poetry reading, he is befriended by one of the most popular girls in the school, Sharon, and he enjoys the poetry reading. However, at the end of the story, he realizes that he lacks the social status associated with being a member of the advanced class.

In responding to this story, the regular and advanced students differed in their responses to the story. The advanced students typically assumed that students were in regular classes not because of their ability, but for lack of motivation. One advanced student noted that, "I have run across many Genes in my ten years of schooling and none of them are in advanced classes even though they should be. The average Gene dresses sloppily and doesn't act like they have a care in the world." Another student said: "I know Gene could make the other class if he just put his mind to it. But he just lays back and puts the front of his cap down and thinks that's a good enough answer." A third student added, "In a 'normal' class it's not cool to be smart; I think Gene isn't using all of his intelligence." These responses reflect the advanced students' adherence to middle-class values, a stance characteristic of Cheryl Reinertsen's daughter's group's response to *Melrose Place* and *90210*.

The Influence of Groups on Individuals' Responses

Once students understand how groups function as microcultures, they can then discuss the ways in which a group's microculture influences individual group members' responses to texts. A central concept here is the notion of stance, which I define as the shared ideological orientation or perspective adopted by group members. Stance, therefore, reflects the group's beliefs and attitudes. For example, stance may reflect a group's shared gender attitudes (Cherland, 1994). In one study of a group of adolescent males watching and responding to a television program, group members deliberately avoided expressions of emotional reactions to characters, particularly female characters, for fear of being perceived by their peers as unmasculine (Buckingham, 1993). They also ridiculed or vilified these characters as "stupid" or "ugly," judgments reflecting their shared macho stance. In a widely cited study of women's responses to romance novels, Janice Radway (1984) found that women would often read romance novels for the purpose of making a statement against the patriarchal control of their spouses. In homes in which women were valued primarily for their work, the very act of reading romance novels as an enjoyable pastime served to assert their resistance to assumptions about their roles and status within their own home.

Students then discuss how these stances shape group members' responses. I share the example from my own research on seventh graders' responses, in which single-gender groups were responding to a "blood-and-guts" survival story. These groups responded according to their opposition to other groups' gender attitudes. A male group of students shared their positive reactions to the detailed descriptions of the story, making intertextual references to their own physical experiences with violence and ridiculing "females" who would not enjoy the story. A second all-female group responded negatively to the story and did not consider it worth discussing. They characterized the story as celebration of "male" values they wish to avoid, making references to sensationalized uses of violence in literature and the media. A third all-female group, who perceived themselves as "better students," was critical of the other two groups for not recognizing and appreciating the story's literary quality, a stance constructed around references to their own previous reading experiences.

These students are using their responses to define their roles or identities in groups. Members of the male group use responses to appear macho to their peers. By appearing to enjoy violence and ridiculing a female stance, they establish their status as being male, defined as being opposed to that which is female.

We also discuss examples of group members who adopt roles that are totally different from their "real-world" roles. For example, members of computer newsgroups or listservs assume identities that represent a fantasy escape from their everyday lives (Turkle, 1995). In participating in the on-line chat rooms of romance, they construct themselves as romantic lovers or provocateurs, because, in these virtual worlds, they do not need to be concerned with actual social consequences. Or, group members may define their role by assuming certain specific functions—as leader, facilitator, scribe, and so forth. For example, in newsgroup discussions of television programs, participants who recount program episodes in an entertaining manner achieve status because other participants value being updated on episodes they may have missed.

Doing Media Ethnographies

When students are familiar with the ideas of groups as microcultures, stances, and roles, we read some examples of media ethnographies (Ang, 1985; Bird, 1992; Brown, 1990; Buckingham, 1993; Jenkins, 1992; Lull, 1990; McRobbie, 1990; Mills, 1994; Palmer, 1986; Provenzo, 1991; Radway, 1984; Seiter, Borchers, Kreutzner, & Warth, 1989; Spigel & Mann, 1992; Turkle, 1995). We talk about the basic purpose of this research, which, as summarized by Shaun Moores (1993) in his book *Interpreting Audiences: The Ethnography of Media Consumption,* is to "understand the lived experiences of media consumers" (p. 32) from their own perspectives as audiences. One popular example is Henry Jenkins' (1992) study of members of *Star Trek* fan clubs. These fan clubs would meet frequently to create their own versions of *Star Trek* programs in the form of edited videos or fanzine stories. These edited videos or fanzines often introduced interpersonal or autoerotic themes into the stories, in which, for example, Spock and Captain Kirk were engaged in a homosexual relationship. Jenkins studied the ways in which these edited versions reflected the groups' own interpretations of the original programs, interpretations that reflected their own, often feminist, beliefs and attitudes. By reading and discussing sample studies, students gain some understanding of how others have conducted research studies.

Selecting Topics for Research and Posing Questions

To select a study topic, students discuss their own experiences with responding to different types of texts, listing questions about their experiences that intrigue them.

For example, one group of students had a strong interest in responding to radio. They recalled their own experiences listening to the radio, noting their preferences for certain stations, disc jockeys, and talk-show hosts. They also discussed the situations in which they listen to the radio—for example, driving to school, doing their homework, or exercising—and purposes for listening—to be informed or entertained, to break up the monotony, to vicariously participate in a talk show, to be a loyal fan and listen to a sports broadcast, and so forth. And, they also noted perceptions of others' experiences—the fact that certain of their friends listened to those stations that only play certain kinds of music or that other friends enjoy listening to certain talk-show hosts in order to ridicule or parody the hosts. They then posed some questions: Which programs do what types of groups listen to and why? What aspects of the programs are appealing? In what types of social contexts do listeners share their responses? How do these responses serve to build social bonds? and How do their beliefs and attitudes shape their responses? All of this helped them formulate questions about these different aspects of the response experience.

Observing Groups

Students then select certain groups for observation. They may observe previously formed groups, such as classes, computer newsgroups, or book clubs. Or, they may create their own groups, asking students to share their responses with each other. One consideration is easy access to groups. Given the usual practice of a group of students renting a video, students may ask their friends to share their responses to the video. Or, students may want to study their younger siblings' responses to television because they can observe and interview their siblings in their own homes. (For examples of ethnographic studies on children's responses to television, see Buckingham, 1996, and Palmer, 1986.) In either case, students should ask group members for permission to study them, explaining the purpose of the study, describing the methods employed, giving them the right to withdraw from the study, and guaranteeing them that their confidentiality will be protected in written reports.

In using written field notes and tape recordings of group discussions, instead of vague, evaluative comments such as "friendly," "outgoing," "talkative," and "emotional," or abstract summaries, students need to use concrete descriptions of behaviors: "Daryl, the smallest boy in the group, began to talk very quickly and excitedly when he described his feelings about the story ending." They record in the margins the time of day and the beginning and end of certain activities—the fact that people move from one activity to the next. In reviewing their notes, they look for recurring patterns or frequencies of behavior, treating their perceptions as a jigsaw puzzle in which certain pieces fall together in certain ways.

In writing notes, students focus on a number of aspects:

- *Setting.* Sensory aspects of the setting or context. Students map which types of persons sit next to whom; for example, in a classroom, certain students may sit in the back of the room while others sit in the front.

- *People.*   The particulars of persons' behaviors, dress, hair style, gestures, and mannerisms, as well as identifying them according to their gender, class, and race.

- *Talk/conversation.*   Recording aspects of the talk/conversations, noting certain words or phrases that are repeated, who talks the most versus the least, and certain turn-taking patterns.

- *Documents, photos, writings.*   Documents, photos, or writings from the people they are observing. For example, members of a fan group may have written letters to their idol or collected magazine articles about that person.

- *Social uses of media.*   How group members are using the media for certain social purposes—developing relationships, impressing each other, defining status, and so forth. For example, male adults may attempt to dictate television program selection for a family, in some cases, by not letting others have the remote control (Morley, 1986). Other studies find that parental authority may be challenged by children's or adolescents' own selection of music, programs, or Internet sites as a way of defining their own sense of independence (Moores, 1993).

Group members may also define their roles through engagement or identification with a text. In a study conducted by one of my students, Aaron Cato (1996), examined the responses of a group of three African American males and a group of three African American females to the movie adaptation of Terry McMillan's novel, *Waiting to Exhale,* which features four strong African American women and their relationships with men. Aaron found that the females identified strongly with the women characters. In contrast, the males were more critical of the negative portrayals of males in the movie, perceiving the lack of positive characters as a personal attack on themselves: "She portrayed us as no good men who were afraid of responsibility" (p. 10). The females disagreed with the males' critique. As one noted, "I don't think it was the down play of African American men in general; it was just those men in particular whom she chose to write about" (p. 11). In response to Aaron's question about whether "the women were unhappy because they didn't have a man" (p. 11), the females argued that the women could achieve happiness without men, whereas the men argued that the women were unhappy "because they could not find a man" (p. 11). These viewers' identification with characters had a strong influence on their responses.

In another study, Rick Lybeck (1996) found that, in viewing a televised baseball game, male viewers who were baseball players responded to the game by vicariously experiencing the actions of the players. They mimicked the ball players when they hit home runs and nonchalantly watched the ball fly as they walked the first few paces to first base. Rick also notes that this male sports talk serves to define their social identities:

> The main feature of the ESPN update was Barry Bonds having hit his 300th and 301st home runs earlier that afternoon. The significance of this was that Bonds joined an elite group of three other players who had in their careers hit 300 or more

home runs and stolen 300 or more bases. A trivia question was put: Who are the other guys? There were three generations of ball players present, two father-and-son combinations, quizzing each other on father-and-son baseball trivia; it truly was a question made for them. The TV medium as focused on in this informal ethnography was something that was *integrated* into a male-bonding setting, but not necessarily central to the bonding. TV enabled the males to extend their baseball enjoyment and to affirm their identities as baseball players following in the footsteps of baseball fathers. (p. 15)

Interviewing

One important phase of a study involves interviewing group members about their responses. Interviews provide an understanding of individual group members' own personal perceptions of the influence of the group on their own responses. For example, a group member may have said very little about a text in a group discussion, but talked extensively about the same text in an interview.

Following are some interview questions that were used in a study of seventh graders' responses to stories in an on-line computer chat exchange using the program Aspects (Beach & Lundell, 1997). One advantage of having students use a chat program is that it produces a printout transcript that can serve as the basis for follow-up interview questions. In this study, students were asked to read through their group's transcript and to "think aloud" their reactions to the transcript. They were also asked to respond to these interview questions regarding their group participation:

- How do you feel about participating in these conversations? Do you feel comfortable participating? How does receiving a lot of comments that are not in order affect you? Recalling the first time you participated, how have you changed? Does your participation seem more or less like engaging in an oral discussion?

- When you are receiving a lot of different messages about different things, how do you decide on what to respond to?

- How did you feel when no one responded to you? When you don't get a reaction, what are you thinking?

- How do you interact face-to-face in an oral discussion group? How does this differ from your participation in the computer group?

- What social roles do you usually play in the classroom or in your peer group? What role do you see yourself playing in these computer groups?

I role-play interviewing to demonstrate techniques for encouraging interviewees to express their thoughts and feelings. Although students prepare interview questions in advance, they should also be willing to "go with the flow" of the conversation with the interviewee. Students tape the interviews so that they have a record of the group member's talk.

Outsider versus Insider Perspectives

In some cases, students are members of the group they are studying. In assuming this role of a participant/observer, students need to reflect on how their own relationship toward that group—as an outsider or insider—shapes their perceptions of the group. As an outsider, they may not be familiar with a group's inner workings and routines. They may, therefore, want to use a "cultural broker" who helps them gain access to the group. On the other hand, as an insider, they may be a fish in water, and they may have difficulty standing back and assuming the Martian stance required to perceive the group as a microculture. They may therefore want to share their perceptions with someone who is not familiar with the group. Ideally, students should embrace both of these perspectives by experiencing what it is like to be a group member and by standing back to assume a spectator stance.

Analyzing the Results

Once they have collected observations, recordings, and information about a group and its members, students then analyze the meaning of these results. In doing so, they are interpreting how group members' responses reflect their shared cultural stance. To define that shared cultural stance, they attempt to discern norms and conventions constituting what is considered appropriate group behavior and talk. For example, in a newsgroup discussion, instances of "flaming," or ridicule of group members, are considered a violation of "netiquette." Although these norms and conventions are generally not explicitly stated, they are implied by members' comments or reactions to behaviors and talk perceived as appropriate or deviant. For example, if someone in a newsgroup discussion does engage in "flaming," another member may admonish that person, noting that such behavior is unacceptable in their newsgroup.

These norms and conventions were evident in Judy Ward's (1996) study of computer newsgroup participants' responses to the television program *X-Files,* a program that portrays two FBI agents, a male and a female, who investigate various governmental crimes. Judy asked participants if they were interested in answering some questions, and thirty-five participants, most of them female, provided her with answers to her questions. When asked what they liked about the newsgroup, participants noted that they "enjoy the discussion threads concerning plot and character development, the 'far out' theories members propose, news about production issues, 'insider information you would otherwise never hear about,' and the stars' talk show appearances."

Newsgroup members demonstrated their allegiance to the group by sharing a common language of acronyms and emoticons, such as :) for a smiley face and :(for a sad face. They also shared common concerns with certain topics and themes, particularly the theme of distrust of government. They regarded certain contributions as inappropriate: making irrelevant, off-topic statements (considered as "dreck" or "drivel"), bashing or spreading false rumors about the two celebrity stars of the show, posting sexually explicit or violent messages, or misusing the newsgroup. Certain members of the group assumed responsibility for monitoring compliance to the group's norms. When a participant began spreading false rumors about the female star of the show, she was immediately castigated and told "either get with it and get some netiquette or please keep your computer turned off" (p. 8).

Members gained status in the group by making frequent postings; by being affiliated with the program; by meeting one of the stars; by selling magazines, scripts, autographs, or T-shirts; or by sharing videos of programs. They also gained status by making intertextual links between the program and other television programs. The practices reflect the value group members place on assisting each other as group members. They also seek out verification of their feelings, asking each other if "someone feels this way" or "am I the only one who feels bad." Based on her analysis of the group members' adherence to certain norms and conventions, Judy inferred that "alt.tv.x-files is a micro culture with its own genre of literature, myths, and mores, embedded in larger cultures of paranoia and distrust of big government and a general fan culture which becomes deeply connected to entertainment icons" (p. 7).

As an alternative to studying a group in the present, students may also write about their own past experiences, with group responses and the norms or conventions constituting their experience in the group. In a journal entry, Staci Banks recalled the experience of a group of female sorority sisters watching the soap opera program *Days of Our Lives* during lunch. She remembers that the seniors, as experienced members of the group, were perceived to have the highest status in the group, although members who "knew facts about past relationships and could fill in gaps for others" assumed some status. Certain norms were operating: Talk was allowed only during commercials, and posing too many questions was considered annoying.

Group members discussed a range of topics having to do with the portrayal of women on both the program and the commercials. Members often applied their own background expertise to these discussions, with psychology majors analyzing character motivations and marketing majors focusing on advertising techniques in the commercials. Banks also fondly recalls these discussions as a time to socialize and make new friends. At the same time, she senses a distance between her past stance assumed in the group and her current, more critical stance regarding soap operas, changes she attributes to changes in her own gender-role attitudes.

Analysis of Text Features

In conducting media ethnographies, students may also describe the particular aspects of texts that evoke or invite certain responses. As part of his study (included in the Appendix) of college females' responses to "Christian" romance novels, Timothy Rohde (1996) analyzed the plot development of 110 mail-order, evangelical novels. He found that these novels contained few references to sexuality, a marked contrast to recent Harlequin and Silhouette romance novels. For evangelical Christians who objected to the trend toward "steamier" romance novels, these Christian romance novels published by the Heartsong Press provided a more "pure" alternative. In contrast to the typical romance novel plot development (Christian-Smith, 1993; Radway, 1984), the Heartsong romance novel heroine initially expresses doubt in her faith. She then meets a "good man," whom she believes is not a Christian. She then experiences a conversion, removing her doubt in her faith. The heroine is rescued from peril by the man, and she learns of his true nature as a Christian. It is only after they marry that they have sex. Although the romance novel is designed to celebrate a woman's role as a nurturer who transforms a more impersonal hero into a more caring person (Radway, 1984), the Heartsong novels are designed to be more didactic and morally uplifting, serving to reify readers' allegiances to evangelical Christian beliefs.

A group of women whom Rohde interviewed responded positively to these novels' "pure" subject matter and plot development. These readers believed that they did not have to be concerned about being "on guard" when reading these novels. Some preferred the historical Heartsong novels because they were set in a past perceived to be less corrupt than the current period. They also responded positively to the novels' didactic messages, noting that "reading these books helped them to grow in their faith as they learned the same spiritual lesson the heroine did." Rohde's analysis of these novels' characteristics helped him explain his participants' responses. This suggests that students, in conducting their media ethnographies, may benefit from linking descriptions of specific aspects of texts to their participants' responses.

Implications for Fostering Reader Response in the Classroom

The results of the students' and others' microethnographic studies have a number of implications for fostering reader response in the classroom.

Aesthetic Engagement as Transformational

The readers and viewers in these studies all shared a "lived through" aesthetic (Rosenblatt, 1983) engagement with texts that served to transform their own sense of identity or self. The readers and viewers in these studies were also using their responses to build social relationships and roles. Through their experiences with texts, these readers and viewers vicariously assumed different roles and stances, which, from a postmodern perspective, allowed them to experiment with different identities. For example, Lybeck's male viewers established their male identities through their shared knowledge of sports. Ward's newsgroup participants established their identities as knowledgeable, loyal fans. Rohde's readers affirmed their allegiance as church members through resisting "hot" romance novels and responding positively to the "pure" Heartsong novels. By adopting different stances and roles through their responses, group members achieved social status in the group. One of the characteristics of these newsgroup exchanges is that the participants define the direction and focus of the conversation. In contrast, in the classroom, as James Reither (1996) notes, "teachers' questions shape and focus the students' study, thinking, discussion, and writing; the teacher's agenda, not dialogic exigency, controls turn-taking; teachers provide feedback on students' work, so that response is routinized; and, of course, teachers assign grades" (p. 49). In the newsgroup exchanges, participants value each others' sharing as contributing to the group's shared, composite experience. Their responses "count as a contribution to the knowing of others who need or can use what the writer knows" (Reither, 1996, p. 52).

This suggests the need to create classroom forums, such as book clubs or computer chat exchanges (Beach & Lundell, 1997), in which students are responsible for shaping the discussions, allowing them to share their ideas as members of a community of readers or viewers. It also suggests the need for teachers, if they are facilitating discussions, to recognize the fact that they need to be open to what Gordon Pradl (1996) defines as "purposelessness"—spontaneous development of conversation not scripted according to a predetermined plan or agenda. In doing so, they are exploring what Pradl defines as a "discourse of possibility" rather than a "discourse of certainty." As he notes, "by seeing our talk in terms of *possibilities,* rather than *certainties,* we come to understand that the way we speak, as much as what we say, has real consequences for participants, who are constantly weighing and choosing among alternative linguistic representations of reality" (p. 104). Students are more likely to be engaged in such discussions when they assume that the outcome of that discussion is not predetermined—that they are mutually constructing knowledge that breaks new ground in their experience with a text.

The Influence of Beliefs and Attitudes on Responses

The readers' or viewers' beliefs and attitudes in these studies have a strong influence on their responses. Lybeck's family television viewers, Ward's newsgroup participants, and Cato's *Waiting to Exhale* viewers drew on their gender-role attitudes to respond positively or negatively to gender-role portrayals. Rohde's readers sought out romance novels that confirmed their evangelical Christian values. This suggests the need for teachers to help students reflect on the nature of those beliefs and attitudes that are influencing their responses. In reflecting on their beliefs and attitudes, students begin by citing reasons for responses. They then explore the assumptions or presuppositions inherent in those reasons. For example, Reinertsen's viewers' reasons for judgments of characters consistently reflected their middle-class, achievement-oriented values. By comparing their own beliefs and attitudes to those of the groups they study in their microethnographies, students may begin to perceive the limitations of their beliefs and attitudes. For example, if a group of students conducted a study similar to that of Rhode's of highly religious readers, by comparing their own, more secular beliefs and attitudes with those of more religious readers, they may, by comparison, better understand their own beliefs and attitudes.

The Relationships between Understanding Real-World and Text-World Contexts

In conducting these studies, students are examining how readers' responses reflect group norms and conventions constituting appropriate responses in a group. In doing so, they are attempting to understand how real-world contexts shape participants' social practices. This requires them to make inferences about group norms and conventions based on observed behavior and talk. Similarly, in responding to text worlds portrayed in literature, students are applying their own social knowledge to infer the norms and conventions constituting those text worlds. Just as Rohde had to construct the world of his religious readers, so do readers construct similar religious worlds in responding to, for example, Hawthorne's short stories. All of this suggests that teachers could help students understand text worlds by having them draw links to similar real-world contexts they are studying in their microethnographic analyses. By explicitly discussing their processes for inferring the norms, roles, rituals, and beliefs operating in real-world groups or institutions, students could then employ a similar process in constructing text worlds. For example, students could observe behaviors in supermarkets or stores, recording their observations of the decor; of clients' behaviors, language, and appearance; of check-out routines, and so forth, and then inferring the conventions, attitudes, and roles unique to that microculture. They could then make similar inferences about the world of the supermarket in "A & P," by John Updike, in which the manager enforces certain norms for appropriate behavior and dress. In contextualizing fictional worlds such as Updike's A & P supermarket, students are drawing on their strategies for discerning appropriate behavior in real-world contexts.

In summary, in studying how others respond to texts, students will better understand their own responses. They will hopefully recognize how readers and viewers become engaged with texts through shared community experiences, in which responding is a social act. Also, in understanding how readers and viewers apply their beliefs, attitudes, and experiences to texts, they will appreciate how their own beliefs, attitudes, and experiences shape their own responses to texts.

REFERENCES

Ang, I. (1985). *Watching "Dallas": Soap opera and the melodramatic imagination.* London: Metheun.

Beach, R. (1995). Constructing cultural models through response to literature. *English Journal, 84,* 87–94.

Beach, R., & Lundell, D. (1997). Early adolescents' use of computer-mediated communication in writing and reading. In D. Reinking, L. Labbo, M. McKenna, & R. Kieffer (Eds.), *Transforming readers and writers.* Hillsdale, NJ: Erlbaum.

Bird, E. (1992). *For enquiring minds: A cultural study of supermarket tabloids.* Knoxville, TN: University of Tennessee Press.

Brown, M. (Ed.). (1990). *Television and women's culture: The politics of the popular.* London: Sage.

Buckingham, D. (1993). Boys' talk: Television and the policing of masculinity. In D. Buckingham (Ed.), *Reading Audiences: Young People and the Media* (pp. 89–115). New York: Manchester University Press.

Buckingham, D. (1996). *Moving images: Understanding children's responses to television.* New York: Manchester University Press.

Cato, Aaron. (1996). *Waiting to exhale ethnography.* Unpublished manuscript, University of Minnesota at Minneapolis St. Paul, MN.

Cherland, M. (1994). *Private practices: Girls reading fiction and constructing identity.* Bristol, PA: Taylor & Francis.

Christian-Smith, L. (Ed.). (1993). *Texts of desire: Essays on fiction, femininity and schooling.* London: Falmer.

Eckert, Penelope. (1989). *Jocks and burnouts.* New York: Teachers College.

Finders, M. (1996). *Just girls: The literate life and underlife of early adolescent girls.* New York: Teachers College Press.

Jenkins, H. (1992). *Textual poachers: Television fans and participatory culture.* New York: Routledge.

Lybeck, R. (1996). *Family members' responses to television news and sports.* Unpublished manuscript, University of Minnesota at Minneapolis St. Paul, MN.

Lull, J. (1990). *Inside family viewing: Ethnographic research on television's audiences.* New York: Routledge.

McRobbie, A. (1990). *Feminism and youth culture.* New York: Macmillan.

Mills, S. (Ed.). (1994). *Gendering the reader.* New York: Harvester Wheatsheaf.

Moores, S. (1993). *Interpreting audiences: The ethnography of media consumption.* Thousands Oaks, CA: Sage.

Morley, D. (1986). *Family television: Cultural power and domestic leisure.* London: Comedia.

Palmer, P. (1986). *The lively audience: A study of children around the TV set.* Sydney, Australia: Allen and Unwin.

Peck, R. (1989). I go along. In D. Gallo (Ed.), *Connections* (pp. 184–191). New York: Dell.

Pradl, G. (1996). *Literature for democracy: Reading as a social act.* Portsmouth, NH: Boynton/Cook.

Provenzo, E. (1991). *Video kids: Making sense of Nintendo.* Cambridge, MA: Harvard University Press.

Radway, J. (1984). *Reading the romance: Women, patriarchy, and popular literature.* Chapel Hill, NC: University of North Carolina Press.

Reinertsen, C. (1993). *Wednesday night is girls' night.* Unpublished manuscript, University of Minnesota at Minneapolis St. Paul, MN.

Reither, J. (1996). Motivating writing differently in a literary studies classroom. In A. Young, & T. Fulwiler (Eds.), *When writing teachers teach literature* (pp. 48–62). Portsmouth, NH: Boynton/Cook.

Rohde, T. (1996). *"I love you; let's pray": The business and "ministry" of the Christian romance novel.* Unpublished manuscript, University of Minnesota at Minneapolis St. Paul, MN.

Rosenblatt, L. (1983). *Literature as exploration.* New York: Modern Language Association.

Schein, E. (1985). How culture forms, develops, and changes. In R. Kilman (Ed.), *Gaining control of the corporate culture* (pp. 17–43). San Francisco: Jossey-Bass.

Seiter, E., Borchers, H., Kreutzner, G., & Warth, E. (Eds.). (1989). *Remote control: Television, audiences, and cultural power.* New York: Routledge.

Spigel, L., & Mann, D. (Eds.) (1992). *Private screenings: Television and the female consumer.* Minneapolis, MN: University of Minnesota Press.

Turkle, S. (1995). *Life on the screen: Identity in the age of the Internet.* New York: Simon and Schuster.

Ward, J. (1996). *Don't watch it alone! An ethnography of the alt.tv.x-file newsgroup.* Unpublished manuscript, University of Minnesota at Minneapolis St. Paul, MN.

A Sample Student Report

"I Love You; Let's Pray": The Business and "Ministry" of the Christian Romance Novel

TIMOTHY ROHDE

Let me describe a new business proposition to you. Let's target women, "primarily women who consider themselves born again Christians" (Heartsong, 1993). We will sell our books primarily through direct mail because there is no retail outlet where our readers would expect to find our products. We will send four novels every four weeks to each subscriber for $9.97 postpaid. I can guarantee that, after three years, you will have more than 20,000 subscribers (Reginald, 1996).

Does this sound too good to be true? It isn't. Let me introduce you to Heartsong Presents. Since its inception in 1993, it has entered a market without competition and has developed more than 20,000 monthly customers. This is incredible growth for a company filling a market that, until 1993, was not being filled by anyone. In other words, it is the first company of its kind, and it has been wildly successful.

This paper is part genre analysis and part ethnography. I am concerned with Christian romance novels and their readers. What are these novels like? Why do readers read them? How do those readers feel about their reading? How are these readers similar and dissimilar to other romance readers?

The Christian Romance as Genre

Serial romance publishing is dominated by Harlequin and Silhouette. Early in their lives, both imprints had a very conservative view of sex and romance—and their readers liked it that way. As late as 1980, Harlequin still shied away from sex, or it featured "consummation" in longer, specifically marketed novels (Brotman, 1980). As romance novels became more sexually explicit—even though some imprints from each publishing giant still maintained the heroine's purity—readers wanted something purer. And it is that type of involvement from readers that makes romance novels huge sellers (Berman, 1978) and a unique commodity: Romance reader involvement and reader loyalty are unmatched in the publishing industry.

I should also draw a specific distinction between serial romance fiction—Harlequin or Heartsong—and romance fiction in general—publishers such as Avon, Warner, and Dell. Although serial romance fiction started out as "pure" and has become a bit more salacious, romance fiction, which came into its own with the direct-to-paperback publication of Kathleen Woodiwiss's *The Flame and the Flower* (1972), appeals to readers who want "erotic-historical romance" (Turner, 1978). These novels typically feature fairly explicit "ravishings," usually repeated or unwanted (at least, at first). Most romance fiction is sold in bookstores; a significant portion of serial romance fiction is sold through direct mail. When romance fiction became "hot" after Woodiwiss's explosion into the book market in 1974, traditional serial romance fiction began to lose business to the more explicit novels featuring "more experienced and worldly women" (Coser, Kadushin, & Powell, 1982, p. 264).

Enter Heartsong Presents—serial romance fiction with a moral purpose. It is both business and ministry. Beaujour (1980) posits that, "The 'good' or righteous novel will therefore indulge in a lot of intratextual transcoding in order to eliminate ambiguity and therefore delimit the range of interpretation allowed to the reader" (p. 345). This is different from the regular romance novels, which "are dirty and powerful because they are, at least on one level, a mimesis of dirt and shares in its power" (Beaujour, 1980 p. 348). Heartsong's novels mean little more than the obvious: they are romance stories in which the heroine finds true love within the context of Evangelical Christianity. When Wayne Booth (1974) describes the reader, he notes that, "Regardless of my real beliefs and practices, I must subordinate my mind and heart if I am to enjoy it to the full" (p. 138). Perhaps that is what separates a reader from a *consumer* of a product: The consumer does not have to subordinate anything—the product is exactly what she or he wants. If it isn't, consumers won't buy it anymore. Readers here must subordinate nothing. The novels cover no new moral territory. Each one is safe, pure, and innocent, never challenging the Evangelical Christian's belief structure or raising questions of appropriateness.

What is a Heartsong romance novel like? It is a safe place, full of prayer and morality. It is also full of desire, wrestled with within the confines of Christian morality. Take, for example, *Sweet Shelter* by VeraLee Wiggins (1993). Candy Hartwell, a construction worker/developer, alternates between love and desire for Jeremy "Chance" Chancellor, a competing builder. When her projects are routinely vandalized, she blames Chance, even though, "God had shown her, really shown her, that Chance would never do a thing like that" (p. 69). In *Sweet Shelter,* as in all the other Heartsong novels I sampled, the heroine fights with herself and with God until finally everything is resolved. Resolution with God brings resolution with the object of her affection. This is not terribly unlike the religious romance epics of the Renaissance.

I have read 110 of Heartsong's novels. Some are written fairly well; others are certainly poor writing. Of course, this sort of judgment is admittedly subjective. Even Steve Reginald (1996), vice president and publisher for Heartsong, admits that, "This is not great literature; it's formula writing." Each novel, in addition to having a predictable plot, features a specific theme woven throughout the story.

Sweet Shelter points out the importance of trusting God even when things look bad. *A New Song* (Yapp, 1994) shows the reader that God wants to heal the wounds of the past. *A Change of Heart* (Lavo, 1995) declares that we must release our anger to God. Indeed, Heartsong's guidelines state, "We are not looking for 'sermons in novel form' . . . One particular biblical message should be threaded throughout if possible" (Heartsong, 1993). The religious theme is important, but secondary to the romance of the story.

Janice Radway found a consistent pattern within the romance novels she studied; she labeled it, "the narrative structure of the ideal romance" (Radway, 1984, p. 134). The pattern I see emerging in Heartsong's novels is a bit different from Radway's. Almost all of the novels I read follow this specific pattern in their plot construction:

1. The heroine has a hidden hurt from the past—usually the death of a parent—for which she blames God.
2. The heroine is removed from her normal environment and placed in a new one.
3. The heroine meets a man she is instantly attracted to, but she denies the attraction.
4. The man is "a good man," but the heroine misinterprets something he does and decides he is a rogue (he is usually also dating—or the heroine thinks he is dating—another woman at this time).
5. Through a sermon, a stranger, or divine revelation, the heroine has a conversion experience with Jesus Christ. This can also be the re-establishment of a relationship that she had as a child but abandoned when the "hurt" in stage 1 happened.
6. Through a crisis situation (an attempted rape, illness, automobile accident, tornado, etc.), the woman is put into peril and is promptly rescued by the man.
7. The man's true nature is revealed and the heroine learns that he, too, is a Christian (or he becomes a Christian, or, in a few novels, he is already a Christian and he learns that she, too, is now a Christian).
8. The man declares his love to the woman, she declares her love to him, and they make plans to marry.
9. If consummation is mentioned, it happens on the wedding night and is called something like "her wondrous initiation into the fullness of marriage" (Lavo, 1995, p. 169).
10. Our couple live happily ever after.

The one notable change from Radway's pattern, aside from the lack of sexual involvement, has to do with the heroine's social identity. As the first stage of Radway's pattern, she sees the heroine's social identity destroyed. That is not always the case with Heartsong's novels. Frequently, the heroine faces an obstacle that makes her relocate, but she is always aware of who she is and expects people to treat her accordingly. Similarly, Radway's final stage is the heroine's re-establishment of her social identity. Heartsong heroines find redemption in Christ and let their social identities take care of themselves (although, consistently, reconciliation with the hero follows soon after spiritual reconciliation).

Another noticeable change was the diversity of careers these women are given. In many novels, the heroine is a nurse, an artist, a singer, or a missionary, but several feature women who are astronauts, construction workers, scientists, accountants, and doctors. Several novels feature women of color, and several feature heroines older than fifty. I am happy that this series cultivates diversity in women's roles, although the guidelines clearly state that a woman can never be shown in any pastoral leadership position.

One of the most obvious differences between a Heartsong novel and other romance fiction is its dual purpose. These novels are not only attempting to entertain—they also attempt to teach. One promotional brochure about the series explains, "They are stories that do more than simply thrill the heart. They truly *inspire*. They don't just move you . . . they change you! " (Heartsong, 1995). The advertisements show women, some young, some older, reading well-worn copies of Heartsong novels with smiles of delight plastered on their faces. Testimonial letters explain how the reader learns new biblical truths ("So very often I find that the lessons your heroines are learning are lessons I need to learn at that particular time as well" ["Enjoy" brochure]) or uses them as therapy ("They've been a blessing to many of the young girls I work with in the shelter for abused and neglected children where I'm employed" ["Enjoy" brochure, 1995]). Therefore, as Radway's readers find romance fiction to be restorative, so, too, Heartsong readers find reading to be redemptive and uplifting. This goes one step beyond regular romance readers—these readers find moral guidance as well as pleasure.

As with any romance novel business, Heartsong authors must write within very strict guidelines. The guidelines list ten very specific "hot topics" that all writers must "steer clear of" at all costs:

1. spirit baptism
2. water baptism (meaning of)
3. time of spirit baptism (at conversion versus second experience of grace)
4. time of water baptism (children or adults)
5. gifts of the spirit (e.g., are tongues still around?)
6. end times (setting dates)
7. Lord's Supper (ordinance versus sacrament)
8. women's ordination
9. Christian perfection
10. transferring qualities of Jesus—or passages in the Bible that refer to Jesus—to heroes in books (This also applies to Mary, Jesus's earthly mother.) (Heartsong, 1993).

All of these warnings seem to fall into issues of theological debate within Evangelical Christianity, or between Protestants and Catholics. The guidelines also warn against using euphemisms like "heck" or "darn," having any of the main characters be divorced, or having a heroine work as a member of the clergy. Writers must portray alcohol consumption as bad, never portray social dancing (although historical dancing can be acceptable), and have their characters modestly dressed at all times. Interestingly enough, the only discussion of sexuality is found in one brief paragraph: "Physical tension between characters should not be overdone. Do not be overly descriptive when describing how characters feel in a particular romantic moment, for example, kissing, embracing, and so on" (Heartsong, 1993).

The "Ministry" of Christian Romance Novels

Cawelti (1976) lays the foundation for serial romance fiction when he states, "The moral fantasy of the romance is that of love triumphant and permanent, overcoming all obstacles and difficulties" (pp. 41–42). He repeatedly uses the term *moral fantasy* to describe the genre, but, when applied to Christian romance, I would have to broaden his term to become moral reality. For the readers of Christian romance fiction, morality and its inherent idealism is assumed to be a day-to-day reality by its readers.

Steve Reginald (1996) says that many of Heartsong's readers don't necessarily define themselves as Christians; they simply want cleaner romance novels. Their writer's guidelines, however, make it clear that the company specifically targets Christian readers. "Most readers were and are buying Harlequins and Silhouettes," he says. Indeed, the covers are designed to strongly resemble those of secular serial romance novels.

Unfortunately, none of the people I interviewed would admit to buying Harlequins or Silhouettes. In fact, some of them didn't even want to be called "romance novel" readers at all. Frances Allen, forty-seven, an office manager and minister's wife, said, "I wouldn't really call them romance novels—they're really historical novels." Sandra Miller, fifty-six, a reading specialist, bristled at the term romance novel. "I *don't* read romance novels," she stated emphatically; "I read historical fiction." Even Reginald concedes that the romance novel tag is problematic—he cites it as a major reason that Heartsong has had difficulty breaking into the retail business. Radway's readers refused to discuss whether or not their novels were sexually arousing; my readers were loath to even consider them as romantic fiction!

A few readers didn't have this problem. Allison Bump, twenty-four, an associate minister of music, readily acknowledged that she reads romance novels. In fact, it is a family affair. "My mother sends me books that are really good, and I read them and then we talk about them. My grandmother likes them too." She didn't seem to care if there was a stigma attached to being labeled a romance novel reader, but she also freely admitted that she used to read Silhouettes, Harlequins, and trade paperback romances before discovering the Christian ones. Sherry Lee, forty-two, a minister's wife, also acknowledged that these are really romance novels that she is reading, but, like Allison, she has memories of reading romantic fiction with her mother at a young age. All four of these women mentioned Grace Livingston Hill—a Christian novelist from the '40s—as one of their favorite authors. Interestingly enough, the company that publishes Hill's work today has recently removed the word *romance* from the covers and now describes them as "books of enduring faith and love."

What do these readers get from reading these novels? That is hard to say. Some of the novels are historical, and while readers never actually articulated it, I suspect that there is a specific reason they sometimes prefer historical to contemporary settings. To the mind of many conservative Christians, the past represents a "golden" time when society was less immoral and generally safer. Therefore, by reading about the exploits of these heroines in the past, these readers are safer than reading about contemporary heroines who would perceivably face the same immoral society the readers face. In this way, the past becomes even more romantic as these readers imagine a time when their conservative morality would not be challenged as stridently as they perceive society to challenge it today.

These readers also like the fact that they do not have to be "on guard" when reading these novels. Sandra was very clear in telling me that she would never read a secular romance novel—or even a secular historical novel—because of the questionable morality. She explained that she could feel "a check in [her] spirit" when something was morally objectionable, and she would then stop reading the book. None of the other women I interviewed were this specific, but they all appreciated the conservative morality that these novels portrayed. Several mentioned that they found the heroine's problems inspiring; they even explained that reading these books had helped them to grow in their faith as they learned the same spiritual lesson as the heroine. (Remember that each novel has a clearly defined didactic moral theme woven throughout.)

Conclusion

I believe that the business of Christian romance has a bright future. Many people I spoke with liked the concept of morally conservative romance novels; a recurring comment had to do with being able to share these with children and grandchildren. If Heartsong can establish the same reader loyalty that other romance publishers have, it should be around for many years. I also expect that some other companies will soon enter into this market and provide Heartsong with competition.

Television's biggest flaw was the mixture of business and ministry; I wonder what role this conflict will play in the evolution of the Christian romance novel. As Heartsong continues to grow and more and more money is at stake, how will the publishers continue to view their "ministry"? Will readers continue to respond so good-naturedly when the price of the novels begins to climb?

Ultimately, the only thing that separates these novels from their secular siblings is their conservative moral stance. Readers of secular romance novels find them restorative; readers of Christian romance novels get "ministered to." Heartsong is both progressive and old-fashioned at the same time. Its heroines can be astronauts but not ministers. They can dance in the past but not in the present. And this is exactly what Heartsong readers love—predictability, conservative morality, and a bit of surprise.

REFERENCES

Beaujour, M. (1980). Exemplary pornography: Barres, Loyola, and the novel. In S. Suleiman & I. Crosman (Eds.), *The reader in the text: Essays on audience and interpretation* (pp. 325–349). Princeton, NJ: Princeton University Press.

Berman, P. (1978). They call us illegitimate. *Forbes, 6*, 37–38.

Booth, W. (1974). *The rhetoric of fiction.* Chicago: University of Chicago Press.

Brotman, B. (1980, June 2). Ah, romance! Harlequin has an affair for its readers. *Chicago Tribune*, B1–B2.

Cawelti, J. (1976). *Adventure, mystery, and romance: Formula stories as art and popular culture.* Chicago: University of Chicago Press.

Coser, L., Kadushin, C., & Powell, W. (1982). *Books: The culture and commerce of publishing.* New York: Basic.

Heartsong. (1993). *Guidelines for writers and editors.* Uhrichsville, OH: Heartsong Presents.

Heartsong. (1995). *Enjoy a brand-new novel of romance and inspiration every week.* Promotional mailing. Uhrichsville, OH: Heartsong Presents.

Lavo, N. (1995). *A change of heart.* Uhrichsville, OH: Heartsong Presents.

Radway, J. (1984). *Reading the romance: Women, patriarchy, and popular literature.* Chapel Hill, NC: University of North Carolina Press.

Reginald, S. (1996). Telephone interview. May 31, 1996.

Turner, A. (1978). The tempestuous, tumultuous, turbulent, torrid, and terribly profitable world of paperback passion. *New York, 13*, 46–49.

Wiggins, V. (1993). *Sweet Shelter.* Uhrichsville, OH: Heartsong Presents.

Woodiwiss, K. (1972). *The flame and the flower.* New York: Avon.

Yapp, K. (1994). *A new song.* Uhrichsville, OH: Heartsong Presents.

Between Readers and Texts: The Work of the Interpretive Community

GEORGE LABERCANE

University of Calgary

A culture is as much a forum for negotiating and renegotiating meaning and for explicating action as it is a set of rules or specifications for action.

—Bruner (1986, p. 123)

Negotiating the Work of the Interpretive Community

When I was eleven years old, I can vividly remember being caught up in the Tarzan books, a series written by Edgar Rice Burroughs (1914, 1915). I was completely taken with the persona of Tarzan, and, having been introduced to the character in Burrough's first book in the series (*Tarzan of the Apes*), I was soon caught up in *The Return of Tarzan* and eventually the entire series. For me, reading became the means by which I was able to enter into the world of Tarzan and live there, not just for one novel but for a whole series of adventures. My encounters were, in effect, a series of rereadings; as one reads through several volumes in a series an effect similar to rereading is created (Hunsberger, 1985). My reading seemed to possess the character of the traveller who, having spent a summer discovering Paris, now wanted to return to explore that wonderful city in greater detail. Having visited the Sorbonne, the traveller now wants to explore the Louvre. As a reader who had opened himself up to the Tarzan series, I was enabled to feel something, to care, to experience action and the consequences. As Rosenblatt (1978) declares, through my transactions with texts, I was enabled to live through the experiences that those texts shared with me.

But what of the work of the interpretive community? How does the reader negotiate the meaning of text with others? I was reminded of this the first time I introduced *The Great Gilly Hopkins* (Paterson, 1978) to a class of education students who had minimal exposure to teaching literature to young children. The students took readily to Gilly and were more than willing to listen as I read to them each time we met (two times a week). In fact, engagement with the text became so intense that a number of students couldn't wait for me to finish the novel; some went out and purchased the book so that they could find out ahead of time what happened to Gilly. In effect, you could say that we, as an interpretive community, had achieved our goals. We were, as a class (an interpretive community), able to engage in a lived-through experience with the text. Our interpretations were "at one" with each other.

Some other activities with the class enjoyed a similar measure of cohesiveness. An "open letter" to Gilly's mother was also effective in that the whole class seemed unanimous in its critique of the mother's lack of concern for her daughter. However, other activities proved, in my view, to be complete failures. Journal responses were clear examples of failed communication. There was simply too much time between my readings and the students' responses. As a consequence, some students wrote full entries, while others simply did not write at all. A similar pattern of behavior surfaced when I attempted to initiate a Community of Readers project with my students in the Wednesday evening class. Although there was a rush of enthusiasm in the initial stages of this in-class activity, it soon became apparent that many were unable to sustain such interest and enthusiasm over an extended period of time. Again, the time length between reading and responding (once a week) could not be sustained, and I was forced, after a month, to abandon the project. Such failed endeavours are, nevertheless, instructive, and it was these kinds of experiences that led to my interest in the topic I have chosen to address: the work of the interpretive community.

I have chosen the term *work* deliberately, in the hopes of showing how readers must first work their way through a text in an active, albeit individual, manner. The idea of passive readers who receive the meaning of a text simply by running their eyes over the print seems inappropriate. Neither does it seem fitting that texts function simply to impose their meaning on an unsuspecting reader. Rather, what seems to fit as a description of reader-text encounters is the idea that these encounters take place along a continuum that exists between a phenomenological account and a socially constructed view that characterizes how readers work together to interpret texts (Bakhtin, 1981).

What I hope to show, then, is that the work of the interpretive community is to help readers break through the wall of silence that characterizes so many reader-text engagements by providing a forum for negotiating the meaning of what we have been reading. A forum does not, of course, ensure that we will come to a complete understanding of that which we find intriguing or confusing. What the interpretive community will do, though, is to show readers that not everyone shares our beliefs and that what we as readers must do is to learn how to adjust our views of what a text means in light of new understandings gained by sharing our viewpoints with others (Dasenbrock, 1991).

Gadamer (1997) provides support for a phenomenological account of reader/text transactions when he says, ". . . neither does the reader exist who, when he [sic] has his text before him, simply reads what is there. Rather, all reading involves application, so that a person reading a text is himself part of the meaning he apprehends. He belongs to the text that he is reading" (p. 340). The reader enters into an "act of constitution," in which both reader and text are set in motion and the virtual text that is created lives somewhere outside both reader and text (Iser, 1978). It is in this sense, then, that I want to begin by arguing that before we can have a communal sense of reading with others, the reader must have a "lived through experience" (Rosenblatt, 1978) with a text or, at least, an ongoing experience of that text while the reader is part of an interpretive community.

Response to literature, therefore, can be viewed as a transaction between reader and text in which meaning represents an act of negotiation between the reader and the text (Iser, 1978; Rosenblatt, 1978). However, this seems to represent only half the picture. What happens when we share the texts we have been reading with others? Engaging with a text is a private affair in which reader and text work together to produce an interpretation; however, there is a more public aspect when readers share their interpretations and test their own understandings with others in the interpretive community (Fish, 1980).

Having entered into a dialogue with the text in which we have become conversational partners with the text, we would naturally want to involve others in the conversation. In other words, inviting other voices into this relationship helps us to extend the range of the conversation to include other members of the interpretive community. In this respect, Probst (1994) argues for the uniqueness of the individual reader and the integrity of individual reading.

Losing the Innocence of Orality:
The Reader in the Text

> "Literary theory has recently begun to show more interest in the uniqueness of the reader . . . , to pay attention to what the reader brings to the text and how each reader goes about making sense of it" (Probst, 1992, p. 118).

The dialogue that I establish in my first encounters with a text are between what the text says to me and the questions that I have for the text. Hence, rather than looking on the act of reading as an analytical endeavour, reading can best be seen as a hermeneutic enterprise in which the aim is to show or disclose the meaning of a subject matter in relation to the whole of which it is a part (Malpas, 1992). Probst (1988), following Rosenblatt's (1983) lead, proposes a series of guidelines or rules for generating and maintaining a dialogue with text. One of these has particular importance for us as teachers: Students must be free to deal with their own reactions. This admonition was never more apparent to me than the comment I read in one Grade Six student's response journal:

> Sometimes I think this book is too slow. It's like when you start a mystery book, for a while nothing happens and then BOOM! This book is taking too long for the boom. (Safina, journal entry, April 2, 1992)

Allowing students the opportunity to deal with their own reactions is risky business, but necessary if we are going to develop readers who have a critical edge to their responses. Sometimes we can achieve a deeper level of response by simply allowing students free rein and encouraging them to question the meaning of the text they are currently reading. Paul's response to *The Giver* (Lowry, 1993) is representative of the quality of response one can achieve with some students who have become deeply involved with a text:

> In Lois Lowry's acceptance speech for winning the Newbery Award, she explained about parts of her childhood. "... I remember still, after all these years, the smells; .... I remember the babes and the toddlers dressed in bright pink and orange and red, most of all. But I remember, too, the dark blue uniforms of the school children—the strangers that are my own age".... When she describes parts of her life in her acceptance speech, I thought about "Coats," not coats that you would wear, but philosophical coats. For example, a problem can wear many coats, and you have to take the Coats off in order to solve the problem. You can do this by drawing things together and making connections.... Sometimes when you remove a Coat, you get information that helps you remove other Coats. Lois Lowry chose to use these kinds of Coats, and by doing this, she enabled the reader to get involved in the book and fill in gaps on his or her own. (Paul, Grade Five, journal entry, 1995)

Teachers can and should leave room in their curriculum for nurturing this kind of response. In addition, there are other ways to help our students develop personal responses to text. Probst states that "students should learn about the processes by which they make meaning out of literary texts" (1994, p. 41). Students often come to class thinking that the meaning of texts they are about to read will be given to them by the teacher or that the meaning of the text lies outside them. Students will need to learn that the meaning of the text is something that they must construct for themselves or as part of an interpretive community. For example, in responding to Safina's comment about the Boom, Mrs. Rolson, the teacher wrote, "If you were the author, where would you have put in the BOOM? Can you see any similarities between the animal behaviour and the human behaviour?"

What Mrs. Rolson's questions did was to force Safina to think seriously about why the text she had been reading failed to excite her and what she might do to make this a more exciting and engaging piece of text. Safina's response to the question is instructive in that it reveals something of her thinking as a writer, "If I were the author I would have done the introduction and not long after I would have put the exciting part in" (journal entry, April 21, 1992). This is in keeping with another of Probst's principles: The teacher's influence should be an elaboration of the vital influence inherent in the literature itself (1988, p. 32). Finally, Probst's other principle—"There must be an opportunity for an initial crystallization of a personal sense of the work" (p. 33)—suggests that we must teach students to develop what Langer (1990) calls the initial envisionment of the work itself. Sometimes this initial envisionment grows out of the student's own sense of identity with the character in the novel. Safina exemplifies this in her journal entry to *Sarah Jane of Silver Inlet,* where she writes,

> I think Sarah Jane would be a good friend because she likes to read (like me) and she isn't stuck up like the other girls at Silver Inlet. I also like this book because it's interesting to find out what avents [sic] happened a long time ago. (Safina, journal entry, 1992)

The act of reading, then, is a private affair, even if we are part of a group (an interpretive community). However, the act of reading is also social in nature and is, as Lewis points out, a complex relationship that entails individuals and the nested contexts that shape literacy practices (1997). Bakhtin (1981) draws this distinction in his demarcation of phenomenology, which deals with the construction and nature of individual human consciousness, and Marxism, which deals with the ways in which human social formations are constructed, and the roles ideology plays in those constructions (Bernard-Donels, 1994). There is, indeed, a tension that exists between these two positions, and it is my intention to explore these tensions in order to find some common ground so that we may arrive at a suitable means for demonstrating and describing the real work of the interpretive community. My purpose here is first to explore the application of Fish's (1980) notion of the interpretive community to classroom practice. Following this, I will present a set of guidelines for delineating the work of the interpretive community. Finally, I will present a number of strategies for teaching response to text within this notion of the interpretive community.

Negotiating Self and World: The Work of the Interpretive Community

> No matter how good the writing may be, a book is never complete until it is read. The writer does not pass through the gates of excellence alone, but in the company of readers. (Katherine Paterson, 1988, p. 37)

In the previous section, I argued for the importance of the student's personal response to text. This is relevant to developing readers' understanding of their own experiences as they evolve in the texts they read. Bruner claims that the imaginative use of the narrative form in literature engages readers in the exploration of human possibilities by situating them simultaneously in a "dual landscape" of both action and consciousness. Stories, he contends, provide a "map of possible roles and possible worlds in which action, thought, and self-determination are permissible or desirable" (1986, p. 66).

The interpretive community, on the other hand, provides readers with another forum for response beyond that which they formulate in their own conversation with the text. Interpretive communities, which Purves (1985) describes as groups bound together by the way they perceive and interpret literary texts, should, as McGinley and Kamberelis state, "enhance their understanding of themselves and their social worlds in a classroom where they [are] encouraged to read, write and talk about personally and socially relevant subjects" (1996, p. 75). It would appear, then, that the work of the interpretive community is to enable readers to act in concert to create, identify, and respond to literature (Purcell-Gates, 1992).

The current notion of interpretive community comes from Stanley Fish (1980). His basic claim is that the reader manufactures the sense or meaning of the text. Meaning no longer inheres in the text but is fully located in the reading community. According to Fish, the interpretive community is a reading public that shares a strategy or approach to interpretation. The text is not an object that can be approached and examined from the outside. There is no metanarrative; there is no truth or story that will encompass and make sense of all other narratives. There are only ungrounded language games and ungrounded interpretive communities. As he states, "The meaning of an utterance, I repeat, is its experience—all of it—and that experience is immediately compromised the moment you say anything about it" (Fish, 1980, p. 82).

In sum, Fish redefines literature, not as an object (i.e., there is no reader-text dichotomy as in Rosenblatt, 1978; or Iser, 1978), but as something that happens when we read. There is, therefore, no preexisting text that controls the reader's response; our texts are our readings, the poems we write. As Fish states, "meanings are the property neither of fixed or stable texts nor of free and independent readers but of interpretive communities that are responsible for the shape of the reader's activities and for the texts those activities produce" (1980, p. 322). Fish's notion of interpretive communities does not, therefore, include a collective of individuals; rather the term refers to a "bundle of strategies or norms of interpretation that we hold in common and which regulate the way we think and perceive" (Freund, 1987, p. 107). In keeping with this notion, Purcell-Gates views the notion of interpretive communities as those in which all members (readers and authors) learn, through social and cultural involvement, the conventions that enable them to create, identify, and respond to literature (1992).

The appeal of this view lies in its emphasis on readers working together to find common ground for their readings and their interpretations. An interpretive community supplies a bundle of common strategies that unite us in our search for understanding. The following excerpt provides us with an example of how an interpretive community made up of four upper elementary school children negotiate their way through John Christopher's *The Prince in Waiting:*

NATHAN: I'm just saying—I'm just mentioning the Duke changed that. They don't call him King, like, like they would.

MICHAEL: But he isn't King. I think they called him Prince but. . . .

NATHAN: All right. If the King dies, then the Prince would then be King. There is no King, so wouldn't the Prince be King then? There is no King. . . .

MICHAEL: I think the Celtic system is a lot different. They don't. . . . They appoint princes and princesses like the ward. He just wasn't there. . . .

NATHAN: I'm the same with Michael. . . . I think some of it's in the past and some of it's in the future.

JORGE: It's in the future.

MICHAEL: It's probably in the future because it has hints of machines. . . .

JORGE: The machines have been abandoned. . . .

CAROL (RESEARCHER):   How else could you tell, besides the machines?

JASON: Well, they said, . . . that their ancestors had big machines that destroyed the earth and so that the spirits forbade them from having machines.

JORGE: I don't think they have the technology any more. . . .

MICHAEL: (refers back to the text and reads) Thirteen year old Luke has no reason to suspect that things will change. Certainly it has been like that for centuries, at least since the year 2000.

JORGE: Imagine making a jet plane in this time.

MICHAEL: Yeah, John Christopher's quite a science fiction person.

CAROL: Why do you think he poses that question or makes it difficult for us to figure out whether it's in the past or the future?

MICHAEL: It has lots of suspense. . . .

JASON: It's sort of like he wants . . . like he writes science fiction and he wants it to be in the future but like it isn't all spaceships and robots and stuff like that . . . like he's thinking like, uh . . . well the future could be like this but it could also be like that.

Within this conversation, one is able to catch the flavor of the work of the interpretive community. In the first instance, negotiation takes place between equals; all participants have an equal voice in determining what the text is saying to them. Even Carol, the researcher, has a voice that is not dominating. The character of this conversation is highlighted by attempts by group members to maximize agreement: Nathan asserts, "I'm just saying. . . . They don't call him King. . . ." Michael replies, "But he isn't King. . . ." Nathan then declares, "I'm the same with Michael."

What I find noteworthy in this exchange is, first of all, the conversational quality of the dialogue. Johnstone states that talk is "as essential feature of the transactional reality" (1993, p. 113). She also claims that "talk reveals a personal monologue to disclose personal transactions" (p. 114). She concluded that conversation is a key element in responding deeply to text.

You will notice that this recorded piece of conversation follows Grice's guidelines for socially acceptable speech, termed "Conversational rules: Quantity, Quality, Relation and Manner" (Grice, 1975; see also Staab, Early, & Hunsberger, 1997).

In other words, the speakers attempted to make their contributions as informative as needed (Quantity); they tried to make their contributions as true as possible (Quality); they attempted to make their contributions relevant to the discussion at hand (Relation); and they attempted to avoid using obscure or ambiguous expressions, to be brief, and to be orderly (Manner). These speakers, then, fulfilled the mandate for effective conversation (Wittgenstein, 1957). However, they also went beyond the mandate for effective speaking; they engaged in what Heath (1983) would call "event forecasting," the making of predictions concerning what would happen next in the story, as when Michael says, "It's probably in the future because it has hints of machines."

In addition, the tentative nature of the language used in these exchanges, points to the effective use of modal auxilliaries ("I think, I imagine . . . , I don't think. . . .") to signal tentativeness or openness to the events being discussed in the novel. Also, in one other comment by Jorge, "Imagine making a jet plane in this time," the speaker invites his listeners to construct a possible world (Bruner, 1986) in which events shatter the pre-conceived notions of what could happen in this particular community. Coates' (1987) research into the acquisition of the meanings of modality suggest these are still not fully developed, not even by age twelve. Nevertheless, the use of such modalities by young children occupies an important aspect of the young child's developing understanding of epistemic modalities. As Coates states, these clusters presage the adult pattern and demonstrate how children in the ten- to twelve-year-old range are able to use modality to facilitate interaction (Coates, 1987).

In this exchange, both the author and the text speak to the community; Christopher is acknowledged as an authoritative writer of science fiction, and the text is consulted for its insights into questions raised by the group.

However, although the foregoing dialogue provides a helpful example of the interpretive community at work, a problem with Fish's confounding the reader-text dichotomy is "Without a subject/object opposition, reader-response criticism disappears and there is no primary consciousness to function as the locus of meaning" (Freund, 1987, p. 108). What seems to disappear is the entire dyadic structure of traditional distinctions, as for example, between ordinary language and poetic language, or between emotive language and scientific language. The reader, imprisoned within community expectations and dominated by the authority of the community, has no means of engaging with the more difficult features of text, such as doubt and ambiguity—features of reader-response theory that are provided for within the framework of Iser's (1978) reception theory and Rosenblatt's (1978) notion of transaction.

Another aspect of Fish's (1980) notion of the interpretive community is that there does not seem to be any practical or methodological outcome to his position. The reader is simply encouraged to utilize the literary competence of "informed" reading provided by the institution in which the reader has studied. As a result, the act of reading loses its powers of resisting the text, revising texts, or even of understanding the power and authority of texts. As Freund states,

Fish has evidently refused to face up to the ways in which the authority of the interpretive community might become grimly coercive or where the appeal to the impe-
rialism of agreement is capable of threatening readers whose experience of the
community is less happily benign than Fish assumes. (1987, p. 111)

I have dealt at length with this criticism of Fish's work, primarily because I
want to incorporate some of Dasenbrock's (1991) critique in a way that I believe
will help us to use the notion of interpretive community in more productive and
fruitful ways. In the first place, it would appear that Fish (1980) and Dasenbrock
(1991) are in agreement that no interpretations can be said to be neutral or objective. All are limited with reference to the beliefs of the interpreter. What we do,
then, when we encounter a text to interpret is to interpret that text on our own
terms. Michaelson's (cited in Dasenbrock, 1991) term for this is "interpretive charity." "Faced with something to interpret, we interpret it so as to maximize agreement, so as to credit the other speaker or the writer with beliefs as much like our
own as possible" (Dasenbrock, 1991, p. 13). This is evident in the following
exchange:

MICHAEL: . . . and blew a hole . . . and blew a hole in the wall. I feel sorry for
the Seer of Innersfield.

JORGE: Yeah, They probably killed their Seer. . . .

MICHAEL: And so, if you disobey the spirits they . . . won't do anything for
you . . . they won't make machines.

JORGE: It sort of sounds like the spirits are telling you [that] you shouldn't
do that but you should fight.

In this exchange the desire to maximize agreement is clearly evident and in
keeping with one of Grice's (1975) conversational postulates. Even the follow-up
comments to this excerpt reveal the attempts by both Jorge and Michael to see the
work of the spirits as a kind of game. (Jorge: "It's sort of like the spirits are these
guys watching at the hockey game." Michael: "Yeah.").

From Dasenbrock's (1991) perspective, charity is not an option; rather, it is a
condition of having a workable theory. Interpretive charity is where you start, but
it is not necessarily where you end up. Fish's (1980) view of interpretation implies
that there is no distance between us and our beliefs. Dasenbrock's (1991) view, on
the other hand, is that we begin by assuming a broad area of agreement on both
beliefs and meanings. However, because beliefs and meanings differ, to some
extent, interpreters soon discover that their assumptions of shared agreement on
beliefs and meanings require modification in places. We must, as Dasenbrock
(1991) argues, begin by assuming agreement because that enables us to find and
make sense of disagreement. Once disagreement is encountered, as members of
the interpretive community, we can adjust our theory about the speaker's utterance or beliefs about language use in order to make sense of a misreading of the

text. To do this, we begin with a "prior theory," a set of assumptions about the dispositions, beliefs, and language use of the speaker/writer (Michaelson, 1984). Dasenbrock (1991) describes these as the expectations that impregnate experience. Then as we encounter the unexpected, we develop a "passing theory," a modified version of the prior theory adjusted to fit what we learned about the other.

In sum, agreement is achieved within the interpretive community as members of the community adjust their prior theories in the direction of what they take to be a provisional agreement between speaker/writer and interpreter. This agreement is not created by the interpreter overwhelming the text by his or her beliefs and values, but by adjusting them to the demands of the interpretive occasion. The adjustment does not, as Fish (1980) would maintain, represent a perfect match. Prior theories and passing theories are, in Dasenbrock's view, both irreducibly plural; they always undergo modification in the situation for which and in which they are advanced (1991).

It can be argued, then, that Fish's (1980) notion of the interpretive community embodies a social theory of response (Beach, 1995). From Fish's perspective, meaning is not the result of a reader transacting with a text; rather, the meaning that accrues is the result of those "interpretive strategies and conventions adopted by readers as members of a particular interpretive community" (Beach, 1995, p. 106). Freund (1987) argues that there is an impasse between attempts such as Iser's (1978) to outline an acceptably complete theory of reading and Fish's (1980) claim that the reader's cognitive activities supply everything—that "we write the texts we read" (Freund, 1987, p. 153). This latter view has been criticized by Dasenbrock (1991) on the grounds that it is a form of conceptual relativism.

Guidelines for the Work of the Interpretive Community

Despite the problems that seem to be evident in Fish's theory, the very idea of an interpretive community is a compelling one and, given the modifications suggested by Dasenbrock (1991), it is possible to develop further guidelines (or guiding principles) for the work of the interpretive community.

Principles

Engagement.   I have borrowed the term from Dale (1997), who stresses the need for a high level of engagement as a critical factor in coauthoring written works. She also argues that it is simultaneous collaboration that leads to the highest levels of engagement. In other words, instead of parceling out portions of text to be read silently, students should be encouraged to create the text together, to work at interpretation as a group process. This is where the tensions in both reading silently and sharing collaboratively can be resolved by carrying out the two activities simultaneously. A high level of engagement does require the teacher to prepare the ground by selecting literature that will secure the interest of the class, by providing the necessary activities that will prepare the ground for successful responding, and by providing a classroom ambience that nurtures and promotes high levels of engagement with text.

Responsiveness.   Teaching responsiveness seems so self-evident that one could easily ignore the idea and move on to deeper and more demanding features of the work of the interpretive community. However, the importance of focusing on responsiveness is that we want to avoid the situation in which the teacher becomes the one who insists on having her students respond to a particular piece of text. In fact, it is the students who are in charge of responding, because this avoids the situation in which "the teacher owns the meaning and rents it out to the students" (Dias & Hayhoe, 1988, p. 7). Moreover, developing a responsive mode depends on the stance we assume when we encounter a text. An efferent stance has its drawbacks because its focus is exclusively on what is to be taken away from the text. An aesthetic stance forces readers to consider what is lived-through in one's engagement with text. In addition, responsiveness, as part of the work of the interpretive community, depends on the willingness of the community to focus on what is lived-through in moment-by-moment transactions with text.

Responsibility.   This term has an ethical connotation to it. Students must read texts in a responsible manner. They cannot simply dismiss what the text has to say and layer over the text's meaning with their own interpretations. Readers have a responsibility to listen carefully to what the text is saying.

In addition to the foregoing principles, I would like to argue for the following set of "rules for responding." Again, the list I have developed should not be considered exhaustive, nor should it be seen as the final set of commandments. Others may see the need for additional rules.

Suggested Rules for Responding

1. All readers in the interpretive community must be given an equal opportunity to have an equal voice in reader/text negotiations. Everyone has a right to be heard.

2. All interpretations are open to negotiation. Interpretive charity is the rule, not the exception, in interpretive work.

3. As the reading of individual texts continues, alternative readings, the forming of tentative hypotheses, inferencing, and so forth should be encouraged. Readers should be actively engaged in constructing prior and passing theories.

4. Readers should be encouraged to revisit sections of the text that were problematic or unclear to re-vision the meanings. This should be done as part of the work of the interpretive community so that collective interpretations might surface. Readers should be encouraged to see the benefits of collective interpretations.

Activities for Promoting the Work
of the Interpretive Community

> It lies within the power of every teacher and librarian to give children rich experiences with literature. . . . We must do more than just teach our students to read. We must help them become readers who are completely absorbed in their books. . . . (Huck, 1990, p. 12)

As I stated earlier, Fish defines the interpretive community as a "bundle of strategies or norms of interpretation that we hold in common and which regulate the way we perceive and think" (cited in Freund, 1987, p. 107). Purcell-Gates presents data that suggest that many young children begin formal schooling with a predisposition, or readiness, for literary response (1992). Added to this must be consideration of the cultural models (Beach, 1995) that children bring with them when they encounter texts. These assumptions about the interpretive community suggest the need to help students reflect on how they, as members of an interpretive community, might work to construct or shape their interpretations using the following activities.

Reflecting on "Gaps" in the Text

The notion of "gaps" in the text comes from Iser's work: "The literary text activates our own faculties, enabling us to recreate the world it presents;" this world is the literary work and is the "coming together of text and imagination" (Iser, 1980, p. 54).

From Iser's perspective, however, making connections is work because the text resists our efforts at synthesis with gaps or indeterminacies that hinder the reader's attempts to comprehend the text's meaning. Gaps vary in nature. They can be the omission of information, ambiguous information, sentences that modify preceding ones, or contradictions and conflicts in the text. Essentially, gaps function to confound the reader, but they are effective precisely because they perform such a function. The net effect of such gaps is to stimulate the reader's imaginative and critical faculties to establish connections—to fill the gaps and construct the literary work (Greco, 1990). The role of activities here is to develop students' awareness of the presence of gaps in the text and to encourage them to question and reflect on these gaps. There are, therefore, three basic purposes at work here:

- to allow students to become aware that gaps in the text are a means of allowing the reader to become an active participant in the reading
- to develop students' awareness of the gaps in their own interpretive processes and the role of active participation in resolving these ambiguities
- to enhance students' use of questioning as an initial step toward highlighting where gaps occur in the text

The requirements for doing this activity are: three relatively short pieces of text of different genres that exhibit textual gaps, chart paper or chalkboard, and sticky notes (enough for five per student). The teacher introduces the activity by discussing how authors, in writing a book, cannot describe or include everything about the setting and characters. The teacher then discusses how readers are left to interpret these gaps themselves. The gaps allow students to become active in the reading process and to bring elements of themselves into the text. In addition, initial forays into gap-filling should emphasize "interpretive charity"—the notion that we agree on what these gaps mean as a starting point for our discussion. Then, as discussion proceeds, points of disagreement, of resistant reading, of the need to construct new intertextual links, should move the interpretive community to revisit our prior theories to propose alternative passing theories of interpretation.

Questions raised by upper elementary students about Chris Van Allsberg's *The Stranger* demonstrate how students' awareness of gaps is heightened:

- Why doesn't he sweat or get tired?
- Why was it so cold?
- Why did the thermometer break?
- Why didn't he get knocked unconscious?

Questions such as these form the foundation from which students can begin to fill gaps. When students preface their comments with words such as "might," "maybe," and "sort of," it is a strong indicator that they are taking the appropriate steps toward filling gaps.

Wandering Viewpoint: Establishing Points of Contact

According to Iser, the text itself can never be grasped as a whole—"only as a series of changing viewpoints, each one restricted in itself and so necessitating further perspectives. This is the process by which the reader 'realizes' an overall situation" (1978, p. 68). Thus, the reader's acts of understanding are grounded by his or her attempts "to build up a consistent view of textual segments as she/he moves between the shifting perspectives of the text" (Freund, 1987, p. 144).

For a text such as *Rosie's Walk* (Hutchins, 1968), used at the primary level, large sheets of construction paper and felt pens would be required. The chart paper could be set up at the front of the class on three easels or affixed to the wall near the teacher's chair. The teacher, in reading through the text, would model "points of contact," helping students see how parts of the story relate to each other. For example, the juxtaposition of Rosie in relation to the fox could be explored by having the children's attention drawn to how Rosie is able to thwart the fox's attempts in practically every page in the text. Again, the teacher could use questioning as a means to draw students into the actions in the text. These thoughts could be modeled on three sheets of paper, with the teacher drawing the children's attention to how each thought establishes points of contact among textual segments.

At the intermediate level, the teacher could read a chapter from an ongoing novel (e.g., *Woodsong*, by Gary Paulsen, 1990), stopping at strategic points to have students reflect on the ideas, images, or thoughts engendered by the text and to discuss with the students how Paulsen's text unfolds as they journey through its landscape.

A variation would be to have students read a chapter of the text silently and comment using sticky notes at points of contact. These could be collated by individual students and used to write responses. Responses could then be shared by small interpretive communities within the class as a basis for developing a series of passing theories of the text's meaning. In addition, points of contact could be written on the chalkboard or chart paper (with page numbers and notes to describe where the point of contact was located in the text). After six or seven points of contact had been listed, students could be asked to write a response based on these points. Written responses could then be shared and discussed as a whole class activity.

Reading against the Grain

Corcoran (1990) argues strongly for the view that conceptions of what it means to read well are far from fixed. As he states,

> What I will unearth in the historical spaces where reading, re-reading and resistance meet are a series of almost stratified zones of reading, which, when penetrated, reveal that the fissures which traverse the text and problematize meaning belong as much to its context of production as to its various historical moments of reception. . . . I want to move the reading subject a little left of centre in order to see what part the developing, historical individual is required to play when the dialectic between structure and agency, initial reading and re-reading, allows for intentional stances of refusal, opposition or resistance. (1990, p. 132)

The aim here is to develop strong or resistant readers, readers who can read against the grain. Beach contends that one of the relevant goals of teaching response is to assist students to recognize that their responses are constituted by cultural models (1995, p. 93). In so doing, readers are enabled to engage in a dialectical tension between their own and others' cultural models.

To illustrate, *The Giver,* by Lois Lowry (1993), provides students with opportunities for resistant reading. The community created by Lowry is one of sameness—a lifeworld where the landscape is devoid of action and culture. This is a text in which students can use a jigsaw strategy to discuss how their particular cultural backgrounds differ from the one depicted in the text. Also, not only are there cultural differences to be explored, there are political differences to be raised. Students could be asked to speculate on what life would be like where the ruling authority dictated the lifestyle of the community.

- What would be the benefits of living in the community depicted in *The Giver*?
- How would you feel about living in a world where memory didn't exist?
- What is it about living in a democracy that forces us to make choices that are oftentimes difficult and dangerous?

Having read *The Giver,* students could then be introduced to *Underground to Canada* by Barbara Smucker (1977), a novel that shows students how life for a different cultural group can be both oppressive and racist. Here students encounter a different world, a world in which sameness is replaced with danger and cruelty, primarily because of one's color. Within the confines of this novel, students are given the chance to interact with a group of children whose circumstances are distinctly different from their own. Similarly, "Thank you Ma'am" by Langston Hughes (1996) is a short story that is set within African American inner city culture. For African Americans in a similar environment, this may be a familiar setting, whereas it is likely to be quite foreign to students of other ethnic or social backgrounds. Using a response journal, children could be asked to take on the voice of a narrator who questions the objective, subjective, and intersubjective elements of the social text that has been created by *The Giver* or *Underground to Canada*.

Constructing Prior and Passing Theories

One of the texts that I have found to be of particular interest in developing what Langer (1990) calls the reader's growing envisionment of the text is Paterson's (1978) *The Great Gilly Hopkins*. At the outset of this novel, we are confronted with a picture of the main character, who is unlovely and generally hostile. Gilly is a foster child who is at odds with society and who is hiding behind a shell of resentment and anger. What I have done with students in my professional-year courses is to read the first three chapters of the text and then have them draw a sketch of Gilly, which is then followed by a brief description of the sketch (in other words, Sketch to Stretch, from Short, Harste, & Burke, 1996, p. 528). We then discuss our varying interpretations; we construct a prior theory about Gilly. Later, after we have read up to the chapter entitled "The Visitor," we repeat the activity and then discuss how our sketches have changed, including our newly revised passing theory about Gilly. Although this is not a new idea, it does help to see how our interpretations of characters change and grow over the length of a novel.

Final Reflections on the Work of the Interpretive Community

The interpretive community is a construct that owes its definition to Stanley Fish (1980). However, I believe that the notion has a much broader interpretation than that originally envisioned by Fish. Interpretive communities are really that domain in which readers are enabled to join in (or, as Corcoran, 1990, says, "to be excluded from") a series of circumtextual and intertextual conversations. An interpretive community should be able to provide a forum for such conversations, for talk about text that will enable readers to share possible worlds they have created with others who have envisioned like-minded creations and who wish to discuss their envisionments with others. In the final analysis, such conversations have the distinct prospect of moving beyond the realm of gentle inquisitions to more enriching experiences with texts.

REFERENCES

Bakhtin, M. M. (1981). *The dialogic imagination*. (C. Emerson & M. Holquist, Trans.). Austin, TX: University of Texas Press.

Beach, R. (1995). Constructing cultural models through response to literature. *English Journal, 84*(6), 87–94.

Bernard-Donels, M. (1994). Mikhail Bakhtin: Between phenomenology and Marxism. *College English, 56*(2), 170–188.

Bruner, J. (1986). *Actual minds, possible worlds*. Cambridge, MA: Harvard University Press.

Coates, J. (1987). Epistemic modality and spoken discourse. *Transactions of the Philological Society 1987* (pp. 110–131).

Corcoran, B. (1990). Reading, re-reading, resistance: Versions of reader response. In M. Hayhoe, & S. Parker (Eds.), *Reading and response* (pp. 132–146). Philadelphia: Open University Press.

Dale, H. (1997). *Co-authoring in the classroom*. Urbana, IL: National Council of Teachers of English.

Dasenbrock, R. W. (1991). Do we write the text we read? *College English, 53*(1), 7–18.

Dias, P., & Hayhoe, M. (1988). *Developing response to poetry*. Milton Keynes, UK: Open University Press.

Fish, S. (1980). *Is there a text in this class? The authority of interpretive communities*. Cambridge, MA: Harvard University Press.

Freund, E. (1987). *The return of the reader: Reader-response criticism*. New York: Methuen.

Gadamer, H.-G. (1997). *Truth and method,* 2nd revised edition. (Joel Weinsheimer & Donald Marshall, Trans.). New York: Continuum.

Greco, N. A. (1990). Re-creating the literary text: Practice and theory. *English Journal, 79*(11), 34–40.

Grice, H. P. (1975). Logic and conversation. In P. Cole & L. Morgan (Eds.), *Syntax and semantics 3: Speech acts* (pp. 41–58), New York: Academic Press.

Heath, S. B. (1983). *Ways with words*. Cambridge, UK: Cambridge University Press.

Huck, C. S. (1990). The power of children's literature in the classroom. In K. G. Short & K. M. Pierce (Eds.), *Talking about books: Creating literate communities* (pp. 3–15). Portsmouth, NH: Heinemann.

Hunsberger, M. (1985). The experience of re-reading. *Phenomenology + Pedagogy, 3*(3), 161–166.

Iser, W. (1978). *The act of reading: A theory of aesthetic response*. Baltimore: Johns Hopkins University Press.

Iser, W. (1980). The reading process: A phenomenological approach. In J. Tompkins (Ed.), *Reader response criticism* (pp. 50–69). Baltimore: Johns Hopkins University Press.

Johnston, C. (1994). *Webs of understanding in response to literature*. Unpublished masters thesis. University of Calgary, Calgary, Alberta.

Langer, J. (1990). Understanding literature. *Language Arts, 67*(8), 812–816.

Lewis, C. (1997). The social drama of literature discussions in a fifth/sixth grade classroom. *Research in the Teaching of English, 31*(2), 163–204.

Malpas, J. E. (1992). Analysis and hermeneutics. *Philosophy and Rhetoric, 25*(2), 93–123.

McGinley, W., & Kamberelis, G. (1996). *Maniac McGee* and *Ragtime Tumpie:* Children negotiating self and world through reading and writing. *Research in the Teaching of English, 30*(1), 75–113.

Michaelson, D. (1984). On the very idea of a conceptual scheme. In D. Davidson (Ed.), *Inquiries into truth and interpretation* (pp. 183–198). Oxford, UK: Clarendon.

Paterson, K. (1988). *Gates of excellence: On reading and writing books for children*. New York: E. P. Dutton.

Probst, R. (1988). *Response and analysis: Teaching literature in junior and senior high school*. Portsmouth, NH: Boynton/Cook.

Probst, R. (1992). Writing from, of, and about literature. In N. Karolides (Ed.), *Reader response in the classroom: Evoking and interpreting meaning in literature* (pp. 117–127). New York: Longmans.

Probst, R. (1994). Reader-response theory and the English curriculum. *English Journal, 83*(3), 37–44.

Purcell-Gates, V. (1992). Roots of response. *Journal of Narrative and Life History, 2*(2), 151–161.

Purves, A. (1985). On the nature and formation of interpretive and rhetorical communities. *Highway One, 8*(1/2), 79–96.

Rosenblatt, L. (1978). *The reader, the text, the poem: The transactional theory of the literary work*. Carbondale, IL: Southern Illinois University Press.

Rosenblatt, L. (1983). *Literature as exploration*. New York: Modern Language Association. (Original work published 1938).

Sardello, R. (1975). Hermeneutical reading: An approach to the classical texts of psychology. *Phenomenological Psychology, 2*, 273–280.

Short, K., Harste, J., & Burke, C. (1995). *Creating Classrooms for authors and inquirers*. Portsmouth, NH: Heinemann.

Staab, C., Early, M., & Hunsberger, M. R. (1997). A teacher's knowledge of oracy. In V. Froese (Ed.), *Language across the curriculum* (pp. 88–107), Toronto, Ontario: Harcourt Brace.

Wittgenstein, L. (1957). *Philosophical investigations*. Oxford, UK: Blackwell.

CHILDREN'S LITERATURE CITED

Burroughs, E. R. (1914). *Tarzan of the apes.* (Rev. 1972). New York: Watson-Guptill.

Burroughs, E. R. (1915). *The return of Tarzan.* (Rev. 1975). New York: Grosset.

Christopher, J. (1970). *The prince in waiting.* New York: Macmillan.

Hughes, L. (1996). Thank you ma'am. In A. Harper (Ed.), *Langston Hughes: Short stories* (pp. 223–226). New York: Hill & Wang.

Hutchins, P. (1968). *Rosie's walk.* New York: Macmillan.

Lowry, L. (1993). *The giver.* New York: Bantam.

Paterson, K. (1978). *The great Gilly Hopkins.* New York: HarperCollins Publishers.

Paulsen, G. (1990). *Woodsong.* New York: Bradbury Press.

Smucker, B. (1977). *Underground to Canada.* Vancouver, BC: Clarke Irwin.

Van Allsberg, C. (1985). *The polar express.* Boston: Houghton Mifflin.

Revealing Warmer Shadows: Tensions in Reader Response

9

NIKI CHERNIWCHAN
Calgary Board of Education

I will always be grateful to Linda F., a colleague, for enthusiastically introducing me one June morning to some ideas she had been trying in her language arts class. With apprehension and excitement, I was finally returning to language arts teaching that September. However, coming back into touch with current practice had revealed that my old thematic units, bags of tricks, and teacher-fronted approaches should best become relics of a former time. Something new and different had emerged and was emerging in the classrooms I had observed. Linda's contagious enthusiasm for this new approach and its underlying theory and her frank and professional sharing of literature, classroom practice, hopes, and struggles gently initiated me into the reader response paradigm. I was set for the challenge. Since then I have not looked back; looking forward has been chaotic, fruitful, challenging, inspiring, difficult, wonderful, and bothersome all at once.

As I read *In the Middle* that summer, Nancie Atwell's (1987) portrayal of her classroom program, with its vivid descriptions of the organization of writers' and readers' workshops and examples of minilessons, conferences, student writing, journals, and classroom strategies, captured me. I was irreversibly impressed with her accounts, which showed me how language arts teaching and learning could be other than how I had previously conceived them to be. I acknowledge the initial idealism I then possessed under the guidance of Atwell's description; it was guidance without which I could not have begun to move into this way of thinking. It was also an idealism that I imagine is requisite at the onset of any (r)evolutionary endeavor. Atwell provided the essential foundation upon which I could begin to build my program, both theoretically and practically. However, I know that from the very first class I taught, I could not help but begin negotiations that respected and reconciled my students, my milieu, and myself with Atwell's writing and with my interpretation of what I thought reader response practice to be. This is not to suggest that Atwell is flawed or that her beliefs are fiction, but that, quite simply, her classroom did not and could not overlay itself onto my classroom in the same ways. I found myself turning to reader response theory as a resource.

As I continued to attempt to negotiate between reader response theory and effective classroom practice, gaps in my understanding, rifts in my practice, and inconsistencies in my thinking and doing more and more began to reveal themselves in subtler and fantastic ways. Emanating from this perpetual negotiation are a myriad of questions that I am certain I am not the first nor only person to ask:

- Do I really value the different points of departure from which each student constructs personal meaning?
- How should I read journal responses, and what determines an acceptable or genuine response?
- Are there wrong responses?
- How should I help my students in the processes of reading and responding?
- Do response activities, particularly journal writing, indeed indicate understanding of and engagement with literature?
- Are students aesthetically engaged with text in my classroom?
- Can I encourage personal response and then justifiably evaluate it?

These are only some of the questions that have arisen for me with time and usage; they are intertwined, elude clarity at times, and certainly spawn more questions.

"As We Accept the Shadow, We Are Naturally Humbled"

Duff's (1993, p. 90) statement relates to grappling with the questions posed previously. In coming to ask, and beginning to answer, these questions by reading academic literature and by ever modifying my approach, two darker realizations about reader response theory and its practice have resurfaced again and again, imploring closer examination. These realizations are not to be feared. I have come to accept that their darkness is not debilitating but is suggestive of warmer shadows in which multiplicity, ambiguity, circularity, and the messiness of reading and life itself muddle and breathe. Although the following two topics can be seen to represent forces that "militate against a reader-centred classroom" (Sheridan, 1991, p. 805), their consideration reminds me of the necessity of remaining humble in order that I may best reconcile the light and the shadow for me and my students.

The first concern began to present itself as I collected, read, and evaluated my students' response journals. The process seemed to be flowing, à la Atwell, with my students reading and responding; however, my evenings at home at my dining room table proved frustrating as I struggled with a lack of evaluation criteria for the variety of journal responses that had been submitted. I chastised myself for not having taught my students how to respond more effectively. Armed with a fail-safe minilesson consisting of examples of good and poor responses photocopied for comparison and discussion, I returned to the classroom the next day vowing to rectify the situation. Although this is arguably good pedagogy, a point of theory niggled at me each time I set out to do this. Reader response suggests that all responses to literature are valuable and should be validated because they are a natural product of having read. Yet, here I was attempting to coerce students into "acceptable" manners of responding. This tension had cast its shadow. The next section is devoted to its discussion.

The second concern arose as I became more conversant with reader response theory and Louise Rosenblatt's (1976) aesthetic and efferent stances to reading. I could truly appreciate her distinction between the stances of reading aesthetically for the pleasurable reading experience and reading efferently for information to be used. However, taking this learning to my classroom proved problematic. I began to wonder if my students indeed were taking an aesthetic reading stance to the fiction assigned in class. I saw my requests for journal writing and other projects as activities I do not anticipate, nor participate in, when I encounter a novel or short story. I wondered whether, in my role as teacher and evaluator, I was compromising my students' aesthetic experiences with literature, whether their school reading was actually something other than what I claimed it to be. This tension located itself in the shadow between reading literature aesthetically and producing classroom work based on one's reading. This concern is discussed further later in the chapter.

Although it would seem most orderly to discuss first the stance a student might take to reading and then comment on the aspect of response to that encounter, in this chapter I have chosen to defy this flow and put the proverbial cart before the horse. My rationale in doing this is that an understanding of how I came to conceptualize response as a learned phenomenon did lay the groundwork for how I have come to think about the stances students may take to school reading. These issues arose for me in the order presented here and, therefore, I have opted to respect and share this progression of questioning and learning through which I have come. Thinking about response and deciding it to be a learned phenomenon did indeed lead me to wonder how that affected the process that precedes it. Despite the awkwardness of the poor horse pushing a laden cart, I remain optimistic that both horse and cart are still progressing forward.

The ensuing discussion is intended to illuminate these concerns and to stimulate thoughtfulness, rather than to explain, conclude, or offer surefire pragmatic recommendations. I sense these issues do not have clear solutions, nor are they applicable to every student, every teacher, or every classroom. They exist in the tenebrious in-between of theory and practice. By speaking in a somewhat critical tone, I do not wish to promote despair or paralysis about a paradigm that I feel offers much to the teaching and learning of reading and literature. I believe that by taking a harder look at the disparities between theory and practice, and the inconsistencies in my own classroom program, I can more seriously continue the ongoing negotiations typical of a thoughtful teacher. Perhaps in these questioning challenges, some of the taken-for-granted movements of current reader response theory and its practice may become more open for me and others, promoting further inquiry, change, and growth. Often that which is worth pursuing is only achievable with difficulty and struggle in the darkness; that which comes easily and is seen as perfect often lacks substance, movement, and life.

Calming the Multiplicity of Voices:
The Natural and the Learned

That literature study should center on the readers and assert the primacy of their responses as central to reader response was, and continues to be, a welcome change in my thinking and teaching. A prevalent assumption in much of the literature is that students' reading and generating meaning will naturally lead to personal response and growth. It is the reader's transaction with the text that is sought, with response being seen as an inherent, universal, or spontaneous extension and representation of that transaction. It has been suggested that "response to narrative is a fundamental human attribute" (Griffith, 1987, p. 67), hinting at innate roots.

Initially I embraced this tacit assumption, only questioning it as it began to show itself in complications in my practice. It seemed reasonable that if I established the classroom requirements for response as suggested by Atwell (1987), specifically in the form of journal writing, then my students would not only enthusiastically meet these requirements but would discover a new enjoyment and kinship with reading and responding. I expected my students to respond with the voices of caring, engaged readers "in congenial talk about books, authors, reading, and writing" (p. 164). After all, I would be permitting, encouraging, and capitalizing instruction on their natural response tendency. I was disappointed and quickly disillusioned with my students' written responses and their attitudes toward reading and responding. Most often the journal entries were trite, unfocused, and hasty, uncovering little about transactions with the texts. In the search to make things right, I vamped and revamped the journal criteria, the literature being read, and my responses, only to discover that the root of the difficulty seemed to be the assumption I held that student responses were naturally occurring phenomena.

Complementing this assumption, but represented more overtly in the literature, reader response theory advocates that the personal meaning-making of students with texts will be unique to each and that each individual's response will be prized and validated by the teacher. Confirmation will be given to each reading of a text. The widely diverse contributions of readers in the oral and written dialogue that emerges in the classroom will be respected and authorized. "We cannot read without actively constructing the text before us, and that is why actual readings vary so much from one person to another" (Dias & Hayhoe, 1988, p. 18). Validating and privileging the multiplicity of voices that arise from reading seems to be a cornerstone of reader response theory. This diversity is seen to be consonant with ways students are believed to read; each student being able to "talk about the possible world of the text which reflects his creation and transformation of that text" (Labercane, 1990, p. 151).

Of particular emphasis is the affective *felt* response, which is seen to be notably indicative of genuine engagement with and commitment to literary text. Valued are the initial "personal, groping reactions" (Protherough, 1987, p. 77) that serve to promote individual development and lay bare for examination the learning and meaning-making processes of the student. "Emotional reactions are an essential and a large component of the literary experience and should not be ignored in classroom teaching" (Dias & Hayhoe, 1988, p. 19). With this most of us would generally agree, particularly with reference to the work of Rosenblatt (1976) and Iser (1978). When readers connect the stories they read to their feelings and experiences, and then are able to express this connection, they are considered to have engaged with text and truly to have read well.

Therefore, presenting and representing this gentle, alluring theoretical paradigm for language arts teachers are four tenets: (a) engagement with literature and responses to it are seen as naturally occurring processes; (b) the "ordinary person reading literature has views and can express them" (Evans, 1987, p. 38); (c) "at last student meanings can be taken aboard as 'legitimate' because they represent personal engagement with texts" (Gilbert, 1987, p. 237); and (d) students' affective responses to literature have worth.

Accepted as such, reader response theory suggests relatively clear guidelines or criteria about what should be valued in English language arts practice. Responses ranging from a heartfelt grunt to the composition of a full-length opus would all be given the same status as a natural representation of an individual's transaction with text. Culler (1982, p. 179) writes that "each reader's reading would be as valid or legitimate as another, and neither teachers nor texts could preserve their wonted authority." Although this seems very reasonable, it promotes a decentering effect that can be darkly uncomfortable. Privileging each student's reading and response as natural, idiosyncratic, and personal does not coincide with schooling's institutional arrangements and its societal centering on norms and standards. Each student's response cannot simply be valued for what it is because then competitive academic ranking of students cannot be achieved. This rift between reader-response theory and the requirements and expectations of education is left to each of us as teachers to reconcile somehow.

Buried in the educational institution, as well, lies a significant premise of teaching that lets itself be revealed in reader response advocacy. That interventions made by teachers in student learning are possible, desirable, and fundamental to pedagogy seems to be rendered trivial and unnecessary in light of the theoretical acceptance of all response. Here I have struggled between valuing the paradigm and heeding my role in the lifeworld of the classroom. Believing that students left to their own innate measures will read and respond in ways meaningful to themselves is at odds with convincing myself that I must show my students the path to successful response through instruction and practice. This vacillation seems to occur continuously on a yearly and daily basis with both gross and fine details of my program. The reader response literature, however, does not entirely leave one to flounder. It is suggested that the role of the teacher be one of informed guide of the process of response, in which "developing a sophisticated repertoire of response options" should be a major goal of literature instruction (Beach & Hynds, 1991, p. 459).

Having students respond to reading is a means teachers commonly employ for assessing students' understanding of a work of literature (Brown, 1987, p. 112). It is also a way of indicating to teachers which students are engaged in the books they are reading. Teachers assist students in developing responses to reading and "train students to produce response statements" (Culler, 1982, p. 65). This suggests that response activities, including journal response writing, are learned forms of discourse and expression; "response" is a construct subject to *techniques* applied by more experienced adults to neophyte students of literature. These techniques are grounded in how individual teachers "see literary meaning as constituted" (Dias & Hayhoe, 1988, p. 19), which then directs their bias to reader response activities and subsequently determines their judgment of what constitutes an *acceptable* response in both form and meaning. These conditions of signification, structure, and style are felt to be needed because students differ in their abilities to articulate their understanding of literary works, and it is "the role of the teacher to help students develop and mature in their responses" (Young, 1987, p. 16). The described nature of response and the role of the teacher all leads to where I find the shadows most disquieting: Is, then, the primacy of individual responses and personal meaning-making upheld if the teacher attempts to enhance, extend, or correct the quality of this naturally occurring phenomenon? Does the intervention by the teacher suggest that spontaneous responses by students are somehow inadequate or wrong and that they require fixing?

Holland (1980, p. 370) suggests that reader response practice "uses the differences in response as an occasion for eliminating difference." This statement would seem to be at desperate odds with the principle of valuing each individual's response, which, in effect, embraces differences. Corcoran (1987, p. 47) refers to enabling strategies and questions to "help students adopt a more reflective stance" in reworking their initial response. This suggests that already there is some understanding, either tacit or overt, of the parameters of the response product. Protherough (1987, p. 77) advises that "telling stories about stories is a form of learned behavior," in which the teacher, as a strong model with appropriate expectations, guides students in determining what information to include and what to omit. Young (1987, p. 153) advocates that "responses can be made both richer and more satisfying" (to whom?) through teacher intervention. I find an irony here in that all difference in response is essentially treated the same. The movement is to making *better* what has emerged, to center it in classroom criteria that calm the roughness of thirty individuals in a group.

Reader response in classroom practice, therefore, can be seen to be treated as a skill to be acquired, more a created system than a natural occurrence. Responses become epistemological pursuits, quests for coming to understand the shape of this type of knowing and discourse, objects to be prodded, adapted, and, in some cases, violated. There does not seem to be a sincere letting go of the responsibility for student meaning-making, a genuine acknowledgement of the natural outcomes of student encounters with literature, nor widespread practice illustrating that variations in response are normal effects of the act of reading. The discourse tradition called reader response seems to have been established, existing in a quantifiable form, and can be seen to boil the theoretically valued multiplicity of voices down to *What does the teacher want?*—essentially a speaking of one voice.

This is a harsh, and in some ways unfair, description of such a promising paradigm, but scrutiny can sometimes be an effective route to reconciliation. Therefore, continuing with this focus, reader response can be seen to have a centralizing or homogenizing effect (Culler, 1982, p. 35), promoting "a monological mode of thought" (Dias & Hayhoe, 1988, p. 12). It tends to value certain responses and types of response over others, at once establishing norms and standards of response and simultaneously excluding responses that are judged inadequate, inappropriate, or wrong. In other words, all responses are not accepted; there are standards. Thus, it can better fit into the institutional setting, which requires these types of parameters and labels. However, by authorizing a certain kind of response writing, students learn "to abandon some stories in favor of others" (Protherough, 1987, p. 79) and have to be taught to understand, feel, and respond as a reader of literature should. This is a somewhat backdoor approach to response. Somehow the response product has taken priority over the process of reading and the coming to respond. This will be discussed further in the next section of this chapter, in which it is asserted that the emphasis on product affects the stance students take to the reading process.

"One has to conclude that any uniformity we achieve in the classroom comes not from the text but from our own skill and authority as teachers—from agreed-upon (or insisted-upon) methods of teaching" (Holland, 1980, p. 366). I find this statement disconcerting, probably because it rings truer than I care to admit. Students surrender some of their right to personal response in classroom encounters with literature. Their responses tend to become contrived and impersonal in their attempts to meet the (c)overt (un)defined criteria of the teacher, who may not be completely in charge of the meaning that evolves but who controls, to a greater degree, the way it is expressed (Dias & Hayhoe, 1988, p. 7). Rising out of theory that I feel stresses process-oriented inquiry and diversity, response seems to have been transformed into a school product uniformly molded for institutionally mandated evaluation and assessment.

As critics of response, teachers must set out to achieve uniformity by first deciding how that is to be defined in their programs. Evans (1987, p. 27) offers that we "teach ourselves to judge the honesty and validity of different subjective attitudes and record those judgments in our assessments." What are the criteria for these types of judgments? Again, the position held by the teacher with respect to reader response theory directs the teacher's role as critic of response. Protherough (1987, p. 85) presents one viewpoint in suggesting that "the chief strategic problems for a teacher are to decide how far it is desirable to preempt certain responses to a text, and to decide on ways in which pupils can be encouraged to formulate their own versions of the story in a narrative that is more than a plot summary." His judgment that retellings are inadequate responses is supported by Atwell (1987) and Rosenblatt (1976), among others. Bleich (1978), however, judges retellings as an important act of recreation, restatement, and resynthesis. These aforementioned scholars are not isolated in their differing treatment of the criteria for acceptable responses, and their suggestions for practice subsequently reflect these biases. What counts as a good response can be said to be directed by the teacher who naturally has a set of personal biases regarding students' thinking about literature. Wide diversity of response cannot be considered because it renders evaluation chaotic if not impossible, and, therefore, students must submit to this homogenization of a natural, personal process in order to succeed in school.

Reader response in practice has high stakes; it is not the rosy paradigm put forth in much of the literature. It seems to require students to learn to play its game as well as possible as a manifestation of school success; to recognize those "institutionally sanctioned and empowering ways of talking about the literary productions of the culture" (Corcoran, 1987, p. 48); and "to explore their reactions intelligently and articulate them successfully for themselves and for other people" (Judy & Judy, 1983, p. 112). Our job as teachers is to communicate and inculcate these skills. This learned behavior, however, in its darkest form, can be seen to privilege the cognitive/rational over the affective/emotional, the impersonal over the personal, the teacher over the student, conformity over individuality, and product over process. It suggests unification and centralization of what ultimately would better be left to plurality and diversity, and unfortunately in doing so, it eliminates possibilities.

What is to be done with the preceding laments? It should be clearly acknowledged that they are indicative of my perceived disturbances and my coming to understand response, initially as natural, then later as learned. I believe that each teacher of reader response has a vested interest in these issues, which emerge in the day-to-dayness of classroom practice. The professional learning arising from my journey to the darker side of this consideration reveals itself more as a mode of thought with which I can approach my practice than as particular teaching methods that are quickly implemented.

I submit that, as a result, I more directly teach students how to respond to literature by addressing diversity, depth, and detail in response journals that are written and submitted at preset times as interjections in the course of reading. Acknowledging obvious criteria such as format, legibility, length, and number of entries (Fulwiler, 1987), I encourage my students to explore such elements as plot, theme, character, and author, as well as to express emotions, thoughts, wishes, and dreams—revelations of self with respect to the text. As individual students attempt or master a response form, that success is celebrated and another uncharted response area is introduced and encouraged. I endeavor to act as their mentor and guide in this diverse exploration of self and text.

Second looks (Atwell, 1987) continue to be an important aspect of response journals in my program. They provide the moments when students enter into conversation with me by responding to comments I have written in their journals. Asking them to come back to and reconsider their initial responses attempts to promote depth and detail in their thinking about what they have read and about how they have responded. Through my comments and questions, I seek to lead students to deeper considerations that may have remained closed to them without an interested interlocutor, and to uncover particulars that when highlighted can take on new shapes and understandings. It is hoped that any new way of thinking about or seeing their reading and responding will eventually become available to them as one of their many response skills in a grand repertoire.

Some students respond naturally and superlatively. They have either already been taught how to respond well to text in the school environment, or somehow, with their understanding of text, school, and life, they are able to produce response products that meet all criteria seemingly in a natural way. The majority of my students, however, require structured guidance—techniques—to assist them in producing this type of discourse after their engagement with literature. My steps in this direction have resulted in more acceptable student responses and generally happier students. They now better understand and can more successfully meet the criteria for responding and, thus, for grading. It does bother me that I used to pretend that I would accept whatever responses students gave me. I feel much more comfortable in the honesty provided by my classroom criteria, which reflects my best reconciliation (and it does seem ever-changing!) of the darker and lighter sides of this issue. I will accept the full-length opus as well as the heartfelt grunt, as long as both are packaged in a manner befitting my language arts classroom and both provide insight into the transactions between my students and their chosen texts.

Rethinking Dividing Requests: The Aesthetic and the Efferent

As already suggested, reader response theory manifests itself in classroom practice in as many forms as there are teachers dependent on their articulations of the theory. There seems, however, to be one significant commonality: students read and then respond to having read, which renders the act of reading a response activity in classroom pedagogy (Young & Robinson, 1987, p. 153). Although most teachers and students recognize free, voluntary reading as generally being risk-free, other more structured forms of reading in language arts carry greater import, and it is on this second type of reading that teaching is commonly focused. The emphasis here is that, in school, reading is usually followed by something—some act, some piece of writing, some assignment for accountability purposes. Reading is rarely ever just left as the act itself. The representation of that act is significant and important school fare. That this seems to be the case has led me to wonder about the repercussive effects of this product on the process, act, and art of reading. This is the point at which this chapter seems to double back on itself. Consideration of how the criteria for a product impact the process that spawns it is circular at best; it can border on being a confusing weaving of thought and rethought.

This second realization, which has been particularly disturbing for me in my encounters with the theory and classroom practice, emerged significantly when I came to understand the nature of response as learned discourse and came to incorporate that understanding into my program. As I settled into giving students more structured guidance with their responses, my wonderings and questions did not cease. Still dark, they are of a slightly different shade: How does reader response as a learned mode of discourse affect student reading of literature? Does having a set of teaching approaches, guidelines, or expectations for engagement with literature and production of "reasonable" responses affect the flow, purpose, or stance of reading? Does reader response treatment of literature enhance student appreciation and enjoyment of literary works? From my reading and observations, it seems that the classroom expectation of response activities has a determining and influential effect on the process of reading and the stance that students take when reading literature under my guidance.

Rosenblatt suggests that in the aesthetic stance, "the reader focuses attention primarily on what is being lived through *during* the reading" (1991, p. 119). Concentration then is on what is being seen, felt, and aroused by the words. Rosenblatt distinguishes this from reading with an efferent stance, in which "attention is focused mainly on building the public meaning that is to be carried away from the reading: actions to be performed, information to be retained, conclusions to be drawn, solutions to be arrived at, analytic concepts to be applied, propositions to be tested" (1991, p. 119). Although both stances are equally important and necessary to being a reader and can be seen to constitute the poles of a continuum, they are different and serve to reach different ends. Rosenblatt advocates that the reader's primary goal with respect to literature is to have an aesthetic experience spawning an aesthetic object as a response (Culler, 1982, p. 75).

Teaching students to adopt an aesthetic stance toward reading and to produce more affective responses to narrative text as indicative of that stance tends to be a priority in the reader-response literature. That the aesthetic mode appears to be valued over the efferent in discussions of reader response is commensurate with the foci on response as a natural process, the validation of diverse responses, and the importance of *felt* response. With respect to student response, "what teachers should be worried about is an attitude that is too literal or dogmatic (or perhaps, too efferent)" (Labercane, 1990, p. 151). This seems to be the bad currency that a number of scholars and teachers feel needs to be driven out of reader response practice. That students read for aesthetic enjoyment and can communicate this in an "artistic response to the artistic work of others" underpins reader response theory (Adams, 1987, p. 119).

But is this indeed the stance most students take to reading and responding in the educational setting of the language arts classroom? What is assumed is that the temporal relation exists as: first students read, then they respond to the aesthetic experience of having read. However, it would seem that in the majority of cases in which literature is treated in the classroom, the expectation of producing a response is introduced to students *prior* to the reading of the text. Response is assumed to be a retrospective account of engagement with text, but in school its inception usually precedes the act of reading, or if not, students certainly anticipate its arrival. By knowing that a response is expected, do students adjust the stance they adopt to reading literature? Is the product of their endeavors a response to reading *for a response*?

For me, this did not beg serious pragmatic consideration until my Grade Nine students and I read the novel *Snowbound,* by Harry Mazer, in a community-of-readers setting. As a group, we decided how much we were to read and what the response-writing expectations would be in preparation for our next class together, when we would talk about the common reading by sharing our journal writing. Although this methodology was not alien to my program, this was my initial attempt at active participation in the community when coming to the novel myself for the first time. As a lover of fiction, I can say that this experience held little satisfaction and could not be likened in process or gratification to my personal reading experiences. Although they were not excessive, I was greatly perturbed by the journal requirements. I consistently felt pulled out of my engagement with the novel as I considered and ruminated what my written response might contain. Forcing myself to continue reading and to leave response until its time was difficult; finally, I simply gave in and began writing in my journal as I read. It could not be said that I was ever "lost in the book," because it was the journal and the response that had control. It was the "information to be retained" and the "actions to be performed" after the reading that directed my experience and my stance. I believe I was reading the novel efferently in order to produce written response; very few aesthetic threads seemed woven in. Although some may argue that my case is not generalizable, I maintain it is indicative of a person simultaneously reading and holding the expectation of response.

Rosenblatt (1976) suggests that the same text can be read either aesthetically or efferently because it is the reader's purpose toward the text that varies and determines the stance taken. However, "Often school contexts unwittingly demand that pupils adopt an efferent stance towards literary texts" (Dias & Hay-hoe, 1988, p. 22). The learned behavior of responding to literature can be seen to promote this efferent purpose for reading because students are expected to "carry away" something from that experience, something that is quantifiable and *counts* in school. Thus, engagement with literature does not automatically or naturally result in aesthetic response, as suggested in some theoretical discussions. Response as a school requirement seems to focus students to that end, and therefore can shift their purpose for reading to an efferent one as it did with me. It would seem that reader response expectations exert control over the reading experience. This is a significant impact of a product on the very process that it is thought to represent.

In the darkest manner, to ask students to read aesthetically and efferently at the same time is a divided request. However, reader response appears to catch students in a type of language game in which an aesthetic object is an expected outcome of an efferent reading of a creative work. To succeed at this game, students come to learn to read literary works as *responders.* The act of reading is compromised and in a sense violated by the expectations that selected aspects of the fictive text have to be taken away and written down for "immediate use in the primary world" (Corcoran, 1987, p. 48). Reader response somewhat undermines its own desires to uncover students' lived-through experiences of reading. In this light, it commands a shift from student processes of reading and meaning-making to the ability to answer that comes out of these processes.

Gilbert (1987, p. 240) asks, "Do students indeed 'learn' how to make their stories sound personal?" It would seem that taking an efferent stance to literature in order to produce personal response discourse would be a form of school learning and would thereby answer this question affirmatively. In a significantly more radical fashion, Brown (1987) suggests that it may not be necessary to read the text at all in order to produce legitimate responses, because the student engagement that is valued is not with the text or reading process, but rather is with the discourse or response. Students, having been taught the discourse style, know what a response should look like before they read the text, and if their purpose for reading is to produce this acceptable response, then it is possible to create a facsimile that would meet the outlined criteria without having read the text. In the extreme, reading could potentially be bypassed in the pressure to produce adequate responses; the goal of school success could win out over the sense perceptions of reading literature aesthetically.

This is certainly a cautionary message to teachers; whether it happens just this way, it is worth considering that students can fabricate responses. Linda F. tells the story of one of her Grade Nine students whom she overheard explaining his journal success to a classmate, "I just write two inferences and a question to get full credit." Although both Linda and I are certain that this student did do the required reading, it nonetheless does demonstrate the risk of this type of discourse being contrived and gamed, and possibly divorced from the act of reading that it is called on to represent.

Reader response activities could be seen to steer the reading of literature, leading students into a type of misreading (or nonreading) of the text. Left alone, students might have read differently. This control seems to be directed by the setting out of criteria for response as a school behavior. The aesthetic or efferent stance and the degree of commitment or detachment students have to a text are "monitored and modified by the presence of an *other* in the person of the teacher" (Young, 1987, p. 7). What students take away from their reading can be seen to be determined in advance by the conventions that are constructed for aesthetic response in light of the teacher's biases. We, as teachers, have a very real impact on our students and the stance with which they approach literature.

If we say then that response represents aesthetic personal reading and transformation, this in a sense contradicts how responses are arrived at in classroom practice and presents a kind of double logic. Students respond as if they are aesthetically engaged with text, and this product is treated as the sign of that engagement, when coming to the product itself can be seen to jeopardize the very engagement that is sought. Students learn to respond to reading for a response. The texts themselves are treated as if they are aesthetic objects, but what is required to succeed in reader-response activities is a more efferent reading of these texts from which a (learned or possibly fabricated) aesthetic response is anticipated. Students are treated as if their role as readers is privileged, yet they are taught and learn to read and respond as responders in order to succeed in school.

All this can possibly invoke for students a "loss of reading faith" (Corcoran, 1987, p. 43) in school contexts because the treatment of the reader and the reading seems contrary to the intent. Students in my classes have shown confusion about what they are doing and about the expectations of reader response. At first I thought they simply did not understand my criteria, as lucidly as I presented them. But the confusion came from a place deeper than that. They sensed they were being misinformed somehow. What I maintained I valued about reading and responding to literature and what I actually valued and counted appeared to be at odds. My students, living in the perennial tension between reading for oneself and reading for another, faced this upheaval, which was further augmented by my opaque practice. I told them to be creative, to react to their reading honestly in their own way, but then their grades reflected my insistence that they meet my program criteria.

As teachers, what can we do to ease this tension? "Our routines of the classroom are enactments of what we believe to be true about literature" (Sheridan, 1991, p. 812). Therefore, as I probe and prod this issue, I am uncertain what form my enactments should take because some of my beliefs have been challenged, and some have collided with other beliefs about reading, teaching, learning, schooling, and assessment. However, I can no longer unquestioningly accept that because students are reading responsively, they are reading aesthetically—a position I once held. Moreover, I believe that by being in the school environment, students will tend to take a more efferent stance to reading in any subject. Simply, if teaching of literature is going to continue in language arts classes, as I believe it should, unavoidably there will be efference. With this recognition, I feel I can move to being more honest with students and myself by establishing routines that reflect these current understandings. What my students and I are doing in our treatment of literature is a school function that is in many ways similar to their reading outside of school, but it has marked differences that I now address boldly and openly. I still wonder how much this straightforward approach helps students with their reading in either milieu, if at all. Perhaps all it does is better ensure their status as trusted learners and partners in the classroom, and placate me in the disjointedness I feel on this issue. For now, this is the most truthful enactment for this place of multiplicity, circularity, and ambiguity: We will read and respond, understanding that each affects and guides the other as woven strands of an intricate process.

"To Come to Reflect, to Come to See Is to Learn"

Hannah Arendt's (1959, p. 84) words hold a special wisdom. If by asking, poking, mulling, or shaking any of the threads of reader response, we can come to see or see differently, then our learning is the outcome (or unlearning, as it sometimes feels when addled with too many apparently contradictory considerations). When this happens to me—and it probably always will when I think hard about response as a learned form of discourse and about the aesthetic and efferent reading of literature—I try to settle myself comfortably into the warmer shadows of the in-between. Willis encourages us to live productively in this place of uncertainty and tension, "in the generative tension between knowing and not knowing" (1989, p. 74). It is not an easy place in which to dwell. It is clearly demanding to be continually re-creating some balance within these recognitions, particularly when they tend to interweave with one another in disturbing and mind-boggling ways. By positioning these darker issues in critical lighting, they can become better reconciled with present understanding and practice in a unique way for each of us—a way that augers well for our particular students and program.

De Man reminds us that "the possibility of reading can never be taken for granted. It is an act of understanding that can never be observed, nor in any way prescribed or verified" (cited in Culler, 1982, p. 224). In a constant, yet always tentative, effort to lighten my way as an educator, there are always more questions:

- How do students benefit from training in response as a discourse skill?
- Are there other ways that reading of literature in school can be evaluated that meet the institutional mandate but that also better respect the aesthetic stance?
- Are reader response activities simply another language game that is being upheld by a societal institution?
- Should I insist on certain formats for student journal writing?
- Does reader response marginalize the act of reading and assert the primacy of the product of response?
- Can reader response be treated as a reliable instrument or sign of student engagement with literary works?
- How can I encourage students to adopt an aesthetic stance to reading, to lose themselves in a book?

Over and over, I answer these questions and act on the answers in practice—for the moment. The only certainty I hold is that there is no panacea for these disharmonies.

One of the keynotes of alchemical philosophy is that all things are related to their darker opposites like "the sun and its shadow" (Duff, 1993, p. 90). The goal involves their reunion, starting with the acceptance of the shadow. Humbly I accept the shadowy tensions of reader response theory and practice. Alongside all the disconcerting considerations discussed here and the rapidly rising questions, I will continue to encourage response activities in my classroom, for I recognize their value in my students' encounters and learning with literature. Although I may never design an elixir of longevity for practice from any of this, the processes involved in the reconciliation attempts have been fruitful. I am grateful for the constantly shifting vantage point the darker side affords me and for the collegial conversations of Linda F., Nancie Atwell, and others. Given the nature of reading and of teaching, I will probably always feel a quiet need to let musings such as these capture me and sit me up straight again and again to bring renewed, reformulated, and reunited integrity to my thinking and my practice.

REFERENCES

Adams, P. (1987). Writing from reading—"dependent authorship" as a response. In B. Corcoran & E. Evans (Eds.), *Readers, texts, teachers* (pp. 119–152). Portsmouth, NH: Boynton/Cook.

Arendt, H. (1959). *Between past and future.* New York: Penguin Books.

Atwell, N. (1987). *In the middle.* Portsmouth, NH: Boynton/Cook.

Beach, R., & Hynds, S. (1991). Research on response to literature. In R. Barr et al. (Eds.), *Handbook of reading research* (Vol. 2, pp. 453–489). New York: Longman.

Bleich, D. (1978). *Subjective criticism.* Baltimore: Johns Hopkins University Press.

Brown, L. (1987). Rendering literature accessible. In B. Corcoran & E. Evans (Eds.), *Readers, texts, teachers* (pp. 93–118). Portsmouth, NH: Boynton/Cook.

Corcoran, B. (1987). Teachers creating readers. In B. Corcoran & E. Evans (Eds.), *Readers, texts, teachers* (pp. 41–74). Portsmouth, NH: Boynton/Cook.

Culler, J. (1982). *On deconstruction.* New York: Cornell University Press.

Dias, P., & Hayhoe, M. (1988). *Developing response to poetry.* Milton Keynes, UK: Open University Press.

Duff, K. (1993). *The alchemy of illness.* New York: Bell Tower.

Evans, E. (1987). Readers recreating texts. In B. Corcoran & E. Evans (Eds.), *Readers, texts, teachers* (pp. 22–40). Portsmouth, NH: Boynton/Cook.

Fulwiler, T. (Ed.). (1987). *The journal book.* Portsmouth, NH: Boynton/Cook.

Gilbert, P. (1987). Post reader-response: The deconstructive technique. In B. Corcoran & E. Evans (Eds.), *Readers, texts, teachers* (pp. 234–250). Portsmouth, NH: Boynton/Cook.

Griffith, P. (1987). *Literary theory and English teaching.* Philadelphia: Open University Press.

Holland N. N. (1980). Re-covering "The purloined letter": Reading as a personal transaction. In S. Suleiman & I. Crosman (Eds.), *The reader in the text* (pp. 350–370). Princeton, NJ: Princeton University Press.

Iser, W. (1978). *The act of reading.* Baltimore: Johns Hopkins University Press.

Judy, S., & Judy, S. (1983). *The English teacher's handbook.* Toronto: Little Brown.

Kelly, P., & Farnan, N. (1991). Promoting critical thinking through response logs: A reader-response approach with fourth graders. In *Learner factors/teacher factors: Issues in literacy, research and instruction.* 40th Yearbook, National Reading Conference (pp. 277–84). Chicago: National Reading Conference.

Labercane, G. (1990). The possible world of the reader. *Reflections on Canadian Literacy, 8*(4), 145–152.

Protherough, R. (1987). The stories that readers tell. In B. Corcoran & E. Evans (Eds.), *Readers, texts, teachers* (pp. 75–92). Portsmouth, NH: Boynton/Cook.

Rief, L. (1992). *Seeking diversity.* Portsmouth, NH: Heinemann Educational Books.

Rosenblatt, L. M. (1976). *Literature as exploration.* New York: Noble and Noble (1938 publication by Appleton-Century).

Rosenblatt, L. M. (1991). The reading transaction: What for? In B. Miller Power & R. Hubbard (Eds), *Literacy in process* (pp. 114–127). Portsmouth, NH: Heinemann.

Sheridan, D. (1991). Changing business as usual: Reader response in the classroom. *College English, 53*(7), 804–14.

Willis, G. (1989). The corpus and the incorporeal of curriculum. *Curriculum Inquiry, 19*(1) 71–96.

Young, C. (1987). Readers, texts, teachers. In B. Corcoran & E. Evans (Eds.), *Readers, texts, teachers* (pp. 7–21). Portsmouth, NH: Boynton/Cook.

Young, C., & Robinson, E. (1987). Reading/writing in the culture of the classroom. In B. Corcoran and E. Evans (Eds.), *Readers, texts, teachers* (pp. 153–173). Portsmouth, NH: Boynton/Cook.

Reading as Coauthorship: A Reader Response Connection to Culture

PAUL BOYD-BATSTONE

Claremont Graduate School of Education

Culture is a story with multiple authors. One's culture is made up of a myriad of experiences, images, sensations, creative solutions, and stories. The artifacts and indicators of one's culture are felt and understood implicitly. The story of one's culture is told and retold explicitly. Children experience their own culture as something in the background—the accumulation of lived-through experience. They express their culture in the games they play, the songs they sing, the images they create, and the stories they tell. According to Louise Rosenblatt (1938/1968), the experience of understanding and interpreting a story is primarily aesthetic. Therefore when children read stories, they respond to their reading with aesthetic images and sensations drawn from the experience of their cultural background.

Efferent versus Aesthetic Reading

Rosenblatt (1986) pointed out that reading efferently—that is, for information purposes—is different from reading a literary work aesthetically. Efferent reading is objectified acquisition of information. An example of efferent reading is reading a set of instructions in a manual or on the back of a medicine bottle. The reader is reading to gain meaning to take away from the reading. In contrast, reading literature is a form of creative expression that is experienced aesthetically. In reading a literary work aesthetically, one responds by evoking feelings associated with prior experience and images illustrating the story. The meaning evoked is contained within the reader's response to the text. An aesthetic response is the spontaneous creation of a new work of art in the mind, or as Rosenblatt (1978) calls it, "the evocation of a poem." As children read, they create a new poem. They feel unique sensations and picture images. They share their own stories orally and in other forms with conversation, writing, music, or visual and performing arts. Reading, therefore, is coauthorship of a text.

The purpose of this chapter is to explore the reader response connection to culture as an aesthetic experience. I will begin with a discussion of how culture affects reader response in terms of sharing power, negotiating culture, and giving voice. Then I will consider how one student expressed her culture aesthetically in a reader response learning environment by looking at the written responses of Erika, a Latina fifth-grade bilingual student. Erika's responses to reading, as expressed in her writing, demonstrate three ways that reader response and culture connect: (1) plugging into another's story, (2) telling one's own story, and (3) connecting to a family story. Erika reads as a coauthor, rewriting the text to include her own and her family's stories.

Reader Response and Culture

In culturally diverse settings, such as schools, students are constantly experiencing aesthetic responses to their world and to their reading, particularly as these experiences are drawn from their cultural background; yet the responses can easily remain hidden. Many students may not be aware of expressing an idea aesthetically. They may not even be conscious of applying a cultural metaphor to explain their way of seeing. Generally in any culture, deeper thoughts and feelings are kept to oneself, so a passing word from a student may be a kind of test balloon. It is said in passing to see if what the student says has merit or is acceptable within the group. If the passing word is ignored or derided, the immediate consequences may be minimal, but silence is the ultimate price of unresponsive instruction. Recognizing and affirming the test balloons of aesthetic responses to literature are ways of spotlighting the many expressions of culture in the classroom.

Aesthetic responses can be as ethereal as air, unless they are made explicit. Students may or may not articulate their responses verbally. Sometimes aesthetic responses surface as a drawing, other times as a groan, and still others appear as a song or a poem. Because schools tend not to respond to cultural differences, deeper cultural metaphors are more easily hidden from learning on the surface unless the learning environment is responsive to the musings of students from diverse backgrounds. Without a response-centered environment, it is virtually impossible to access the culture of the students for instructional purposes.

Sleeter and Grant (1994) identified a number of approaches to multicultural education ranging from deficit myths to empowerment. My understanding of multiculturalism is more than a benign statement of "everybody is okay." I see multiculturalism as an issue of culture and empowerment. Multiculturalism in an educational setting is a process of sharing power, negotiating culture, and giving voice (Darder, 1989). A response-centered approach to teaching connects reading to culture, because culture is a story understood most deeply in the realm of the aesthetic.

Sharing Power

In Spanish, the word for power, *poder,* connotes not so much domination, but authority to know and to do—to have authority as in authorship. My use of the phrase "sharing power" carries the idea of being an author of knowledge and action. Sharing power in the classroom means that knowledge and action are shared by the teacher and students as coauthors of the curriculum. Being powerless means passively accepting instruction as handed down from teacher to students. It is not authoring one's ideas and actions; it is being acted upon. Sharing power in the classroom is sharing the authority with students to act as coauthors of their learning and their lives.

In the classroom, the teacher is the one who initially establishes the environment for reader response and the stance students will adopt in their responses to text. If the teacher's stance is predominantly efferent, the students will follow the teacher's lead and read for informational purposes. In other words, they will read in order to obtain the correct answers on a test or some other assessment tool. Therefore, when a teacher establishes an efferent stance, the classroom environment becomes a place for accommodation to the culture of the teacher and for subordination of the culture of the students. However, if the teacher is predominantly interested in connecting the text to the students' lives, aesthetic reading comes to the forefront.

In reader response, the students' aesthetic experience connects the multiple worlds of children (Dyson, 1990) to their reading. The primary vehicle for bridging the written word across the students' multiple worlds is dialogue (Freire, 1970). The conversations among students and with their teacher open up places for instruction (Tharp & Gallimore, 1989); such dialogue also allows opportunity to integrate learning across the curriculum. Quality literature that reflects the students' lived-through experiences can be a touchstone to connect reading to culture. Reading literature adds to the dimension of the realm of the aesthetic (Rosenblatt, 1986). And when classroom instruction explores students' aesthetic readings of literature, there takes place an inclusive process that invites a wide range of understandings and divergent thinking. Reader response calls on all individuals to share their knowledge and experiences and to actively join in the development of their own learning. Students from diverse backgrounds, by bringing to bear their own particular cultural knowledge and experiences, are able to enrich the experiences of others who may have only a singular set of experiences to contribute to the reading act.

Negotiating Culture

Sharing knowledge and action, especially in classrooms in which the teacher may not necessarily share the cultural backgrounds of the students, requires a significant degree of cultural negotiation. The teacher needs continually to ask the students, "What are you thinking?" "Is this what you mean . . . ?" "Are there other ways to see this?" Cultural negotiation means both that the teacher is actively listening for ways in which the students' cultures permeate their understanding of their reading, and that the students are freely investigating and expressing their cultural knowledge. Frequently the role of teacher shifts from instructor to colearner as the students explain their thinking. In reader response practices, the raw substance of an initial response to a story is clarified and made explicit in an atmosphere of cultural negotiation. Sometimes a student may make an association to a text that appears on the surface to be completely far afield, but, on closer examination, that association may actually be a culturally embedded way of understanding a text. Even though an association may be foreign to the teacher or students from different cultural backgrounds, very insightful thinking is taking place. Additionally in culturally diverse classrooms, the teacher and students can function as cultural mediators of meaning as these meanings are expressed by students of differing backgrounds. Essentially, reader response invites cultural negotiation as a way of affirming how each one thinks and comes to an understanding of a text.

Giving Voice

Sharing power and cultural negotiation would be feeble concepts if they did not result in giving voice to the students. Giving voice is threefold: validating the students' aesthetic responses, developing articulate expressions of their aesthetic responses, and making those expressions public. Validating students' aesthetic responses is a function of power sharing and cultural negotiation. Giving voice begins with fostering a classroom environment in which teacher and students genuinely listen to each other's ideas, feelings, and imaginations. The nitty-gritty of classroom instruction takes place within the process of giving voice. Part of giving voice is teaching the conventions of writing and editing. Another part is exploring creative ways to bring student responses to full and articulate expression. Both aspects of giving voice are hard work. It is mental work to dig for a unifying metaphor in a student's myriad of responses. It is work to edit a story with a student so that the revision communicates the intended meaning. Reader response is time-consuming and is in a sense like the effort put into mining for ore and then refining the gold. Once a student's response has been formed into articulate expression, it begs to be made public. Making a work public can take many forms, from a class or schoolwide presentation to full-scale publication of the work.

Giving voice is an act of drawing out what is inside so that others may respond. Each student responds uniquely to a story according to his or her own cultural experience. If a student's culture is to be validated in school, instruction must be response-centered. When an individual develops an articulate voice, the voicing calls for a response from those around. The extent to which a student's aesthetic response is included in the classroom is, therefore, an indicator of the degree of multiculturalism practiced at school. Response-centered instruction takes on a transformative role then, as students realize the value of their lived-through experience, their ideas, feelings, and imaginations, and become authoritative with their own story. Reader response connects to culture by sharing power, negotiating culture, and giving voice to aesthetic responses. Culture is a story with multiple authors. Responding to culture in the classroom is recognizing the readers as authors who write their own stories.

Erika, a Fifth-Grade Coauthor

Erika is a bright and delightful Latina fifth-grade student in a bilingual classroom in an urban school district in Southern California. She does not come from a wealthy home. Her father works as a laborer, and her mother stays home to care for the family of six children. Erika is the firstborn in her family and carries the responsibilities of being the oldest. She must help baby-sit and make sure that younger siblings get ready to go to school. She helps with meals and laundry and, in keeping with the burden of being the oldest, she is expected to keep her brothers and sisters in line. She is literate in both Spanish and English and takes schooling very seriously. Erika loves to read, and much of what she reads she associates with her family. Her responses to stories often include references to members of her immediate and extended family. Even when she is thinking in terms of fantasy, her family is inserted into her aesthetic responses. Erika's family is her initial connection to her cultural understanding of a text.

During the school year in which she was one of my students, Erika and I had numerous discussions about the stories she was reading. She took a special liking to two Mexican American authors, Sandra Cisneros and Victor Villaseñor. She readily identified with the first-person accounts of life in *The House on Mango Street* (Cisneros, 1989), and she was caught up by the fabulous family tales of *Walking Stars* (Villaseñor, 1994). Erika's responses to these books provided a wealth of opportunities to write creatively. Her written expression itself is worthy of publication, but for the purpose of this chapter, her writing gives insight into ways that cultural expression emerges in her responses to what she has been reading. I have identified three ways that Erika connects her culture through reader response: plugging into another's story, telling one's own story, and connecting with a family's story.

Plugging into Another's Story

Erika selected Sandra Cisneros' (1989) book *The House on Mango Street* to read for a literature study project. She immediately identified with the experiences of Esperanza Cordero, a young girl growing up in a *barrio* in Chicago. Erika did not read the book sequentially. She sampled vignettes at random as they caught her attention. She was immediately taken by "A House of My Own" (p. 108), Esperanza's poetic longing for her own space in this world. Erika and I discussed the vignette, and she shared how much she wished she had a place of her own without the invasion of all her brothers and sisters. I suggested that she look at the book again and then write her own poem about a house of her own. Here is Erika's poem in response to Cisneros' (1989) vignette:

A House of My Own
by Erika Tamayo

Not a flat.
Not a little house in the front.
Not the manager's house.
Not my sister's house.
A house all on my own
with my yard and my bed and my pretty bears all around.
My books and my stories waiting for me to pick them up and read them.
My two shoes waiting under my bed.
Nobody to run after.
Nobody to mess up my homework.

Only a house as quiet as quiet as a church when nobody is inside,
a space for myself to go,
clean as my house when my sisters and brothers are in school.
A house all of my own.

If you look at the original version of "A House of My Own" (Cisneros, 1989), you will see that Erika closely followed Cisneros' style and format. It appears that Erika took out certain words and simply inserted other words that more closely matched her own experience. For example, where Cisneros writes "Not a man's house. Not a daddy's. A house all my own." (p. 108), Erika inserts, "Not a manager's house. Not my sister's house. A house all my own. . . ." Obviously, for Erika the problem of dealing with siblings is much more pressing than the gender issues that Cisneros raises. This is not to juxtapose sibling rivalry against gender inequality; it merely demonstrates how Erika personalizes the reading of the vignette by inserting her brothers and sisters as the source of her frustration. The story functioned like a cloze exercise, with blank spaces to fill in. Erika adapted Cisneros' story using a kind of one-to-one correspondence of ideas as she plugged her life into the text. Plugging into another's story is probably one of the simplest ways to resource the culture and experience of students. Telling your own story takes aesthetic responses to another level.

Telling One's Own Story

As Erika continued to read *The House on Mango Street*, she was amazed at how the book touched her life. The story "Chanclas" tells of the embarrassment of having to wear old, worn-out saddle shoes (*chanclas*) to a dance party, because Esperanza, the protagonist, did not have time to buy new ones. In Cisneros' account, Esperanza overcomes her embarrassment when her uncle insists that the two dance and they dazzle everyone with their spectacular dancing. Not so with Erika's story. The embarrassment of being compared to other girls is too much for her, and she stays on the margins of the party, even though it means refusing her cousin's invitations and being a wallflower all night long. She is left with a lesson to be learned and a story of her own. Here is the personal story that Erika wrote (without further editing).

Chanclas
by Erika Tamayo

Once my uncle Jesse invited us to a party and he said, "It's going to be at my house on Saturday at 1:00 o'clock." And then we said, "OK, we'll be there." Then he left to go to his house.

It was Saturday morning, I was getting dressed. I was just about to put my shoes on and I said, "Oh no, I don't have any shoes." I told my mom, "Mom, I don't have any shoes." So she said, "You have to wear whatever you have."

"What? I'm not wearing those old shoes!" I yelled. So my mom said, "It's too late to go buy new shoes, Miss Erika." I said, "OK, ok, but I am not going to get out of the car." As she ironed my clothes she stopped and stared at me. She folded her arms and said, "that is your choice for shoes. Now don't say that they are old. Well, they are a little bit old; but you can still wear them, and the people won't say anything." "Okay, okay, I won't say they are old, and I will not stay in the car." And away we went to the party at my uncle's house.

When we got there, my uncle Jesse and my other uncles were cooking *carne asada* and the day passed it was time to cut the cake. (My cousin Jesse Jr. was going to be two years old.) Jesse and his mother cut it and everybody got a piece.

After we ate the cake, the music started. My uncles brought out their own C.D.'s of a lot of *bandas,* like *Banda Machos* and *Banda Maguey* and *Los Pajaritos de Michoacan.* They were getting ready to dance all night long. All my uncles danced with their wives and my parents were dancing while I was taking care of all the kids.

My mom and my dad stopped dancing and came to pick up my little brother, Danny. My cousins waited me to dance, but I didn't know which one which one wanted to dance with me, because they were all shy, except for Chava.

We call him "Chava," but his real name is Salvador. He is seventeen years old. He's not too tall because he came from Mexico. (Well it's the truth. They are not so tall when they come from Mexico, or maybe from other places. *Chava se va a los bailes.* Sometimes my cousin Araceli gets mad, because her father lets Chava go to dances, but not her. He's a good soccer player. My other cousin, Efren plays in a Saturday league with Chava. I don't know if they are on the same team, but my father takes them to play.) Chava had been dancing with Gabi, *una muchacha que le gusta.* He had nice boots made from rattlesnake skin. Gabi was wearing burgundy, *tercio pelo* shoes *con tacon alto.* The shoes matched her tight, burgundy dress.

I looked at my *chanclas.* How embarrassing to have those shoes. I felt like crying in frustration for not having time to go buy shoes. I wanted to run away and go home. I wished I had stayed home. But just then, Chava asked me to dance, because Gabi got tired.

I said, "no, I don't want to dance right now." So he asked me and he asked me; but I said, "no" every single time. Then he asked Gabi if she wasn't tired anymore. And she said, "Nope!" So they danced till five in the morning.

We all slept from five to seven and then we went back to our house. My mom didn't say anything right there, because she was sleepy. Later on when she woke up, she said, "you learned a lesson: check everything before the party so we will have everything including party shoes."

This story from Erika's life, as confirmed to me by her parents, paralleled Cisneros' story but went off on its own direction. With the first draft, Erika told the bare-bones outline of the story. She could have easily kept the rest of the many details to herself, but I decided to ask very pointed questions about what happened in the story, such as, what kind of shoes was your Cousin Chava wearing? and how was Gabi dressed? Pressing Erika for rich details transformed the story from a quick rendition of an embarrassing night into a vivid tale of the inner struggles of an eleven-year-old girl. Rather than sterilize her account with all words in English, I encouraged Erika to pepper the text with words in Spanish that better communicated her meaning. Once again, her family emerged in her response to a story. Sharing the power to be an author, Erika negotiated her meaning with me and gave voice to her own story.

Connecting with a Family Story

Plugging into another's story and telling a personal account begin to mine the ore of one's culture, but when an author taps into an old story—a story told and retold within a family—the writer begins to strike gold and connect deeply with a culture. Later in the year, I showed Erika a copy of Victor Villaseñor's (1994) collection of stories based on his own family's oral tradition, *Walking Stars*. Villaseñor's *Walking Stars* combines magic and reality as a way of understanding his life and the lives of the members of his mother's and father's families in Mexico and California. Many of the stories are based on Villaseñor's interviews with his grandmother and his grandfather.

I simply asked Erika to take a look at the book and later to tell me what she thought of it. A couple of days later we sat down together and she began by telling me about the first story in the book, "The Smartest Human I Ever Met: My Brother's Sheepdog" (Villaseñor, 1994, pp. 15–18). Erika explained how the sheepdog magically saved Villaseñor's brother's life. According to the book, Villaseñor's brother was dying of leukemia in San Diego at Scripps Hospital. On a critical night, the dog went *"crazy-loco,"* running to the hills and barking at the sky in an effort to intercept his brother's soul. I asked if she had ever had a dog or a special pet, and she said, "No." She liked the book, but our discussion was not particularly engaging, so I asked her to do the same thing as Victor Villaseñor: to interview her parents or grandparents about any magical family stories that they had heard. The following is a story that Erika shared with me the next day (with original spelling).

> *The Ghost Treasure*
> *by Erika Tamayo*
>
> In a ranch called "El Puerto" in Purépero, Michoacán [Mexico] my two uncles, Amador and Roberto, planted corn and took care of horses and cows. One night when my uncles were in bed they were ready to sleep in the silence of the night. They heard the sound of a horse's stampead. It stopped at the head of their beds. They heard the stampead two or three times that night. And they asked one another, "what was it?"
>
> At last they went out to see what happened. They saw that the horses were as quiet as the stars in their corral, and the cows as calm as when they were eating. So my uncles asked themselves again, "what happened?"

Some people told them that there was a ghost that had a treasure hidden in that ranch. But they never heard the stampeading horses and never knew what it was.

I think that the ghost was looking for the treasure. It was late Friday night and my grandpa had heard about the treasure before. In fact, the day before my grandpa was looking for it. He had been digging into the ground of the the corral with a shovel and a weeding tool. He only found an old, gold coin with Benito Juarez on the face. No one had ever owned one of those coins before. It was one-of-a-kind.

When my uncles heard that there was a ghost who had treasure, they were very scared. They never heard the stampeads again; but they only slept there until somebody burned it to the ground.

When Erika handed me a draft of this story, I had two reactions. First, I was intrigued by a real ghost story floating around the family. Second, I noticed that after the first paragraph, the handwriting had changed and I became suspicious of the authenticity of the story. As teacher, I asked her why the handwriting had changed. She responded that her mother had been telling her the story, but she noticed that Erika was not getting it down correctly, so her mother grabbed the pencil and began writing the ghost tale. In addition to the account of the ghost ranch, I asked Erika to write what she thought about it, to put herself into the story. That afternoon, I talked with her mother about the writing. Apparently, the homework assignment of interviewing Erika's parents involved the entire family in telling stories about experiences in Mexico. Everyone in the family sat around the kitchen table that night as Erika struggled to capture her parents' stories in print for the first time.

Reading for Erika took on the form of authorship. As she read quality literature, she told her own life in the forms of plugging into another's story, telling her own story, and connecting to a family's story. The springboard for her learning was the quality literature from Sandra Cisneros and Victor Villaseñor, and the substance of her learning was Erika's own responses to their work. The reader response connection to Erika's experience ushered her culture into the classroom. She shared the power (*poder*) to influence the classroom curriculum. Her responses formed the basis for cultural negotiation. Her writing also expressed her voice. She became a coauthor with Cisneros and Villaseñor as she told her own story and those of her family.

Conclusion

Reader response connects to the story of culture. Reading literature is a creative experience of retelling a story in one's mind. Students' culturally based readings are expressed primarily in the realm of the aesthetic. Though grounded in cultural understanding, aesthetic responses are unique to the individual, so that in culturally diverse settings aesthetic reading is a way of inviting multiple interpretations of a text. Efferent approaches to reading are focused on gaining information from a text. In classrooms that take a predominantly efferent stance, students tend to accommodate their understandings to the dominant culture of the teacher and the school. In contrast, response-centered learning environments treat reading as a creative act of making one's own story. Using student responses as the substance of the learning treats the students as coauthors of what they read.

A response-centered classroom is one in which students share power as authors of their learning. They speak authoritatively as they share their lives and understandings. In the process of sharing aesthetic responses, cultural negotiation takes place between the teacher and the students, as well as among the students. Reader response calls on the teacher and the students to shift their relationship from the single direction of instructor to learner to a more dialogical relationship of colearners and cultural mediators. The product of sharing power and negotiating culture is the advent of giving voice to the students. Giving voice involves validating student responses, developing articulate expression of the students' aesthetic responses, and making their work public. In this way students' cultural interpretations become a central object of study when reading literature; giving full expression to those interpretations is the collaborative task of teacher and students alike.

Erika demonstrated how a student interprets her reading aesthetically. She developed an understanding of Cisneros' and Villaseñor's writings through the lenses of her own family and culture. On one level she expressed her responses to *The House on Mango Street* by plugging into another's story. Erika simply took certain words out of the text and inserted her own, which reflected her own predicament and desire. On a deeper level, Erika springboarded from the text to tell her own story. Her original story paralleled that of Cisneros, but it was definitely her own rendering, containing a wealth of cultural images and understandings. She understood how Cisneros felt about dancing in *chanclas,* but she told the story the way it took place in her own life. Finally, Erica connected the story of Victor Villaseñor to a magical tale of ghosts on a ranch in Mexico. The experience of capturing a family story in print acted to bring the entire family together around the table. Erika tapped into an oral tradition in her own family and placed herself in the story. Culture is a story with multiple authors. Erika responded to her reading as a coauthor with the power to write authoritatively, negotiate her culture, and give voice to her own story.

REFERENCES

Cisneros, S. (1989). *The house on Mango Street.* New York: Vintage Books.

Darder, A. (1991). *Culture and power in the classroom: A critical foundation for bicultural education.* New York: Bergin and Garvey.

Dyson, A. H. (1990). Weaving possibilities: Rethinking metaphors for early literacy development. *Reading Teacher, 44*(2), 202–213.

Freire, P. (1970). *The pedagogy of the oppressed.* New York: Contiuum.

Rosenblatt, L. (1968). *Literature as exploration.* New York: Noble & Noble. (Original work published in 1938).

Rosenblatt, L. (1978). *The reader, the text, and the poem: The transactional theory of the literary work.* Carbondale, IL: Southern Illinois University Press.

Rosenblatt, L. (1986). The aesthetic transaction. *Journal of Aesthetic Education, 20*(4), 122–128.

Sleeter, C. E., & Grant, C. A. (1994). *Making choices for multicultural education: Five approaches to race, class, and gender.* New York: Macmillan.

Tharp, R., & Gallimore, R. (1989). *Rousing minds to life.* New York: Cambridge University Press.

Villaseñor, V. (1994). *Walking stars: Stories of magic and power.* Houston, TX: Piñata Books.

CHAPTER

11

Resistance to Reading in School

CAROLE COX
California State University, Long Beach

This chapter begins and ends with Elizabeth, a child who voices resistance to reading in school. In the beginning, it describes results of a study of Elizabeth's and other children's responses to literature from kindergarten through fifth grade in one urban school in Los Angeles. In the middle, it shifts to an unexpected finding that Elizabeth, among many other children in the study, feels frustration, resentment, and even anger about the way teachers have co-opted control of book choice and time for reading by replacing reading with writing and other activities and by marginalizing student response to literature. In the end, it presents a tool for response-centered teaching with literature that begins, rather than ends, with a child's personal response. Also, there is a final suggestion from Elizabeth on how teachers should teach with literature.

Elizabeth and Other Children Respond to Literature

Even though she is in fourth grade and really almost a little too big for a "lap reading," Elizabeth sighs contentedly and leans against me as I read the story *A Chair for My Mother* (Williams, 1982) aloud to her in the school library. We're alone, however, and she seems to luxuriate in the intimacy of a one-to-one reading session with an adult. Before I begin to read, I tell Elizabeth that she can tell me anything she wants about the story at any time. She began immediately on page 1:

> How old is she? I think she is my age. No, I think she's seven or eight. When does this take place? Her pants look like the '70s or '80s. They have bell bottoms, well, not exactly bell bottoms, but it looks like the '70s.

Elizabeth has been a participant in a longitudinal study of children's responses to literature that I have been conducting in one culturally and linguistically diverse urban school in Los Angeles since she and the other participants were in kindergarten (Cox, 2000). I felt that a key to understanding how to teach with literature was a description of elementary school children's natural, unprompted responses, especially as this pertained to reader stance toward a literary work. The purpose of this study was to identify and describe emergent categories of stance toward a literary work from a theoretical perspective and to analyze and compare these to discern differences over time.

Understanding reader response is important because literature-based teaching has been advocated as a cornerstone of literacy development, kindergarten through twelfth grade. Over the last few decades, there has been a growing body of research on response and a renewed interest among educators in the exploration of theoretical frameworks for teaching with literature (Marshall, 2000). Reader-response theories, in particular, have gained importance in literacy instruction because they are primarily concerned with how a reader makes meaning from an experience with a text (Beach, 1993). The field of literary criticism in general is concerned with meaning making, but it has shifted from a focus on finding the meaning in the text to more fully understanding the process by which readers, as critics, go about making meaning. Although reader response theorists do not all agree on how the process of understanding literature is shaped in transactions among readers, texts, and contexts, they share an underlying assumption that meaning is not found solely in the text. They have also become increasingly interested in how response theory might influence classroom instruction and in exploring sociocultural perspectives on literary response (Galda & Beach, 2001).

Among reader response critics, Louise Rosenblatt's transactional model of the reading process (1978), in particular, has interested educators. Rosenblatt calls the reading process a transaction during which a "live circuit" is created between the reader and the text. During this transaction, readers assume a stance; that is, they focus their selective attention in different ways. A reader's stance represents how a reader organizes thinking about reading according to a more efferent or more aesthetic framework. During a more efferent reading, the reader focuses attention on the information to take away from the text—for example, reading the label on a medicine bottle to find out the correct dosage. During a more aesthetic reading, the reader focuses attention on a more personal, private experiencing of the text—for example, reading a novel and picturing yourself as one of the characters. A more efferent reading focuses on what the book says, whereas a more aesthetic reading focuses on the associations, feelings, attitudes, and ideas that the book arouses in the reader. Because Rosenblatt's writings have influenced thinking about teaching with literature (Clifford, 1991; Farrell & Squire, 1990; Sipe, 1998), the transactional theory was the beginning point of analysis of children's stance in this study.

Several patterns have emerged. Stances categorized as more efferent were focused on the text itself, demonstrated by attention to print and language, content, explanations, and analysis. Stances categorized as more aesthetic focused on the personal experiencing of the text demonstrated by attention to favorite parts, associations, hypothesizing, questioning, and performance. The majority of responses in kindergarten through third grade were aesthetic (71.6 percent), and aesthetic responses were more varied than efferent. Furthermore, efferent-type responses, usually associated with goals of traditional reading instruction such as recognizing words and explaining a character's actions, occurred more frequently embedded in more personal aesthetic-type responses than alone or with other efferent responses. Both the more aesthetic and more efferent responses were mutually embedded in these data. There was a consistent pattern of dynamic interplay between efferent and aesthetic stance consistent with the continuum metaphor for stance used by Rosenblatt as a to and fro positioning movement along a fan, finally settling on one predominant stance. This finding also supports a three-dimensional construct such as Benton's (1983) description of stance as "a shifting viewpoint," Bruner's (1986) "possible worlds," and Bakhtin's (1981) notion of the reader's dialogic relationship with the voices imbedded in the text.

The proportion of aesthetic to efferent responses remained the same for kindergarten through second grade. By second grade, efferent responses increasingly focused on explaining a story. Any attention to print in the text occurred when children chose to read aloud. Most children were reading independently at this time and often asked to read to me. They asked questions when they did not know a word or had a question about its meaning. There was a marked increase of aesthetic responses by third grade. At this time, efferent responses had all but disappeared except for explaining the story. Students in fourth and fifth grade increasingly focused their attention on the ways a story pertained to their own lives, suggesting the importance of directing students to this inner, secondary "story world," which Benton (1992) argues should be the basic subject matter of classroom literature lessons.

Students who consistently responded most fluently also consistently challenged the story, and this tendency increased through the grades. In a phenomenological view of the reading process, Iser (1978) has described what active readers do as "filling in the gaps" of the text as they "share the game of the imagination" (p. 108). When a state of tension seemed to exist for these young readers due to the ambiguity they felt about the story, they confronted the text and hypothesized multiple explanations of possible solutions to resolve the conflict they seemed to be experiencing, drawing on their own fund of personal experience to confirm or disconfirm several possible understandings of the story. Bakhtin (1981) explains that all utterances are dialogic—multivoiced, "contradiction-ridden, and tension-filled" (p. 272)—and especially so with novelistic discourse reflecting the strained coexistence of diverse social, historical, contextual, psychological, and developmental forces within language. There are no neutral words or forms. Readers appropriate the word—"take the word and make it one's own" (p. 294). The reader's stance toward a text makes entry into this dialogic and tension-filled world of literary meaning-making possible.

Goals of traditional reading instruction, such as understanding words and story meaning, were most frequently met when children tried to break through the boundaries of the text. This relative emphasis on personal, engaging, even confrontational response, therefore in no way excluded opportunities for becoming skilled in using the more public, lexical, analytical, and abstracting components of reading. In fact, it mirrors the shift in reading research from concern with basic competence, to cognitive processes involved in reading comprehension, to acknowledgment of the active role of the reader, and the importance of prior experience. Especially by fifth grade, students in the study only briefly brushed the story in their spoken responses, choosing instead to talk about their own lives. Even though by middle school literature instruction focuses increasingly on a close reading of the text itself, it appears important at this age to help readers seek links between stories: Life as literature is to be fully realized as a means of personal exploration for students (Appelman & Hynds, 1997; Hemphill, 1999).

Implications of the finding of this study would be for teachers to first direct children to take a more aesthetic, personal stance toward literature, rather than first directing their attention to text or print. Focusing on the personal experience of the text, encouraging students to address things they find anomalous, and accepting diverse responses could provide a rich medium of growth for reading and language development, as well as for literary understanding, critical interpretation, and self-knowledge through transactions with literary works (Commeyras & Sumner, 1998).

Hade (1992) maintains that the one who controls stance controls learning. Although reader response theorists have provided theoretical metaphors and models as frameworks for examining literary processes, it is essential that these theories be tested through research studying these processes as they occur in the real world. Benton (1983) remarks: "If we can translate these (theoretical) details . . . into an instrument for the descriptive analysis for what writers and readers actually do, then we shall go some way towards an understanding of literary processes" (p. 74).

Elizabeth and Other Children on Reading Inside and Outside of School

Something of interest has unexpectedly emerged from my sessions with children, and it points to the gap that often exists between theory, research, and real-world practice. Children have begun to tell me what reading is like for them both inside and outside of school. I first noticed this tendency in third grade. Elizabeth and others were now competent readers and most wanted to read. In my sessions with them, however, these children began to express resistance to reading in school, describing how for them, reading had been co-opted by teachers. Many expressed frustration with teachers who limited their reading choices and their time to read self-selected literature, and who consistently required them to do an activity such as writing after reading. For example, Elizabeth told me:

> I like to read a lot. I'm reading *Scared Stiff* and *The Ghost in the Window* from the library at home. . . . I don't like reading at school very much

because I don't have very much time. Like when I'm home I can read all I want. I can't at school. . . . I hate reading in school because you have to read what they make you. The only time I like reading in school is when the teacher's reading aloud and we can read along, or when we can read for fun—which is never. We never have time to read. You have to write down the stupid thing (She sounds very frustrated and is practically crying). I hate that. You gotta write down everything you do. I don't get how that is reading. And one time I told the truth and she put it wrong. She said 'What was your favorite part? And I didn't have a favorite part. I said I just liked the whole thing and she counted it off. So I have to make up something, which is real dumb. Writing answers to questions instead of reading is the dumbest thing in the whole world. I love to read at home. My favorite authors are Betsy Byars and Lois Lowry. I'm reading the Anastasia books. My favorite series books are *The Babysitters Club* and *The American Girl* series.

On another occasion she compared reading in school to book burnings in Nazi Germany:

I love to read. It's my favoritest thing in the whole world. If there was no such things as books I'd die [spoken dramatically]. 'Cause it's not fair if nobody invented books. I'd be so mad. I'd invent a book. What if suddenly that really mean guy . . . Adolf Hitler . . . What if someone like him came and took away all the books in the world? I'd be so mad I'd say, "You're the stupidest, ugliest, meanest person in the whole entire world." I'd punch him in the nose. . . . If somebody as mean as Hitler took books away I'd beat him up.

I sensed these feelings about reading in school had been building up in Elizabeth over time, resulting in this small explosion while we talked. She was ready to punch Hitler in the nose if he took books away. She was not joking, and I don't think she meant Hitler. I sensed real anger here. Note that Elizabeth was an extremely successful student, from standardized test scores to report cards and other school performance assessments. She wanted to read but felt she couldn't in school.

Other students echo Elizabeth. Cassiopea is another avid fourth-grade reader who has told me she reads a lot at home. Her grandmother, who is raising her, takes her to the library and buys her books, but she works hard all day and does not have time to read to her, so Cassy reads on her own. Her comments are usually to the point:

I don't like to read in school [said adamantly]. Because we only get to have the same time of reading and when I get to the very goodest part, we have to stop reading and do something else.

Fourth grader Jennifer said:

> I feel that most of the kids at home like to just read for fun, because they feel like sometimes with school, they tell you only to read this, but when they read for fun, you read all this and sometimes at school they make you stop at a certain chapter and it's really hard. I feel that most kids even could finish if teachers let them. If teachers would let you read more it would help you be a better speller.

I don't think Jennifer was that concerned about spelling, but she was fishing for a rationale to support her complaint about time to read and had lost faith that time for personal reading was a priority in her school. However, she knew that becoming a better speller was a priority, so she used that as an arguing point (and a good one actually supported by extensive educational research).

Jacy was always happy to see me come to read to him. However, from about third grade on he would wait patiently for me to read the story, make one seemingly obligatory comment while I read, pause, and then launch into an extended monologue on his personal reading at home. In fourth grade, he told me about reading *Nintendo Magazine;* numerous *Goosebumps* books; books on lizards, snakes, and dragons; *Marvel* comics; and *Mad* magazine at home. When he finished, I asked him about reading in school: "I'm not reading anything at school."

Like Jacy, Becky waited patiently through the reading, but after one comment about the book, she talked extensively about the lack of choice of books in school. Her responses in fifth grade were similar. Her complaints were that "Sometimes we only have like five minutes where everybody reads"; it wasn't quiet enough; the teacher assigned books and you had to take notes and "she wants to know what page you're on, and do homework . . . "; and too often reading literature was to get information, for example, assigned reading of *My Brother Sam is Dead* (Collier & Collier, 1974) to learn about the American Revolution. I was reminded of Louise Rosenblatt's article in *Language Arts* (1980), "What facts does this poem teach you?"

Eduardo, a native Spanish-speaking student in a bilingual classroom, is an emerging English language learner who can and likes to read in English. He doesn't, however, like all the writing he has to do during and after reading. Writing is more difficult for him than reading at this point in his biliteracy development: "I love to read, but I don't like to write down information, I like to talk about books now." Elizabeth makes the same point: "I don't see how writing is reading."

Many students in this study from third through fifth grades complained repeatedly about lack of choice in the books they could read and discuss in school, limited time for self-selected reading, doing things other than reading, and what they thought teachers really meant when they asked students to respond to literature. Below the surface of an apparently successful reading program in this school was student resistance to reading instruction in school even when the program's spin was literature based and reader responsive.

Time, Choice, and the Nature of Response

All these children are speaking to the point of who controls choice of books and time spent reading in school. They do not feel that they have enough choice or time, and they have no control. Both explicitly and implicitly, they blame teachers. They are able to generalize about the relative importance of time spent on various school tasks: Reading will make you a better speller. Writing isn't reading. But they also know they are not in charge of their choices and time, and they dutifully—if resentfully—fulfill the many tasks associated with reading literature that the teacher assigns. Not, however, without cynicism. While observing a teacher-directed library visit one day, I sat next to Colleen, an avid reader and dramatic speaker. She always hugs herself when I come, proclaiming, "I love it when you come and read to me!" The teacher told them to pick a book and read it, and then she gave them prompts for responding to it. Most of the library time was spent writing about what they were reading. The teacher talked throughout the period, telling students what she expected them to do before their library time was over. She had gone over the directions for writing yet again and asked, "Are there any questions?" Colleen leaned over to me without taking her eyes off the paper she was writing on and whispered, "Yeah. Why are you taking the fun out of it?"

As I have listened to what many of these children have told me, it has become apparent that, at least for this group of children in this school, key issues in reading and teaching with literature are institutionalized practices of lack of student choice of books, lack of time to read, and doing other things such as writing, reflecting the notion by many teachers that response is an activity you do or something you make after reading, rather than the experience you have while reading. Correlated to this lack of time and student choice in reading is an overreliance on commercial reading programs with class sets of books, teacher's manuals with extensive "teaching ideas," and "integrating" literature with other activities. Although these are often considered "best practices" in reading, the result in this school has been, according to what children tell me and my observations in their classrooms, that teacher-directed thematic approaches to literature limit children's book choices to those related to the theme and limit their time to actually read books because they are busy doing something other than reading or talking about their reading experiences. In this instructional model, response frequently does not reside in the reader's experience of the text, but rather in a concrete artifact such as writing in a reading journal, answering a set of questions in writing after reading, or constructing a puppet. Just reading is limited. I saw virtually no time allocated for children to simply and freely talk about their response to literature unprompted by the teacher.

The result for students who can and want to read and talk about their experiencing of a text is resistance to reading in school. Reading has gone underground, outside of school. It's possible that, because students feel a lack of control over reading choices and time, they are not fully engaged in reading instruction. It's also possible that teachers, sensing this lack of engagement, may feel students need more, rather than less, prompting and guidance with regard to choosing and responding to literature, because students may have resisted many teachers' over-reliance on teacher-directed reading activities that leave them little time to actually read. They may feel they need to "help" more: give them more book lists; more, rather than less, direction for their independent reading; and more cookbook ideas for activities after reading. Take one soda can, one styrofoam ball for a head, cloth, and pipe cleaners, and spend hours making a doll of a character in a book. Unsolicited ideas from students in my study, however, suggest that students are not less engaged in the reading-response process, but in the reading program. This resistance cuts across many personal variables: gender, native language, culture, class, and taste in books (Cox, 1996; Cox and Boyd-Batstone, 1997).

Where should control of choice and time for reading reside in a supposedly literature-based program? With the teacher or the reader? What do teachers want students to do when they read books? Jim Zarrillo and I found that a group of teachers considered experts at teaching with literature were basically atheoretical (Zarrillo & Cox, 1991). Their instruction went unfettered by any guiding principles. Teacher's manuals for commercial programs, idea books, and in-service sessions were the source of their ideas for teaching with literature. Response was seen as an artifact such as writing or a puppet, rather than what a child was thinking during reading or a verbal expression or discussion of those thoughts.

Response Record: A Tool for Response-Centered Teaching with Literature

During the course of this study, I have found that students readily engage with literature, making personal connections and developing interpretations of a text. Their curiosity extends beyond the pages of the book, however, and they often ask questions and express interest in situating the story in a broader context. I have also often found these to be more insightful and sophisticated than what a teacher might expect from a child. Teachers might do well to allow time for verbal response and discussion pointing to things students know or would like to know. An open-ended discussion could be followed with an aesthetic question or prompt: "What did you think of the book? Tell me about it." Students' questions could lead to learning in a broader context. These could be recorded in a concept cluster about the book, with time given to following up and finding answers to questions that intrigued them. However, it is not necessary to do this every time a child reads a book.

For example, I read *Song of the Swallows* (Politi, 1948) to Carlos, a native Spanish-speaking student who was in a pull-out primary language-support program. This book is a Caldecott award-winning book set in the mission San Juan Capistrano in California. The main characters are the elderly mission gardener and a young boy who helps him. The plot follows the anticipation of the return of the swallows to Capistrano. It was quickly discernible that Carlos clearly understood the story. He knew the setting, characters, plot, and problem. No problem.

Furthermore, most of what he said when asked what he thought focused on personal connections to his own experience and situating the story in his world. The result was a seamless discussion, not only of the story itself, but also about the mission and how California has changed from the time of the setting of the book in the 1940s, a comparison of life in Mexico and the United States, the status of immigrants, his feelings about being a bilingual student, his dream of going to college and taking care of his parents, and guns, gangs, and life and death in Los Angeles.

Some of these topics might appear in a teacher's study guide for this book, although a writer of these guides might guess most to be too mature, serious, or even inappropriate for his age group and for consideration in a school setting. But there is no guesswork on that account here. These are all actual responses. Carlos' high school cousin, a good student and successful athlete, had just been killed in a drive-by shooting on a sidewalk outside his school. For Carlos, the topic of gangs is all too real and relevant, and in this school district, education about gangs is a regular part of the curriculum. I'd also be willing to guess that an author of these guides and many teachers would not have had a similar experience or be able to relate to it on a personal level, or even consider it appropriate for third-grade students. This is a dangerous side of life, but it is the life many students are living. How can we know of the possible meaningfulness of such experiences for students in discussions of literature if questions and prompts for teaching with literature are limited to those of the teacher or teaching guides?

The question to be considered here is what to do about response to literature in the classroom. How do we reconcile the many complex aspects of reading literature, the theoretical or atheoretical approaches to teaching with literature, and the real responses of real children in the real world? Can we move from guidelines for thinking about literature prepared by someone other than the reader, and often the teacher—such as a writer/editor for commercial reading programs and study guides—for the student in the classroom? Can we give students choice in reading, provide time to read, and build in time for them to think and talk about their reading experiences? The practical issue, of course, is how does the teacher plan and organize for instruction if all students do is read and talk.

The Response Record is a planning tool for your consideration for using students' responses as the center of literature teaching and for planning further reading and responding to literature. It is based on my experience as an elementary teacher, many years of listening to the responses of the same cohort of children in this longitudinal study, and my own experiences as an avid child reader and the parent of same. I have filled it in using Carlos' response to *Song of the Swallows* to show how it might be used while listening and talking to a child about a reading experience (see Figure 11.1). It not only allows for noting their personal response, but also for checking for understanding of the story and for developing a personal plan for further experiences with literature for that child. The child's talk about the book, rather than the book itself, then, is a jumping-off place. There is also space to do a quick check for understanding during this open discussion so students essentially can "test out" of the often-extended questions that a teacher would ask after a reading to make sure they have understood the story and that often precede or preclude moving on to discussion of personal response. It has space to note responses from both a more aesthetic stance, with a focus on personal experiencing of the work, and an efferent stance, with a focus on the text itself. From this information, a teacher can discuss with a child next steps in reading, which may include writing activities or may also plan for just more reading. It may include reading for information or may lead to more reading and talking with the teacher or other students about what has been read.

FIGURE 11.1   Response Record

	Date:
1. Reading Context	*Teacher reads aloud to child* Book: *Song of the Swallows* Student(s)/Group: *Carlos* Ask Open Question: *What did you think of the book?* While student responds, note focus on: 2) Personal Experience, 3) Text Itself, 4) Story Understanding (as needed)

2. Personal Experience	*When we did missions I did San Jose.*
	    Pretty mission. Pirates back then?
	Nice pictures.
	    Looks like St. Anthony, the church I go to.
	    Like in Ontario where we went, lot of cows, it stinks, my cousin lives there, we play soccer.
	I like horses and dogs.
	    Grandpa has horses in Mexico, Guadalajara, I ride 'em, never fall off, no smooth roads, rocks
	    Kids can drive there. I know about gears going down but not up.
	    We got a little puppy. Rottweiler. Star. He looks like white and brown mixed together. My sister says he looks like a star at night, a little white.
	We came from Mexico; I got papers; we're American
	    My dad wanted work, pay is better here, sometimes bad for them, immigration officers try to get them, jump the fences, capture 'em, put 'em back, wonder if it's worth it, some of my friends don't have papers some joined the army to get papers, but you could get killed with a gun
	Dad says never grab a gun, stay away from gangs
	    Three cops live near me and tell me don't wear baggy pants cause gangs will shoot me, they shot my cousin.
	    He never was a gang member, my buddy, good in school, prom king, buried him in his baseball uniform
	    He was a peacemaker, didn't want problems. Mexican people get in a fight with white or black he'd say why fight, most people are the same, he wrote a poem about dying the week before
	    They were just driving by, fooling with a gun, yelled at him, he started running, shot him in the back in cold blood in front of a church, it's not right

FIGURE 11.1   *(Continued)*

2. **Personal Experience** *(continued)*	*I will stay in school and help my parents* *My dad would be mad if we ditched, I go to summer school, I will get a good job* *When I grow up I want to give him a Corvette or Lamborghini, not a Honda, and a house in Mexico* *If you're bilingual you can get a job helping doctors, they pay you a lot of money*
3. **Text Itself**	*Where is this?* *That's what California used to look like? Is this the road? They don't have horses like that any more. There's gardens there. Do they charge to go into the mission? About how much? The boy helps the old man garden. The old man teaches him and tells him about the swallows. The birds are nice there. One fell down and they held it real tight* *Las Golondrinas means swallows in Spanish* *It was sad for them at the end when the swallows left but when they came back he was happy. They always return.*

4. **Story Understanding** (check or note)	Setting	Characters	Plot	Mood/Theme
	mission	*old man*	*swallows return*	*happy–return; sad–leave*
	California	*young boy*	*swallows leave*	*life goes on*

5. **Next Steps** (check or note)	Reread Read more: *The Nicest Gift* by Leo Politi; *Smoky Night* by Eve Bunting; *L.A. Riots; horses, Mexico, soccer* Talk more: Who—*teacher, pair with Eduardo (who is reading Gary Soto)* When—*next week* Find out more: What—*What does a Lamborghini cost?* How—*Check on the Internet* Things to do: *Bring poem cousin who was shot wrote. Read Gary Soto poetry with Eduardo.* [Make other notes as appropriate.]

Suggestions for Using the Response Record

1. Reading Context. Is this an individual conference with a student or a small group discussion? Was the book read aloud by the teacher, with the student, or did students read and discuss with each other or teacher? These would depend on age and reading ability of students. Note not only title but background. Was reading of book tied to a class theme? Self-selected? Other factors? For example, librarian did a book talk, student ordered from a book club, was referred by a friend, or book was the current rage, such as *Goosebumps*.

2. Personal Experience. Teacher jots down primarily aesthetic responses, such as what interested student, links to personal life, or intertextual links.

3. Text Itself. Teacher jots down primarily efferent responses, such as information found in the text, explanations, and comments on words. This also provides verification of items in Story Understanding.

4. Story Understanding. If necessary, check off, or note comment or question. If clear understanding of text has been indicated, focus on student's ideas while reading.

5. Next steps. Make plans with students based on their response and your discussion together. Students can reread book; read more on the same topic, the same genre, or books by the same author; discuss further by talking to others who have read same book, author, or genre and form an interest group; find out more, such as answers to burning questions; or for selected books do activities such as writing, art, drama, or thematic projects.

These are all possible options. It is not necessary to form a group or to do an activity after every reading. Probably the best thing would be to read it again or read another book and plan time for another response-centered talk.

Time is an issue. One teacher cannot meet with every student every day, but a teacher can meet on a rotating, regular basis with individuals, or meet with small groups who are reading the same book, books by the same author, the same genre, or books related to a theme.

Remember also the comments of children who repeatedly complained that they didn't have time to read because the teacher was talking, or telling them to write or answer questions. What they wanted was to be able to choose books and have time to read them. When a teacher is talking to one child or a group, others read. From these discussions, both teacher and child focus on the child's experience of the text as a basis for further reading and experiences with literature.

Elizabeth on Teaching with Literature

When Elizabeth was telling me how unhappy she was with the lack of choice and time in reading in school in the fourth grade, I asked her what she would like to do about reading literature in school. She did not hesitate:

Read it! [Emphatically, followed by a long pause here]. Think about it. You don't have to talk to anybody. I like thinking. After I read a book I think for a million years, and then go back and read my favorite pages again. Sometimes I read through a book really fast, and then I go back and read my favorite parts again.

I also asked her what she would do about reading and teaching with literature if she were the teacher:

I'd just say "Read this book. Go read whatever book you want and if you want to come tell me about it you can or if you don't, just think or just go do something else like read it again or read another book." I'd make it so that you'd bring as many books as you want and just read, read, read all day.

REFERENCES

Appelman, D., & Hynds, S. (1997). Walking our talk: Between response and responsibility in the literature classroom. *English Education, 29*(4), 272–97.

Bakhtin, M. (1981). *The dialogic imagination.* (Emerson & Holquist, Trans.) Austin, TX: University of Texas Press.

Beach, R. (1993). *A teacher's introduction to reader response theories.* Urbana, IL: National Council of Teachers of English.

Benton, M. (1983). Secondary worlds. *Journal of Research and Development in Education, 16,* 68–75.

Benton, M. (1992). Possible worlds and narrative voices. In J. E. Many & C. Cox (Eds.), *Reader stance and literary understanding: Exploring the theories, research, and practice.* Norwood, NJ: Ablex.

Bruner, J. (1986). *Actual minds, possible worlds.* Cambridge, MA: Harvard University Press.

Clifford, S. (1991). *The experience of reading: Louise Rosenblatt and reader-response theory.* Portsmouth, NH: Boynton/Cook.

Collier, J. L., & Collier, C. (1974). *My brother Sam is dead.* New York: Four Winds.

Commeyras, M., & Sumner, G. (1998). Literature questions children want to discuss: What teachers and students learned in a second grade classroom. *Elementary School Journal, 99*(2), 129–52.

Cox, C. (1996). Literature-based teaching: A student response-centered classroom. In N. Karolides (Ed.), *Reader response in the elementary classroom: Quest and discovery* (pp. 29–49). Mahwah, NJ: Lawrence Erlbaum.

Cox, C. (2000, April). *Reader stance towards literature: A longitudinal study, K–6.* Paper presented at the meeting of the American Educational Research Association, New Orleans, LA.

Cox, C., & Boyd-Batstone, P. (1997). *Crossroads: Literature and language in culturally and linguistically diverse classrooms.* Columbus, OH: Merrill/ Prentice Hall.

Farrell, E., & Squire, J. (Eds.). (1990). *Transactions with literature.* Urbana, IL: National Council of Teachers of English.

Galda, L., & Beach, R. (2001). Response to literature as a cultural activity. *Reading Research Quarterly, 36*(1), 64–73.

Hade, D. D. (1992). The reader's stance as event: Transaction in the classroom. In J. E. Many & C. Cox (Eds.), *Reader stance and literary understanding: Exploring the theories, research, and practice.* Norwood, NJ: Ablex.

Hemphill, L. (1999). Narrative style, social class, and response to poetry. *Research in the Teaching of English, 33*(3), 275–302.

Iser, W. (1978). *The act of reading: A theory of aesthetic response.* Baltimore: Johns Hopkins University Press.

Marshall, J. D. (2000). Research on response to literature. In M. L. Kamil, P. B. Mosenthal, P. D. Pearson, & R. Barr (Eds.), *Handbook of reading research* (Vol. 3, pp. 381–402). Mahwah, NJ: Erlbaum.

Politi, L. (1948). *Song of the swallows.* New York: Macmillan.

Rosenblatt, L. M. (1980). What facts does this poem teach you? *Language Arts, 57,* 386–394.

Rosenblatt, L. M. (1983). *Literature as exploration* (4th ed.). New York: Modern Language Association of America. (Original work published in 1938).

Sipe, L. (1998). The construction of literary understanding by first and second graders in response to picture storybook read-alouds. *Reading Research Quarterly, 33*(4), 376–78.

Williams, V. B. (1982). *A chair for my mother.* New York: Greenwillow.

Zarrillo, J., & Cox, C. (1991). Efferent and aesthetic teaching. In J. E. Many & C. Cox (Eds.), *Reader stance and literary understanding: Exploring the theories, research, and practice.* Norwood, NJ: Ablex.

12 Writing in Response: Reflections on Learning How

DAVID L. E. WATT
University of Calgary

In the dark gray evening
I can see a faucet slowly dripping
Into the mouth of a large
yet soft and
gentle creature.

—Julie (Grade 5)

One of the greatest challenges that faces a reader response approach to teaching is that of finding a way to make the acts of writing as intellectually enriching as other explorations of the lived-through experience. A traditional approach to the purpose of writing might easily relegate it to an after-the-fact record of our experience. Yet the goals of writing in response are far grander. They are equally responsible for enriching the intellectual engagement. For writing in response to be compatible with the goals of a reader response approach, it needs to:

- be an integral part of the exploration and enrichment of the reader's mind (insight, empathy, imagination, and intellectual connections) and voice (ownership, risk taking, tolerance for ambiguity, and specificity of detail);
- support the development of a critical and creative sense in response to literature;
- help establish the commonality of experience in a community of readers and the uniqueness of individual responses;
- provide new and intentionally planned explorations for expression; and
- offer another means of assessing the signs of development in the response process.

It is almost axiomatic that a reader response approach to teaching will concentrate on enriching the respondent, in the belief that the respondent is the source of the richness of future responses. It is not today's response that is the primary focus of this approach, but rather the process of learning through an exploration of personal reaction and through the process of exploring ways to articulate that reaction. Writing is not really about recording the known, but about exploring the new. Unfortunately, some of our most common practices around acts of writing and response actually work against the goals of engaging and enriching the respondent.

I think that many of us, who have been attracted by the learner centeredness of a reader response approach, have held to an underlying belief that absolute freedom in writing will promote quality of individual thought. We have aspired to maximize freedom in the choice of reading material, in the exploration and discussion of topics arising from the reading, and in the form and substance of oral and written response. The belief is, in part, a reaction to the stifling effect that sometimes occurs in more-conventional approaches to teaching literature, in which the focus is on guiding students toward an approximation of a particular authoritative interpretation of the text (usually the teacher's) while practicing the conventions of organization, spelling, punctuation, sentence structures, and word choice. However strange it may sound, absolute freedom in the articulation of written response is far from a liberating force in the learning process. In fact, the apparent freedom can often result in limited exploration.

When we ask students to write a response in whatever manner they wish to what they have just been reading and discussing, it is surprising how little variety occurs in the types of response and in the form that those written responses take. It is as if the group members quickly and silently work out a safe way to proceed and then uniformly adhere to those expectations. The more often we prompt students to respond freely, the more entrenched the expectations for an acceptable response become. Eventually, they seem to coalesce around a centralizing tendency: a set of unspoken rules and expectations about what can be expressed. If left unchecked, this tendency toward the safe response can produce in us an uneasy feeling that we are perfecting mediocrity, rather than enriching the intellectual potential of our students. Under these conditions, students' writing shows very little sign of having risked the exploration of individual reactions and, more often than not, appears to be emulating a response that the writers believe will match the teacher's expectations, even when these expectations have explicitly encouraged students toward individual exploration.

Providing students with direction (and sometimes instruction) in ways to explore and articulate their thoughts is one way of demonstrating the degree to which we recognize and value the expression of individuality. As students become familiar with different ways of exploring and responding, they are in a better position to create personal responses without relying on the safety offered by the centralizing tendency in response. Direction may not be freedom, but it does encourage students to explore their personal reactions, and it can produce greater variety in the responses than might otherwise be found.

The role or purpose that we assign to writing also affects the kind of engagement we can expect. Sometimes we relegate writing in response to the status of a written record of the discussions or grand conversations that may have just occurred in the community of readers. Directions like "take out your journals and write about what you have been discussing so far" often meet with a foot-dragging resistance by the students and a teacher's sense that, although writing may be more difficult and tedious than talking, it is one of those things that students need to do to improve their conventional literacy skills. Typical reactions from students are echoed in such phrases as "We already said everything that we wanted to say. Why do we have to write it down?" and "I don't really have anything else to say, so I don't know what to do now." There is something obvious and compelling about these pleas, something that would suggest the need for writing in response to be far more than a written record or a necessary exercise in discipline.

Writing, or any form of text creation, is an equally important aspect of articulating one's critical and creative sense. Fortunately, writing has its own intellectual riches, and a reader response approach brings its own contributions to directions in writing. By providing students with directions for their written exploration, we can help make visible both the commonalities across responses and the uniqueness that individuals bring to the process.

What Reader Response Approach Brings to Writing

The reader response approach brings two different views to the world of writing. One lies in the exploration of different stances that we can hold in articulating a response. The other involves the kind of connections that we can make between the text that we have read and the one that we write in response.

The idea of exploring a reader's stances as suggested by Langer (1992) is one way to highlight how we as readers move ourselves in and out of our reading experience, or engagement with text. Her approach allows teachers to engage in the direction of written responses during the process of reading, helping to break the tendency to relegate writing to an after-the-fact status. Langer (1992) has described these different stances cryptically as:

- being out and stepping into an envisionment
- being in and moving through an envisionment
- stepping back and rethinking what one knows
- stepping out and objectifying the experience

Langer's description of a reader's differing stances offers valuable richness to the directions we can take in developing writing engagements.

Being Out and Stepping In

We can help students consciously formulate responses to their personal reactions to that part of the reading process that parallels their entry into the text. Individual reactions to "stepping in" are likely to be expressed in different ways, but by keeping a record of the common experiences that surround an initial engagement with text, we can help readers articulate a much-overlooked component of the lived through experience and deepen their ability to fold these experiences into their later interpretive responses to text. Techniques as simple as posting a written record of the unspoken thoughts, questions, and emotional reactions to being out and stepping in can develop a common awareness of the process and provide students with a sense of their uniqueness within that common experience.

Metacognitive activities are particularly useful for helping students understand what they have learned from a writing engagement. Merely asking students to keep a daily record, consisting of only a few lines, identifying something they learned today that they didn't realize yesterday, can provide a rich source of insights for discussion. The insights add a dimension of conscious discovery to the thoughts and emotions that surround the process of stepping into a text. Students' writing about the process of being out and stepping into engagement with a text provides us as teachers with an opportunity to recognize and value the characteristics of mind (insight, empathy, imagination, and intellectual connections) in the development of their critical and creative senses. Directing students to reflect on their thoughts about learning, on what transpires in the mind as they wait for engagement, or on other topics that enhance reflection can itself act as a means of deepening the response and sparking grand conversations, which might otherwise be relegated to insignificance.

Being In and Moving Through

Once students have entered the world of the text, the flow of their reading and the nature of their reactions change. Characters take form. Readers become partisan members of the text. They race over some spans of text and crawl painstakingly over others. The reader's imagination fills gaps, develops expectations, and constantly revises those expectations. Within the minds of the readers, there are ebbs and flows of possible meanings, allegiances, and interpretations as they move through the text. The experience is not a start-to-finish straight line of interpretation, but rather one that is filled with competing possibilities, abandoned interpretations, and an emergent sense of understanding. This ebb-and-flow process of establishing what has been called the horizon of possibilities is a rich source of exploration for response writing. The meanings that readers create with texts include all the possibilities of wandering viewpoints, even those ideas that may have been abandoned along the way. As readers, certainly as efferent readers, we quickly dismiss the value of the road not taken, of abandoned interpretations, of emergent understanding, as an integral part of the lived-through experience. Yet, as others have recognized, this is a process that is filled with "the making and revising of assumptions, the rendering and regretting of judgments, the coming to and abandoning of conclusions, the giving and withdrawing of approval" (Fish, 1980, pp. 158–59). However, without specific directions to the contrary, our minds tend to favor the final version of what a text means. Being able to articulate the breadth of our thoughts as we moved through a text can deepen the texture of our response to our lived-through experience.

Being In and Stepping Back

Most of us, as readers, pause in our reading from time to time. Some of the places that we stop provide us with "vistas" that we feel are worthy of a moment's reflection to envision and explore the imaginary view arrived at through reading. Keeping track of where we pause and the thoughts that pass through our minds contributes to the stepping back dimension of the response process. The use of a technique, suggested by Peterson & Eeds (1990), in which students put sticky-notes into the text at points where they stopped to imagine and then jot down a question or a few descriptive words, can help to open up the possibility of exploring commonality and uniqueness in how and where students step out of the text. It is surprising how often the pause points are common to different members of a reading community. Guided written exploration of common vistas can help readers deepen their understanding of the reading process by making them aware of the impact that the text has on their reading.

Stepping Out and Looking Back

This stance within the response process is by far the most commonly explored in classroom settings. It is here that as teachers we seek evidence of insight, empathy, imagination, and connections that demonstrate a critical and creative sense of the interpretation and the reading experience. How we explore the connection between these reflections and their expression in written form comes with its own set of possible directions. As teachers we can guide the process with decisions that promote the internalization of a critical and creative sense. Here, Probst's (1992) view of writing "**from, of** and **about**" the text offers a new set of choices.

Probst has suggested that the exploration of text through writing can be characterized as taking one of three general forms. We can write *about* the text; a form typified by conventional expository exploration of the *issues, events, attributes, and relations* that arise from the interpretation. We can write *of* the text, pursuing an issue uncovered in the text (the human condition, freedom, survival, etc.), or an event (acts of kindness, cruelty, decision, etc.), or an attribute (youth, wisdom, suspicion, etc.), or a relation that connects any of the issues, events, or attributes to each other, motivating us to explore our own beliefs beyond the confines of the text itself. We can also write away *from* the text, using some aspect of the text as a point of departure for the creation of a new text that may only have a tenuous connection to the text that evoked our creative response.

It is this last form of exploratory writing from the text that has always intrigued me. I am sure that we have all felt and witnessed moments when the text has acted as a source of inspiration for exploring one's own thoughts in a similar manner. However, moments like these do not normally arise without some direction to support the initial engagement. One way of supporting the introduction of this form of creative response is to scaffold our entry into creativity, through an activity as simple as creating something new with the *powerful words* and images of a text.

Scaffolding an activity around powerful words can start by having students scan over a text they have read, looking for words or expressions that resonate for them in some personal way. These words act like the anchors for an unarticulated response. At first, the search for powerful words or phrases can be a confusing idea, and the choices are likely to include words that have semantic power (i.e., strength as a feature of the word—steel, hurricane, etc.) rather than connotative power. However, once a group is comfortable with the process of recognizing powerful words, they can begin the creative and exploratory process of arranging them on paper, joining ideas into new images that may or may not echo the substance of the original text. The potential for arranging and rearranging, for adding words and discussing the intended effects, leads to a sense of personal ownership over the new ideas that emerge in the writing. With some direct guidance into simple writing decisions like line arrangement (in which each line is placed in relation to the other lines), line length (the effects of breaking lines or thoughts at unexpected places), and dramatic repetition (the impact of repeating selected words or phrases), it is possible to attach a new dimension to the creative act of writing away from text. The common ground of the original text supports each writer's ability to appreciate and interpret the choices and effects by others, in what soon begins to take shape as a community of writers who can recognize and value their differences.

The greatest hurdle that faces us in exploring what a reader response approach can bring to the process of writing is the demand that it places on us as teachers to creatively and critically explore and expand our own sense of the lived-through experience. At least, the combination of the stances that help us understand how we move in and out of our engagement with text and the connections that we can make between reading and writing throughout the process provide us with a framework in which to develop teaching ideas in ways that can be distinguished from the traditional goals ascribed to the engagement-in-writing activity.

What Writing Approaches
Bring to Reader Response

The field of writing research brings a richness of experience in instructional models and approaches that can benefit the goals of reader response teaching (Watt, Hunsberger & Labercane, 1999). Writing process approaches are actually plural, rather than singular, though we often focus our attention more on the cognitive approach of managing the writing process of our students through engagement in a series of steps that represent the movement from initial engagement to published product. The various approaches to the teaching of writing can be distinguished from each other on the basis of the principle that they hold in greatest esteem. In my own thinking, I have short-handed the differences into labels: *think–write, talk–write, see–write, read–write, write–write,* and *rule–write.* For example, the think–write approaches privilege the idea that you can make writing richer by thinking about it. Talk–write schools value the development of voice and are directed by the idea that you can make writing richer through different types of talk. See–write schools privilege the active development of the senses as a means of deepening the quality of writing. Read–write tends to advance the idea that reading engagements are a fundamental source of richness in writing. Similarly, write–write focuses on writing about one's writing, and rule–write prioritizes the value of conventions in the process.

As individuals, we are likely to privilege certain approaches over others, but whichever we favor, the quality of our instruction relies on our ability to provide repeated opportunities for engagement and chances for our students to watch us as we engage with the same writing activities that we are asking them to try. When we make visible the process of exploring our thoughts in a variety of genres, styles, and perspectives, we provide students with the power to make meaningful choices in their search for self-expression. We can make the process visible by first modelling the process, then jointly negotiating a group response, and finally engaging students in the individual pursuit of responding. This method of modelling, negotiating, and independent engagement provides its own forum for discussions about the writing process. Overcoming our initial reticence is essential. To teach writing we must write, and more to the point, we must model the intellectual process in plain view of our students if we are to demystify the relationship between thinking and writing. Otherwise, we are in danger of passing on to our students our own reticence to risk and explore the world of writing.

Some Ideas from Different Approaches

The limits on the ideas that we can develop for meaningful writing engagements are equal to our own creativity. In this next section, I illustrate some ideas arising from exploring three different approaches to teaching writing: see–write, think–write, and talk–write. They are meant to provide students with a common direction for exploration and creation so that they can learn from each other and appreciate the commonality and uniqueness of their responses.

See–Write

> The five senses are the five doors . . . the first step in writing well is to establish the habit of observing. (Allen, 1982, p. 20)

> Observation is not simply good use of the eyes. It is the ability to find what is significant, what is thought provoking, what is of human interest, in persons, places and books. (Hammond, 1983, p. 8)

The see–write approach to writing (Allen, 1982; Hammond, 1983) might better be called sense–write. It involves not only sight, but all of the senses. The thrust of this approach is that by developing our students' abilities to observe deeply we can unlock their potential to interpret the world around them and therefore enrich their writing. Our imaginations are powered by our senses, and by consciously exploring our senses, we deepen our ability to envision what we unconsciously see.

C.O.D.E.: Perception and Interpretation.   Often students have difficulty under- standing that perception affects interpretation. This is as true for narrative and descriptive writing as it is for explanatory writing. Teaching students to "see" makes them aware of the role of perception and interpretation in their responses to reading. Whether as reader or writer, there are always decisions (often uncon- scious) about the content, the detail, the order and, ultimately, the essence of what is seen by the mind (Richards, 1990).

- *Content.*   Which people, places, and things will be included and which omitted?
- *Order.*   Given the choice of content, how should we choose to order our view of the picture? (near to far, sense to sense, center to edge, most important to least important, person to person, inside the picture to beyond, etc.)
- *Detail.*   Given the content and order, how much detail should be included? Will it be the same level of detail for every element?
- *Essence.*   What makes the particular selection of content, detail, and order hang together? In a word, what is the essence of the image? What words would help carry this essence in each sentence?

A teacher might then lead a class through this process in the following way.

1. Content: From a large picture, visible to all the students, ask students to name "things" that they can see in the picture and that they can imagine outside the pic- ture's perimeter. List them on either side of the picture.

2. Content: Discuss how difficult it would be to include all the items if you were going to paint the picture with words. With the help of the students, choose a lim- ited number of things (three or four) to be included.

3. Detail: From the content list, discuss with the students ideas that might be included about the content items. Explain the idea that they can change the picture they are writing by choosing to write more about one thing and less about another. One level of detail, roughly speaking, is one sentence about the chosen content.

4. Order: Begin to engage students in a discussion of the order in which they want to describe the content. Let them know that there are a number of ways to think about ordering where their eyes are attracted and what their thoughts reflect. From their choices, choose one.

5. Essence: Every good picture has an essence, a word or phrase that captures the overall feeling of our reaction to the picture. Collect several possibilities in a mind map to let students see that while everyone can sense an essence, there is no single essence. Explain that they can sprinkle essence into every sentence by choos- ing to use words that carry that feeling.

As with other types of learning, it is valuable and enjoyable to ask students to keep a record of what they learned from trying something new to them. Here are some examples of statements from a Grade Four class.

- "When I look at a picture, I can pick what to write."
- "I learned to write more creatively."
- "I learned to use my imagination and to see more than what is there. Even what is outside of the picture. It's like the picture starts to move."
- "I was able to write my own story from what I already knew."

These kinds of statements give us as teachers a much better idea of what was actually learned and where we may need to scaffold greater attention to achieve our future aims.

Word Bowl

See–write: Creating images in the mind can spark creative writing by giving it a place to start.

A word bowl approach to creating images works wonderfully as a bridge between vocabulary enrichment and an appreciation for the intellectual process of activating imagery. Steps involved is this approach are:

1. Pick words from a single text or from a collection of texts and place them into two different lists, one for modifiers and one for nouns.

2. Ask students to make the most striking or unusual image by combining one word from the list of modifiers with one word from the list of nouns. You can scaffold this step by having one group of students pick modifiers and another group pick nouns, then randomly combining them until you get a few pairs that create appreciable images, according to the students.

3. Explore the power of the two-word image by asking students what they see, hear, and so forth in the images that are presented, and by asking about what they think when the images come to their minds and what similarities and differences they hear in the descriptions of others.

4. Ask students to make three pairs of images and order them in a way that they think creates a bigger image. Allow them to join the three pairs together with as few words as possible to create a poetic image.

5. Discuss what students imagine as they hear the poems of others.

6. In future word bowl activities, add lists of adverbs to create three-word images.

Here are two lists of words taken from the novel *The Cay*, by Theodore Taylor. These words were selected by a teacher (Nilsen, 1999) and her students.

Modifiers

violent	scorched	twisted	gnarled	sweet	tearful
terrible	motionless	gusting	cheerful	forgotten	silent
slobbering	shattering	broken	howling	greasy	hissing
juicy	deafening	empty	desperate	clear	sticky
vicious	noisy	cool	melting	empty	sour
searing	locked	ringing	spinning	blind	dark
stiff	cloudy	dry	dreamy	nasty	painted

Nouns

cat	boy	eyes	hand	man	island	water	voices
hurricane	ocean	sand	sky	scorpion	snake	langosta	fire
sea grass	stars	hut	sun	moon	raft	father	mother
friend	hair	birds	back	storm	beach	rope	clothes
chocolate	coconut	fish	tree	hill	rock	knife	smile
treasure	mat	claws	lies	rescue	shore	wind	rain

The discussion of what students see from each of the multiple images allows them to share common and unique aspects of their responses. Here is a sample from the Grade Four class as they share their thoughts after a written response from the word bowl.

> ALI: I see a wolf howling. . . . I can hear him. . . . He's lonely and he's out-side. The stars are his eyes.
>
> TEMON: Yeah, and his eyes are . . . or the stars are dry because it's cold. He's outside in the water in the storm. There are . . . um . . . the water is white like in a storm. What is that?
>
> ALI: I know what it is but . . . well, I think they are on an island.

Think–Write: Writing about Thinking

> "It is not only wasted effort in practice but indefensible in theory to attempt to teach students to write without educating them." (Booth & Gregory, 1984, p. 11)

The think–write approach (Flower, 1981; Murray, 1984; Scardamalia, Bereiter, & Fillon, 1981) dominates our present-day understanding of conventional ways to teach writing. With its focus on managing the writing process through steps and strategies, cues and examples, it has become almost synonymous with the idea of process writing. Most models that outline steps to follow in developing a piece of writing are indebted to Linda Flower's early work. Although newer models may have modified the number of steps or altered the focus slightly (e.g., brainstorm, plan, draft, revise, edit, publish, and celebrate), they still advance the general premise that by engaging in a series of steps in a process, we can teach students to best manage their writing and maximize the quality of the final product. In Flower's initial list of steps, we can see the origins of most of the process approach models commonly used in classrooms:

1. explore the rhetorical problem
2. make a plan
3. use creative thinking
4. organize your ideas
5. know the needs of your reader
6. transform writer-based prose into reader-based prose
7. review your paper and your purpose
8. test and edit your writing
9. edit for connections and coherence (Flower, 1981)

Although this approach clearly subscribes to the notion that thinking about writing will improve the quality of writing, there is an equally valuable contribution from the think–write school that reverses the relationship—writing about our thinking can improve our thinking.

Our minds are like a layered repository of our past and present abstract ideas: We are the sum of all that we have thought. Often, it is difficult to express what we currently think about something without first exploring what we once believed about that topic and why that made sense to us. Educating the mind is, in part, a process of activating our earlier thoughts in order to trace a path toward the explanation of our present ones. This type of think–write activity can help students understand the value of activating their memories in a way that will enhance their ability to articulate their responses to what they are currently reading and living.

1. Explain to students that writing can be a powerful means of tracing how and why we each think the way we do.

2. Based on something that the class is reading, begin to identify abstract values that are important to the story (something such as friendship, truth, the unknown, love, magic, bravery, etc.)

3. Ask students to think of a time not so long ago when they used to believe something different about this idea than they do now. Explore some of their reactions and their old reasons for those ideas.

4. Ask students to write a paragraph for their "memories journal" describing what they used to believe, when they believed it, and why that made sense to them then.

5. Share these ideas with the class to establish the commonality and uniqueness of the community's exploration. Then ask students to think of a time even further back when they had a distinctly different understanding of the idea. It maybe that they search for the first time they can ever remember thinking about the idea. Discuss *the when, the what,* and *the why* as a group.

6. Now ask students to explore what they think today by writing an explanation of their present ideas as if they were steps in a path that starts with their earlier beliefs. Again, these ideas can be shared across the group and in light of the common reading.

Talk–Write

> My first concern is with voice. The human voice underlies the entire writing process . . . it has a driving force. (Graves, 1994, p. 162)

Talk–write approaches (Bruffee, 1980; Moffet, 1983; Graves, 1994) take a slightly different stance toward developing a writer's sensitivity. Here the focus is clearly on the value that exploratory talk and collaborative discussion bring to the quality of writing. Many of the writing engagements center on group writing, talking through decisions, sharing and incorporating ideas, or creative talking and writing through constructive activities such as drawing, building, and acting.

Within this approach, the idea that students benefit from the development of their voices is key. Writing is seen as a version of a person's inner speech. Teaching writing from a talk–write perspective involves developing students' awareness of the value of voice, conscience, and audience in their response process.

Often when we ask students to write about something, they tell us, "I don't know what to say." Sometimes it means they don't know how to choose what to say from a vast and unorganized collection of thoughts. Sometimes it means that they don't know what their thoughts actually are. Whatever the reason, they do not hear an inner voice that guides their writing. They are suffering from writer's block, which prevents them from exploring their ideas. By using others in the class to act as their inner voice, writers are free to respond to the questions they pose, writing sentence by sentence, without knowing the overall direction of the writing.

Writer's Block

1. Gather the writer and three class members, who will act as the writer's conscience, around each flip-chart station in the classroom. Explain that the writer can only write one sentence at a time, and the conscience needs to think of questions to probe the mind of the writer.
2. Start the "blocked writer" with a sentence prompt on a large piece of chart paper. This gives the teacher an opportunity to set the initial direction of the exploration. Base the prompt on something that you want students to explore as a result of a particular shared reading.
3. The writer is not allowed to talk and may only respond in writing. Be sure to limit the writer to one sentence.
4. Once the sentence is finished, the writer stops. One of the three people acting as the conscience reads the sentence aloud, and another asks a question that she or he wants to explore.
5. The writer responds by addressing it in one more sentence.
6. Continue the process for five to fifteen minutes, until the page is filled.

7. Repeat the process with others, offering suggestions for modifications to the kinds and quality of the questions and the formality of the voice. Ask them to make it more conversational or more like a letter, for example. Make both the writer and the conscience aware that there is a difference between the conscience (the participants in the conversation) and the audience (people who will read it later). Therefore, they need to think about future readers, to make their text sound more like a paragraph and less like questions and answers.

8. Once students become comfortable with the process, use it to share the viewpoints of different groups. Students quickly learn from reading the texts of others how best to approach the process.

9. As the need for more than one sentence begins to arise, introduce elements of punctuation (the comma, semicolon, brackets, dash, etc.) that can give the writers more room and will have an effect on the voices they create. Resist the temptation to increase the number of sentences in each turn in favor of lengthening effects that can be achieved by combining ideas in a single sentence.

This activity requires several attempts before students become agile at responding in this manner. Once students are comfortable with the process, you should notice that the texts begin to sound less like questions and answers and more like connected text. The direction provided by the questions is dynamic, rather than static. Although it can't be predicted ahead of time, the text responds to the kinds of things that the audience would want to know about. Even after a single attempt, you are likely to get learning statements such as these, from a Grade Four class:

- "I learned that when I am stuck, I can ask myself questions and then answer them."
- "I liked being the brain and getting to ask questions I wanted to."
- "I learned that sometimes you don't need to know where you are going as long as you have questions."

Pyramid Discussions

Learning collaboratively is especially important in writing because writing is a process of making judgements continually. (Bruffee, 1980, p. 104)

One of the most difficult tasks for a teacher in a community of readers is to keep discussion focused in the various groups so that there is a degree of commonality and yet room for uniqueness. Exploratory talk is essential to developing grand conversations and, when discussion is working at its best, it helps learners to

- sort out their thinking
- clarify meaning
- explore related ideas

- suggest possible answers
- negotiate meaning and intention
- link events in some way
- look for causes and reasons
- interpret and reflect on experiences
- exercise imagination
- establish ownership of ideas
- refine the expression of their ideas (adapted from Kessler, 1994)

Structuring pyramid discussion (Jordan, 1991) can provide the necessary scaffolding to get ideas shared across the classroom.

1. Create a list of ten to twelve statements, principles, predictions, ideas for enjoying literature, and so forth. You can either create the list yourself or guide students in creating the list.

2. Ask students to individually select three items from the list according to what they think are the most important items, for them.

3. Review the choices that students have made and then pair students together (ideally with another person who shares only one of their choices). Give the students five minutes to discuss their choices and to negotiate a common agreement on a list of three items.

4. While students are discussing their ideas, walk around the classroom, listening to the language that they use to express their agreement, disagreement, concessions, and general negotiation. You can use this information to make students aware of how they negotiate meaning and to improve the next round.

5. Once you are ready to move on, take the pairs of students and join them to other pairs to go through the same process. This time, go around the classroom listening for any impact that the language focus has had on the discussion.

6. After several repetitions of the same process of joining groups to groups, ask for a list of all the choices and write them on a board with the most convincing argument that each group heard for each point and the most powerful argument they heard against that point.

7. Have students pick the three points that they would like to use to explain their opinion and one point that they think is a good one but that doesn't agree with their view.

8. Ask the students to explain their new views in their response journals, including the one contrasting point. Be sure that they try to explain why the point is a good one, but why they don't think it is as valuable as the others.

This type of talk–write activity allows for a discussion of how we can tolerate ambiguity within our own beliefs and yet still hold to our personal insights.

Assessing the Development of
a Critical and Creative Sense

Internalizing a critical and creative sense is a long, and possibly never-ending, process. For some students, the development of a critical sense appears to happen intuitively, as if there were an innate understanding between critical acumen and creative ability. For most students, intuition, or what Jerome Bruner equates with the phrase "paradigmatic imagination," is the consequence of explicit direction about what to explore consciously and how to begin the articulation of that exploration. As teachers, we help to set the shape of the new exploration, in which the students let their imaginations loose. If we are to claim that the development of a critical and creative sense is indeed related to our teaching efforts, and not merely the side effect of putting students and books together over time, then it falls to the teachers to orchestrate some of the states of "borrowed consciousness" (Dixon Krauss, 1996) that allow students to explore and articulate their personal response in new and meaningful ways. Although students may borrow the consciousness of another, their responses represent the products of their minds and voices and affect the depth of their future engagements with literature.

Mind and Voice

Enriching the mind is fundamentally about teaching toward four kinds of intellectual engagement: insight, empathy, imagination, and intellectual connection. Voice, on the other hand, involves the development of a heightened articulation of four other individual qualities: ownership, risk-taking, tolerance for ambiguity, and specificity of detail.

As teachers, we can promote the development of insight in several ways. We can guide students through a conscious consideration of their internal and unarticulated responses, encouraging them to seek out the intricacy and detail of their reactions and probing deeper into their subsequent thoughts. We can support their exploration of how the text evokes those reactions, and we can help them discover the commonality and uniqueness that exist in their shared interpretations. Most importantly, we can explicitly recognize and value the pursuit of insight, whether it has to do with the self, with others, or with the text.

Empathy, on the other hand, is the kind of intellectual acumen that keeps any critical sense that is driven mostly by insight from becoming unbendingly critical and myopic. Without empathy, it is possible for crisply logical insight to become insensitive and detached from the lives of those who fill the pages of the possible worlds of literature. Empathy starts with the ability to write oneself into a text and to feel the current of mixed emotions that bring a text to life. However, it also includes understanding the emotions of personal life through our experiences with text. Part of the development of empathy involves making space for the interpretations of others by discovering the integrity that lies within those interpretations.

Imagination and the confidence to use it lie at the heart of the response process. It is through imagination that readers create and layer the possible worlds from which they gain the qualities of insight and empathy. Becoming aware of what we imagine, of the detail that our imagination supplies to the reading process, and of where that imagination can take us enriches the ground from which our insights and empathies spring. A vibrant imagination let loose within the paradigm of characters, situations, and plots is the source of the intuitions that deepen the critical and creative sense. It is what moves the process of interpretation from exegesis to hermeneutics.

Often, students envision much more than they immediately recognize. The imagination fills their minds with images, sounds, textures, and feelings that go largely unnoticed and unheralded in the more conventional discussions of literature. By supporting the exploration of their visions, it is as if we help them illuminate those images as they develop the power of imagination, moving away from an impoverished imagination and toward an educated one.

How imagination inspires insight and empathy is a cavernous question, inside which Bruner's idea about the nature of intuition as a form of paradigmatic imagination casts a modicum of light. By directing students to consider ideas in ways that they may never have thought of, we help to construct the many paradigms, or contexts, in which they can explore the world of their own thoughts. It is in the exploration of ideas within a paradigm or context that refinements in the quality of thought occur.

Part of the richness that we attribute to the mind is the degree to which intellectual connections are made across or among the things that we have experienced in life and in print. Intellectual connections develop through a web of associations that accrue as the personal canon of a reader's or listener's experience increases. Some connections are to either real or reported experiences, whereas others are to texts or images. Lyrics from songs, lines from movies, voice qualities from TV characters, billboard ads, photos, art, and even the voices of others can create the fabric of intellectual connections. By recognizing and valuing the diverse nature of intellectual connections that our students bring, we increase the likelihood of their occurrence in the response process. Intellectual connections lie at the heart of an individual's sense of personal identity as a reader. Our aspirations for enriching the mind of the respondent can, in part, be guided by exploring tenuous connections in novel ways.

Like the qualities of mind, the qualities of voice are essential to the development of a critical and creative sense. The ability to actively and intellectually engage with text is complemented by an ability to articulate a response. At first, a student's engagement with the text can be unarticulated or under-articulated. Their reactions are often deeper than their responses, but their sense of voice is tentative. The development of a voice can be mediated by teaching toward four qualities of articulation: ownership, risk-taking, tolerance for ambiguity, and specificity in the detail. The quality of ownership is one that can be most easily explained as the difference between saying what one believes and saying what one assumes the expected response should be. Often students say what they think the teacher wants to hear.

The quality of risk-taking is what lies behind the confidence to articulate uncertain ideas, or ideas that differ from others. In the absence of risk-taking, students tend to offer responses that do not stretch their thinking. A tolerance for ambiguity, on the other hand, is a quality that allows a person to articulate present beliefs even though there may be conflicting thoughts. Rather than providing a response that is insensitive to the conflicting gray ideas, readers are able to tolerate the ambiguities of responses while still being able to put forward the details of their interpretations.

Finally, the quality of specificity of detail is evident in responses that are able to articulate how they occurred and what aspects of mind and voice have led to the holistic response to text. When the qualities of voice are only moderately developed, responses tend to sound somewhat impersonal, overly generalized, uncertain, and mediocre—in other words, safe. As a result, the responses provide little in the way of intellectual engagement and little that would merit a return to them for further discussion. They become a final artifact in our teaching process, rather than a rich part of the response process.

Teaching toward the qualities of mind and voice allows us to assess the development of those qualities. My attempts to assess growth in the areas of mind and voice have resulted in a pair of guides that I have found useful to the process. I have tried to discern between satisfactory engagement and excellence by seeking different degrees of each quality in students' response writing. My only word of warning to others who may also find the idea attractive is that it is essential to first teach toward the qualities before looking for signs of development. Tables 12.1 and 12.2 outline the qualities I have come to associate with mind and voice. For each quality, I have included some of the characteristics that distinguish the development of these qualities in students' writing.

Teaching toward the enrichment of mind and voice is more of an art than a science. After some struggles with the idea of whether it was even possible to teach such abstract notions, I have come to conclude that in our teaching, we need to recognize and value occurrences of the eight qualities daily, in our classrooms, by:

- phrasing our questions in such a way that we use the eight qualities artfully (e.g., What would be a less insightful way to view that? What would be a more insightful way? What is the riskiest thing someone could say about the importance of that event? What ideas in your imagination are beyond the text?)

- probing students' responses with genuine interest, in an effort to understand rather than realign their thinking

- allowing them to explore with text for signs of these qualities in the characters and events

- assessing directly and only the development of the qualities of mind and voice in response writing (There is a place for more conventional assessment, but for recognition and value to have the greatest impact, writing in response must privilege them.)

TABLE 12.1   Assessing the Quality of Mind in Reader Response Writing

Quality	Signs of Development	
	Satisfactory	*Excellent*
Insight	**Dependent Insight** ■ few signs of unique insights and a reliance on text inferences ■ a willingness to probe individual thought, but only with direct support ■ inconsistent ability to focus on potential insights ■ inability to retrace the development of their thoughts over time	**Conscious Exploration of Insight** ■ active consideration of personal reactions and intuitions about their logical outcomes ■ ability to recognize and ground their unique responses in the commonality of group responses ■ a belief in the value of their own insights ■ clear sense of the development of their own thinking
Empathy	**Self-Oriented Thought** ■ a single, though sensitive, point of view ■ a quickness to judge ■ a limited ability to speak from the perspective of feelings ■ a closeness to plot and a distance from characters	**Other-Oriented Thought** ■ the ability to write themselves into the characters and situations ■ the ability to see multiple and conflicting perspectives ■ the ability to temper insights with empathy for others ■ the ability to think like another
Imagination	**Externally Generated** ■ able to engage in guided imagery but less aware of the role of imagination in self-directed reading ■ a reliance on external sources (pictures, book covers, etc.) in forming imagination ■ imaginative detail often limited to visual elements	**Internally Generated** ■ able to create detailed possible worlds with their imagination ■ able to detail an array of sources for their imagination ■ able to set a context, and redefine a topic ■ can use imagination independently to respond to a question ■ can appreciate the imagination of others
Intellectual Connection	**Circumstantial Connections** ■ most connections are tentative and may lack depth ■ the range of intellectual connections is limited largely to common occurrences ■ limited sense of articulation and detailed vision	**Integral Connections** ■ a willingness to seek connections ■ clear signs of connections from both life and literature ■ signs of uniqueness ■ an ability to make further connections independently

TABLE 12.2   Assessing the Quality of Voice in Reader Response Writing

	Level of Development	
Quality	*Satisfactory*	*Excellent*
Ownership	**Lack of Ownership** ▪ few signs of the internalization of ideas ▪ confident, but not engaged ▪ a tendency to converge on a centralized response ▪ limited ownership of ideas and language	**Desire to Accept Ownership** ▪ originality within a defensible context ▪ ownership of ideas; writers are engaged with the text and with their own ideas ▪ a belief that their ideas merit discussion ▪ clear sense of personal voice
Ambiguity	**Comfort with Absolutes** ▪ little acknowledgment of ambivalence, dilemma, ambiguity, uncertainty, possibility, inconclusiveness, or subtlety ▪ a quickness to judge ▪ limited recognition of differing views ▪ a perception that response means right answer	**Comfort with Ambiguity** ▪ aware of subtlety ▪ enjoys and gains insights from ambiguity ▪ seeks a balanced view ▪ can incorporate the views of others into their personal response ▪ able to appreciate gaps between interpretation and text. ▪ able to pose grand questions
Risk-Taking	**Need for Certainty** ▪ reluctance to explore or try on new ideas ▪ a reliance on past response achievements ▪ limited variety in response	**Need for Exploration** ▪ willing to extend their own ideas and those of others ▪ comfortable with a variety of response approaches ▪ able to set a context, redefine topic
Specificity	**Need to Assert or Generalize** ▪ generalized language and ideas ▪ little sign of elaboration ▪ limited sense of articulation and detailed vision	**Ability to Support or Specify** ▪ comfortable responding of, from, and about texts ▪ clear signs of intertextual connections in response

Adapted from work by Alberta Learning. Internal Document, Curriculum Branch, 1993.

Assessing the development of individual response is as important to the goals of a reader approach as is attention to the exploration of the lived-through experience. How writing in a reader response approach supports the development of these goals is surely among the grand questions.

REFERENCES

Allen, T. D. (1982). *Writing to create ourselves: New approaches for teachers, students and writers.* Norman, OK: University of Oklahoma Press.

Booth, W., & Gregory, M. W. (Eds.). (1984). *The Harper and Row reader: Liberal education through reading and writing.* New York: Harper and Row.

Bruffee, K. (1980). *A short course in writing: Practical rhetoric for compositions courses, writing workshops and tutor training programs.* Boston: Little, Brown.

Bruner, J. S. (1986). *Actual minds, possible worlds.* Cambridge, MA: Harvard University Press.

Dixon Krauss, L. (1996). *Vygotsky in the classroom: Mediated literacy/instruction and assessment.* New York: Longman.

Eeds, M., & Wells, D. (1989). Grand conversations: An exploration of meaning construction in literature groups. *Research in the Teaching of English, 23*(1), 4–29.

Eisner, E. (1972). *Arts in education.* Chicago: University of Chicago Press:

Eisner, E. (1985). *Learning and teaching the ways of knowing.* Chicago: University of Chicago Press.

Fish, S. (1980). *Is there a text in this class? The authority of interpretive communities.* Cambridge, MA: Harvard University Press.

Flower, L. (1981). *Problem-solving strategies for writing.* New York: Harcourt Brace Jovanovich.

Graves, D. (1994). *A fresh look at writing.* Toronto, Canada: Irwin.

Hammond, E. R. (1983). *Teaching writing.* New York: McGraw Hill.

Jordan, R. (1991). Pyramid discussions. *English Language Teaching Journal, 44*(1), 58–70.

Kessler, C. (Ed.). (1994). *Collaborative language learning.* Portsmouth, NH: Heinemann.

Langer, J. (Ed.). (1992). *Literature instruction: A focus on student response.* Urbana, IL: National Council of Teachers of English.

Lazar, G. (1993). *Literature and language teaching: A guide for teachers and trainers.* Cambridge, UK: Cambridge University Press.

Maley, A. (1997). Creativity with a small "c." *The Journal of the Imagination in Language Learning, IV.* Jersey City, NJ: Center for the Imagination in Language Learning.

Moffet, J. (1983). *Active voice: A writing program across the curriculum.* Upper Montclair NJ: Boynton/Cook.

Murray, D. (1984). *Write to learn.* New York: Holt, Rinehart & Winston.

Nilsen, M. (1999). *Educating the imagination: Cultivating independent thought and imaginative writing in intermediate level ESL students.* Unpublished research paper. University of Calgary, Calgary, Alberta.

Peterson, R., & Eeds, M. (1990). *Grand conversations: Literature groups in action.* Richmond Hill, Ontario, Canada: Scholastic Tab.

Probst, R. (1992). Writing from, of, and about literature. In N. Karolides (Ed.), *Reader response in the classroom: Evoking and interpreting meaning in literature* (pp. 117–127). New York: Longman.

Richards, J. (1990). From meaning into words. In J. Richards (Ed.), *The language teaching matrix.* Cambridge, UK: Cambridge University Press.

Rosenblatt, L. (1978). *The reader, the text, the poem: The transactional theory of literary work.* Carbondale, IL: Southern Illinois University Press.

Scardamalia, M., Bereiter, C., & Fillion, B. (1981). *Writing for results: A sourcebook of consequential composing activities.* LaSalle, IL: Open Court.

Watt, D., Hunsberger, M., & Labercane, G. (1999). Music and ideas: Enriching written response. *English Quarterly, 31*(1 & 2), 21–31.

INDEX